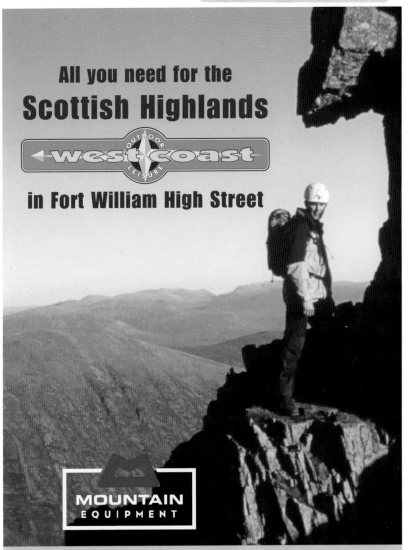

THE SCOTTISH MOUNTAINEERING CLUB JOURNAL

| Vol. XXXIX | 2004 | No. 195 |

A FIST FULL OF STEEL
(Repeating the all hardest mixed routes in the world in a season)

By Scott Muir

THE winter season of 2002-03 had been fantastic. I had spent the whole season, 49 days on the trot, climbing blue ice and enjoying good weather. It had been a period of learning and discovering new techniques and exploring what drove me to climb. The November before, I had nearly been killed with Rick Allen on the 2500m North Face of Baruntse 7101m in Nepal and this experience had really shaken me hard. More so than any other near death situations on Greater Range mountains I'd been in. It had been far too close for comfort and I knew it had ended seven years of adventure in the big mountains. Someone once said to me that a year out every now and then probably doubles your chance of surviving. I listened, knowing that I'd be back recharged in a few years with new drives goals and motivation.

This now left a big gap in my climbing – walking back to Lukla, I had a new mission, and that involved pushing myself technically and physically to the limits of my capabilities in winter. I turned to the big Continental projects that had really inspired me over the years, knowing that they offered big delicate ice, huge roofs and a different style from that which I was used to in Scotland. I wanted to experience pushing myself without the chances of dying in the process. Not the so called 'Scottish Hardman' approach, but one that would allow me to climb harder, more technical and physical rock and ice than was available at home. Maybe the danger aspect isn't always as present as it is at home, but it's still there for sure (shit gear on Stevie's pegged routes like 009 and on Mauro 'BuBu' Bole's pegged *Mission Impossible M11*, gear that has been there rusting for more than six years, yes these knife blades bow at you and you're upside down!) nor is their any mountaineering access or descent problems - I'd had my fill of that for a while.

I guess my other reason for going abroad was that it was almost impossible to get a good run at routes in Scotland, the experience of just getting going and then doing nothing for weeks held no excitement or interest anymore. Right now I wanted it hard and fast.

Welcome to the Machine M9, Pema M9, Die Another Day M9+ in Italy - routes that I thought might be outwith my current ability level and outwith the period of time that I had abroad that year, passed surprisingly quickly, but not without a battle. The battle involved new rules and tactics. It was very hard to accept falling in winter, something I was told never to do. I also had to adopt redpoint tactics and monkey about roofs, rigging and de-rigging gear, something again I never did in Scotland. The locals helped a lot with all this, but they still laughed heartily at my prehistoric kit, at the time Freney's, 'Top Wing' Comp tools and 'Rambo - Comp Mono' crampons with those click on spurs, top kit at home. What topped off the joke was my full gore suit and 20 layers of base clothing. This was a whole new world for a simple Scottish winter climber.

Looking out from the Haston Cave (Valsaveranche – Italy) across the road stands the *Mission Impossible* roof, a roof that Bubu couldn't believe had been missed. It's so obvious and so awesome. What is really impressive is that he had the vision to go there in the first place. I stood underneath it and looked with my mouth on the floor. I had the same feeling looking up at it as I did when I get shown a big mountain objective. I knew I'd be back for it. I thought - M9 to M11 is some jump in difficulty and it is. I believe that most climbers in the country, with a change in attitude and style, could get up M9 with some effort and training, but the next step is massive.

It took a whole summer at Birnam getting fit before I would be ready for the next winter. Nothing can prepare you for the full body thrash you get mixed climbing abroad, it is just so different, and you aren't going to get up anything without being route fit. I am not a person that finds climbing very easy, I would not even say I am very talented, but I work very had to achieve what I want to. I always have direction and drive and plenty of self belief and this often make up for a lack of natural ability. Thus this summer, spent on *Too Fast Too Furious* D12 at Birnam was a period of my life where I had to remain focused on my end goal - to repeat all the hardest sport style mixed routes in the world in a season. Although unconventional to most, this route stands as a bench mark for anyone aspiring to the top routes on the Continent and success on it will definitely set you up for a good season abroad. If you don't like it – don't do it, simple really!

December in Canada was fantastic, the start of the season on December 6, climbing most days when it wasn't thankfully 27°C below. With Canada having one of the best seasons on record it was desperate trying to stay focused on the Cineplex *(No, not a big movie theatre - cutting edge mixed climbing location in The Rockies Ed.)* and contender for the hardest mixed route in the world *Musashi* M12. With a few flashed M9s and M8s in the bag I was going well, but not quite well enough and in the end I pulled my ropes to go home, having fallen off a mere two moves from the ice four times. Each attempt on *Musashi* required a full day's rest. Never have I tried so, so hard on something and walked away empty handed, knowing that it was only a matter of time. But the plane was departing in 12 hours and I had to be on it to start part two of the season.

It was now December 26, and a sprint from the plane followed by a frantic drive north brought me straight to the 'Ice Factor' where I set routes with Dave McLeod till 2am the next morning in time for the Dry Tool Competition. Still burst from jet lag, we managed another night's route setting for the speed and technical ice competition before attending the 'Winter Ethics' debate. This was very poorly attended given the level of concern shown in the chat rooms. Anyway, those who did attend did make progress, regardless of the wide misrepresentation of information floating around about who said what and who wanted that. The gossip mongers would be far better making an effort next time to appear if they are so concerned, rather than assuming and twisting stories wildly. Distance or location is little excuse if folk are truly interested. Those that genuinely couldn't make it will be pleased to hear that a revolution will not take place and the doom of Scottish Winter Climbing is not nigh, maybe this is more likely to happen from the weather than anything else!

With the animated Simon Richardson and Chris Cartwright thankfully both involved in the debate and giving their usual respected views, it was unlikely to run out of control. The discussions will continue I'm sure, openly, and with respect for different demands and styles currently practised in climbing world-wide and without the exclusion of any one aspect!

Next stop, Switzerland, was fantastic, with generally good conditions at Kandersteg. Chris Cubitt, Matt Spenceley and Dave McLeod all pulled off impressive repeats at the same time, creating a great atmosphere alongside Stefan Siegrist, Simon and Samuel Anthamatten, Ueli Steck, Harry Berger, Robert Jasper, Innes Papert, Hans Lochner and later Mauro Bole and Anna Torretta. A place truly on fire. Saas Fee and my first World Championships was interesting with an early bath for me, for touching a line in competition blindness. Still climbing after the fault, I got jumped on and pulled off by three belayers tugging the rope, very ungraceful. At least the wild Saas Fee party could be enjoyed on both nights! My attempts at the speed competition went well placing middle pack, but the 'Rat up a drainpipe' standard was not fast enough to beat the Russians, who somehow managed to half my time.

Mission Impossible and *The Empire Strikes Back* beckoned in Italy. It was now the start of February and we hit conditions perfectly. Within days both routes had gone like a dream. No longer would I have to listen to the *Mission Impossible* ring tone on my phone or look at the screen saver on my computer reminding me of my goals for the year. 'Mission' is truly a contender for the best mixed route in the world, being spicily pegged, the only line on a huge crag and fully futuristically out there! 'Empire', just a brilliant all inclusive line, inspiring climbing back then from Stevie Haston and well ahead of the pack in difficulty and seriousness for the day. It is still one of the best hard routes in the world

As the season crept on, keeping the momentum going was getting harder by the day. I often had down days where progress was slow, however, these were usually the days that I learned the most. In some ways, Greater Range climbing felt psychologically easier, as normally on my trips there was only one objective and only two weeks plus walk-in and out to deal with it. On this project there seemed no end, with every route very close to my physical and technical limit, so many of them to complete and in so many countries. Often it was stressful having others on the routes, as they would break holds, meaning that sequences would change, making routes a grade harder and changing the intricate sequences already learned. Each time this happened it could cost a day. Not time that was readily available.

After working the brilliant 'Performance Seminar' at Glenmore, the brainchild of George McEwan, I headed straight off to Colorado to meet up with mixed local guru's Ryan Nelson and Rich Purnell. These boys have moved on from what Jeff Lowe started out in Vail and Ouray adding the hardest mixed lines in America. They were both great guys to watch, with massively different styles and strengths. Ryan a stamina man and Rich a bouldery, power merchant. It was a great experience doing the route that provided great inspiration for me, *Octopussy* M8, Jeff Lowe's first big exploration into new wave mixed was awesome and very serious. A now poorly pegged roof leads to a very delicate and not easy stalactite that, if it breaks, you will break your legs on the slab below. So much for sport mixed – Respect.

Flashing *Goldline* M10 at Skylight area Ouray and the next day doing *A Fist Full of Steel* M11 and onsighting *Dizzy with the Vision* at the same venue, finished a brilliant tour of Colorado. The icing on the cake for this part of the trip was a flash of the now famous Stevie Haston *Wild Climbs* series route *Reptile* M10, which I managed leashless, the only beta being the television program. Routes don't get more classic or any more wild – a desert island route to rank with 'Mission' and 'Empire'.

Canada – well, it was like coming home – the last blast and arriving just in time to miss the Festival. Everything was quiet, meaning that myself and Rich Purnell who had joined me for the Cineplex had it to ourselves. *Musashi* M12 went first, Redpoint this time, now feeling strong and cruising. All that was left was the hardest mixed route in the world *The Game* M13. It had seen some action already and in December I'd held Ben Firth's ropes while he worked it, so I had some beta. This helped as, on my first go, I made the 8ft first span, the wild swing and almost out through the second. I knew it would go quickly, but I now had only days left. Rich sent it quickly as it suited his style perfectly, proving that you didn't have to be 6ft 6ins to make the crux moves. Both of us could use the smallest of directional body tension holds to catch the lip 50% of the time, eliminating the random throw that got across the second blank downward 9ft span roof. It was now late March and I was tired, no one wanted to go ice climbing anymore and I spent a demoralising few days without a partner. On my last day it was all or nothing and, on my second go, I latched the lip, pulled up, hooked through the now half-an-inch thick ice on the slab above, rocked up, pumping bad. Got my weight over my foot and started pushing. With literally my right leg straight, a no-hands rest and the route in the bag, one second away, I ripped the ice off the top of the rail. With a loud scream of "No," I somersaulted, ripping the sheath and three strands of the core clean off my rope as it caught in my crampons. Dying on the last route would have been an interesting conclusion to the season.

So that was it – I couldn't claim a full ascent of *The Game* M13 – but I was damn close and it's easily in the bag next time.

I got on the plane wholly satisfied at having had the best season of my life and ready to come out harder next year. I am excited by the prospect of getting back into Trad. Scottish winter now, with Dave's *Cathedral* setting the pace for things to come. On arriving home, Ally had told me we'd be getting a new kitchen, little did I know until I sat my bags in the living room, that I'd be fitting it! The battle had only just begun.

Route List:

Musashi: M12: Canada – Multiple attempts.
Too Fast Too Furious: D12: Scotland – Multiple attempts.
Mission Impossible: M11: Italy – second Redpoint.
Empire Strikes Back: M11: Italy – second Redpoint, Pitch 1/2.
A Fist Full of Steel: M11: Colorado – second Redpoint.
Tomahawk: M10+/M11: Switz – first Redpoint.
White Out: M10+: Switz – first Redpoint.
Tool Time: M10+: Switz – first Redpoint.
Reptile: M10: Colorado – Flash.
Goldline: M10: Colorado – Flash.
Captain Hook: M10: Italy – first Redpoint.
Power Limit: M10: Switz – Flash.
Orgasmo: M10 – Canada – Flash.
Power Bat: M10 – Switzerland – first Redpoint.
Slice of Scheiss: M10 – Switzerland – first Redpoint.
Twin Towers: M10 – Switzerland – first Redpoint.
Pink Panther: M9+– Switzerland – first Redpoint.

Misery: – M9 – Colorado – Onsight.
Fatman and Robin: M9 – Colorado – Flash.
Quazy Moto: M8+ – Colorado - Onsight.
Mojo: M8+ – Canada – Onsight.
Octopussy: M8 – Colorado - Onsight.
Dizzy with the Vision: M8 – Colorado – Onsight.
Amphibian: M8 – Colorado – Onsight.
Samurai: M8 – First Ascent – Switzerland – Flash.
Shagadelic: M7+ - Canada – Onsight.
Seventh Tenticle: M7 – Colorado – Onsight.
Frigid Inseminator: M6+ – Colorado – Onsight.
And many more below M6+.

This year's project would never have been possible without the support of my sponsors who dug deep to support and believe in my goals. Although supposedly uncool, to give thanks and highlight these companies, I would like to do it here and thank them for putting money back into our sport, which I feel is highly under-valued and under-funded by our National body Sport Scotland. Climbing has better placed athletes than many other sports and this is sadly overlooked – hopefully, this will change and people like Malcolm Smith will receive the money and support they rightly deserve.

Mountaineering Council of Scotland Expedition Grant; Red Bull; Scarpa; Grivel; Thorlo's – Mountain Equipment; Edelrid Ropes; Tiso and The Ice Factor.

A NEVIS INTRODUCTION

By Morton Shaw

THE bodies made no sound as they fell, or none that we could hear 100m. back and out of sight round the ridge. We were stopped and arguing about where we were. The clouds had parted briefly and it seemed to me that we were looking down into Glen Nevis. Robin however was certain that we had not yet crossed the descent route. We agreed to differ and carried on round the ridge and onto a steep snow bay. The snow was hard and crampons scratched as we crossed the slope. In the middle my eye caught sight of a Silva compass stuck vertically into the snow at my feet, barely visible in the swirling spindrift. My first reaction was pleasure, a win, a trophy. My second less avaricious and more fearful as my eyes followed the slide marks down.

We had left the hut relatively early, cramponing from the start up to the Garadh. This was my first time on the mountain in winter. There was no one else in the hut and no sign of anyone else on the mountain. It was midweek in the Sixties. We were a party of four. My brother and two of his friends from Ullswater.

Garadh Gully was straightforward and led into the great bowl. The light was silvery grey and the buttresses reached upwards into the clouds. I had a great feeling of awe and smallness. A discussion of where next was had. I hovered on the periphery not really part of the decision-making process. A decision made, we traversed huge snow slopes across to the Comb and into the gully.

The height gain in the gully was in direct relationship to the volume of spindrift coming down and by the time we reached the last pitch it was difficult to see, with the holds filling in as fast as they were excavated. The last 50ft. were awkward. Straight up, then a rising traverse rightwards out of the protection of the gully walls and into the howling wind and snow. It was difficult to make out any features and by the time we assembled on the plateau we were white, the ropes like hawsers and my sense of elation replaced by a feeling of unease.

Another discussion, shouted this time. Number 4? No. The tourist track. Maps flapping. Hands cold, compasses adjusted. Eyes stung by the granules of ice swirling about our heads. We set off, still roped, compasses in hand and trying to follow the bearing.

That was when I picked up the compass. I showed it to Robin and pointed down the slope. The light was fading but there was no decision to be made and cautiously we started to crampon downwards towards the drop, noting as we went that there were two slide marks which started apart and then came together to make one. The slope seemed to steepen as we stood contemplating the inevitability of it all.

Rope length followed rope length as we moved, usually together but occasionally belayed, as the gully dropped in short steps. About five rope lengths down a voice could be heard from the blackness below. Robin said: "At least one of them is alive." I registered nothing, my mind totally focused on staying upright and alive.

The gully narrowed again with several short vertical sections and then eased a little into a bowl. In the gloom we could make them out, one standing applying First Aid to the head of the other.

Their story was remarkable. They, like us, had stopped to check the compass. The one behind had tripped taking the other by surprise and pulling both of them down the slope. The injured one despite a helmet had been knocked unconscious early in the slide. His partner had tried to brake but had been unable to stop their combined weight and lost any control, being slalomed at ever-increasing speed from side to side of the gully. When they reached the narrowing he was airborne as he came over the steps and landed in the bowl on a projecting rock which he had the presence of mind to push the rope over. He continued to slide but the rope held and they came to a stop.

The next drop was not a short one!

We patched them up as best we could, lots of pain and some blood but nothing that seemed life threatening, and made our way off the hill in the darkness, moving like crabs as we threaded a route from gully to buttress and back to gully. It did not seem straight-forward. As we lost height the wind dropped, the snow stopped and colour came back into the world in the gleam of the torches. The grass was an intense shade of green.

Eventually, some time after midnight we forded the river, reached the road and then the Youth Hostel. Police were called and interviews held while we awaited an ambulance. We had felt competent while on the hill, now it seemed embarrassing. The presence of a policeman somehow suggested wrongdoing. The one light point for me was the police asking occupations – three Outward Bound instructors and an apprentice accountant. See! It wisnae ma fault mister.

The other two went to the Belford while we had to beg a cell in the police station. Later that day Robin and I returned to the hut to pack up the gear and ferry it back down.

The injured climbers were released from the Belford a couple of days later and we slunk back to civilisation.

The Ben has been kinder to me since.

A HARD RAIN

By Mike Jacob

PRESSING buttons on the cheap car radio merely elicited a variety of crackles and a hissing voice from the loudspeaker. Stopping in a litter-strewn lay-by near Fort William to pull up the aerial, grimy lorries swishing past in clouds of dirty spray, made no difference. Like the radio, which could only get medium-wave, he couldn't think on the correct wavelength so gave up and concentrated on the road. The signs told him what he knew by heart...Onich... Ballachulish...

He drove slowly eastwards through Glencoe, going home. It was February, late afternoon and he could still see the gloomy hills, the snow high up keeping company with the freezing level on Bidean, and pick out the lines of climbs on Aonach Dubh. These mountains had given him every reward but had also sought out all his ambiguities. Misty wraiths drifted around the cold dark crags as he leaned forward to peer up at them and large raindrops, like tears, spattered sadly on the glass inches from his face. It was a sombre scene of dampness, wipers and headlights. How he yearned for something that would return colour to this world of black and grey and bring back the feeling of being glad to be alive. His reflection, a peculiarity of the flat windscreen of the ancient Volkswagen, glinted back at him. Was he looking out or in?

Was it that long ago that life – and for life read climbing, they were interchangeable – had been fun? He had been one of a group of young climbers and hangers-on based in Edinburgh. They climbed hard, lived life to the full and things seemed to happen with no prompting. Events came fast upon each other's heels and all you had to do was just react to them. No decision seemed particularly difficult to make or of any great significance. It seemed natural that he and Malc would climb together as often as they could and that meant virtually every weekend and holiday. Ever since, as young and impetuous novices, they had got talking to each other at Allt-na-giubhsaich in Glen Muick and headed off together up Lochnagar on a day of low cloud and snowfall, this was how it had been and how it always would be. It didn't matter to them that they had been avalanched below the Pinnacle Face and carried nearly to the lochan, with no-one else in the corrie to witness the event. Somehow Malc had lost the rope in the churning, compressing lumps of snow, so, in an act of defiant bravado they had then soloed Gargoyle Chimney.

Over the following years there developed a kind of silent consensus between them, partly due to their complementary abilities but more to do with a natural symbiosis of character and the empathy that is born of experience and danger faced together. They both loved the anarchic lifestyle associated with mountaineering, savouring the rewards that came from their achievements in extreme situations. He had argued with friends, particularly women, that no other relationship could touch the ultimate trust of this kind of partnership, unaffected by any kind of sexuality, of death faced together. This may have been true – their climbing commitment was absolute – but was it because, or in spite of, the fact that there was no voicing of feeling between them? So, while they communicated totally in one sphere, there was an unspoken boundary beyond which they never ventured in another.

Time passed…and the earth spun its subtle web of change and threw in a bombshell for good measure. Lucy and he had lived together for a couple of years and had then married. She was slim with long dark hair, a musician with a soft-spoken Harris voice. He knew, deep down, that it wouldn't solve the conflict within him but he really fancied her. The relationship was a good one, with the emotional intimacy that comes from shared interests, but there just weren't enough of them. She enjoyed walking but wasn't a climber and despaired of the vanity surrounding much of the climbing scene. Having to curb his desire of trying to share his indivisible adventures with her and deal with the immediate pressures of his work as a molecular biologist at the Roslin Institute would start the erosion, the crispness of the memories would start to blur despite his efforts to relive every transient moment. So, when they weren't climbing somewhere overseas, he would meet his friends midweek at a local crag or the wall, discuss this or that move afterwards in the pub, sink an imaginary banana-pick into the bar-top and plan the next trip, the next fix.

Lucy had grown tired of this self-indulgence and increasingly led her own cultural social life as a professional musician playing in an orchestra. This meant many trips away. He didn't like her absences and tried to persuade her to change jobs but she accused him of selfishness and double standards. He thought that she seemed to find more fault with him, trivial matters became brooding bones of contention and developed into long-running arguments. Then, just as he had started to think about facing up to the inevitable, of reappraising his priorities, the decision was taken out of his hands. He saw her one lunchtime, Lucy and another man in Prince's Street Gardens, holding each other close. He felt weak with shock and disbelief, a bitter taste at the edges of his tongue, like the time a timber-wagon had forced him to spin from the road and write off the car. There had been the inevitable furious confrontation with Lucy, everything that could be said was said, he had chosen climbing as a way of life and it excluded her. Tearfully, and with a heavy heart, she left him and went to live in Glasgow. She didn't tell him that she was pregnant.

He felt a gnawing sense of loss but worse was to come. Malc announced that he was moving to Switzerland, initially to earn easy money as a ski instructor in winter and then pursue his career as a surveyor with a civil engineering firm based in Geneva. That was it. Another decision easily made. He envied Malc, not just for the move but for his total control, his uncomplicated, unquestioning drive, his calculated decisions that always came up trumps as though he had some innate vision of his life ahead. Before he left they went out drinking with the lads, and then Malc too, despite the arrangements to meet up and climb together in the future, effectively walked out of his life. This time, everything that could be said remained unmentionable.

For a while there was venom in his climbing but the circle of friends was fragmented and he found that he had been left with a deep resentment. He felt betrayed – but by whom? He was in an emotional void, the emptiness that was the logical end to the failed relationship with Lucy left him floundering. One of her accusations kept niggling him – that he acted as though it was a weakness to reveal his feelings and that it was impossible for anyone to really get to know him. In his climbing circle he was known for his determination and resolve, traits which Lucy translated as stubbornness and an inability to compromise, and he knew, deep down, that she was right.

As if all this wasn't bad enough his integrity was challenged at work. He had been an important member of a team that was pioneering research in genetic engineering and he was very uneasy about the direction that the earlier results were taking them. Eventually, at loggerheads with the rest of the group, he was called to a meeting with the Institute's director and was given a more technical role in a different department. He felt sure, however, despite all the self-doubt about his inability to compromise, that his moral stance was correct.

In the past when he went climbing he had left any problems behind. Now they began to accompany him. He first noticed it when, alone on the Aonach Eagach on a wet weekday in October, he had looked at a buttress looming ahead in the mist and his legs had turned to jelly. He couldn't relax, he couldn't overcome his lack of confidence and had used the weather as an excuse to turn back, feeling wretched. And then, on a visit to the Lakes, the same thing happened, runners every few feet, clinging too tightly to the holds, calves in spasm, he wasn't in control although his partner hadn't noticed anything until he lowered off.

Around that time the dark dreams had started, fresher in his mind than real memories. A black cobra uncoiled onto the bed so that he jerked awake soaked in sweat. The image of a young boy with blonde hair and blue eyes, dead in a frozen ditch with a sheet of ice, like glass, slicing through him holding his body half-in, half-out of the water, haunted him. Was this a horrible omen? Who was he? He dreamed about numbers ending in zero so, as a test, he bought a lottery-ticket and was relieved when it did not win. Previously, when he was off-form, he had climbed through it but now the more he climbed, as though climbing could drive out the demons within, the more established the gripping fear became.

In keeping with his mood, he went to the most isolated hills. Driving back from Galloway he felt a sense of utter desolation, of not belonging to anywhere or anything. He saw the damp, decaying oak leaves at the edge of the road and felt like one of them, browned-off and dying, with no attachment to the roots of life or the strength and security of a sturdy trunk. He suddenly realised what a double-edged pastime he pursued – no longer did he find pleasure in the hills, thrill in the mountains or euphoria after a climb. The event left him with such a powerful feeling of loss that he remembered the precise point on the road, near the small granite-quarrying town, from then on. When he got home he threw his boots in the back of a cupboard and sat down to write a letter of resignation.

With the constraints imposed on him by a different job, he stopped climbing and took up dinghy-racing on the Forth. For a while, his mood improved, but it wasn't long before the chilling presence of omens lay in the pit of his stomach yet again. Ian, an old friend with whom he had once sailed the Hebridean seas in a wooden gaff-rigged cutter and who could make his clarinet stomp with traditional Clyde Valley Stompers jazz joy as the boat rocked to the tapping waves, was crushed to death by his own Harley motorbike on the roadside bend near the small granite-quarrying town in Galloway.

The phone call had come out of the blue. Malc was back in Scotland for a couple of weeks and had managed to get a booking at the CIC. He wouldn't take, 'no', for an answer and his infectious enthusiasm won the day. They had agreed to meet at the hut despite the poor forecast and he had spent hours hunting out his gear from its various places of storage. The Allt a' Mhuilinn bogs were as awful as always, as he floundered from one to the other. There were only a few folk at the hut, still the same as he remembered it, although now there was a windmill to help keep the place a bit less damp. A couple of hours earlier, Malc had arrived from Speyside where he had been surveying for the refurbishment of a major distillery and together, just like the old days, they prepared a meal. However, there was an awkwardness between them as they searched for some common ground.

There was an atmosphere of quiet contentment in the hut as people murmured to each other. They sat in their favourite corner and Malc pulled out a bottle of malt whisky and fetched a couple of glasses from the rack, wiping them with his sleeve. Gradually, with the help of the alcohol, they grew easier with each other and recalled past times. Slowly, the conversation came round to more personal matters. This was something new and he felt a sense of discomfort but Malc clearly had something that he wanted to say and was persistent.

"I heard that you'd stopped climbing. I didn't believe it. Was it true?"

"Oh, yeah, sort of..." His voice tailed off as he thought carefully about his next words.

"I guess I was a wee bit depressed...you know..."

"What, about Lucy?"

"Aye, I suppose...and work too. You moved on and I couldn't. Instead of success I just seemed to have one failure after another. It just all got to me...I thought the problem was climbing but it wasn't...it was something in me...still is..."

"You know, Rob, there's nothing *wrong* with that. You're allowed to fail. You always did have such high expectations...don't get me wrong, we did some great climbs, but when I went to Switzerland I could feel the pressure lifting. Yeah, I still do good routes but I don't push it..."

"No, it wasn't that...it wasn't the danger. I read something the other day that Freud wrote, about how we can derive intense enjoyment only from a contrast and very little from a state of things. I hadn't given it any thought before..."

"Well, that's what the ascetics say, isn't it? To achieve true happiness you have to experience true pain." He poured some more whisky into the glasses.

"I'm not sure that I believe it myself, though having just flogged up here no wonder this place feels like heaven."

They both laughed.

Malc continued: "That's all very well, and I can understand how they distinguish between pleasure and happiness, but life has plenty of other arenas for Freud's contrasts...doesn't it?"

"Aye...I guess..."

Malc was coming round to what he had wanted to say.

"I saw Lucy the other day. She was playing at a concert in Aberdeen and we went for a drink afterwards. She was asking about you." He paused and studied his friend's face.

"Did you ever see her again?"

"No...never did."

"Did you know that she'd had a child?"

"Christ! No, I didn't know. Probably that bloke she was messing about with."

"No, I don't think so, Rob. That didn't last any way. You know what she told me...she would have contacted you but she didn't want to come between you and climbing...she gave me her telephone number. Do you want it?"

"No...I couldn't...not now."

But Malc shoved a bit of paper over the greasy table anyway and he carefully put it in his pocket.

"Why did you change your job?"

"Oh, it's a long story...do you remember all the fuss about Dolly the sheep, you know, the first cloned animal?"

"Yes."

"Well, that was just the tip of the iceberg. There was all sorts of other stuff going on. It wasn't just sheep…you know, we all had to give tissue samples. At first it was pure science but then the Ministry of Defence got involved in the funding."

"Eh, why them?"

"Yeah, you might well ask. It may seem strange but most soldiers don't actually like killing – think of the military advantages if you could clone a load of the best psychopathic squaddies. Look, there's big multinational money in this business now. The latest thing is to clone, say, muscle cells and then put them back in the donor…athletes, footballers…no drugs tests…it's a can of worms. There's no stopping it now, it'll all come one day."

"Is that why you left?"

"Yes."

"What happened to Dolly?"

"They had to kill her in the end. No one really understands it but she had all sorts of problems caused by premature ageing. The Director sidelined me because I wouldn't sign the Official Secrets Act and they couldn't guarantee that my cells hadn't been used, so I decided to quit. It was just a matter of time…"

"You know, Rob, you're about the only person I know who really lives by his principles. I couldn't have done that."

"Well, look where it's got me."

They sat in silence for a while looking into the bottom of their tumblers. Eventually, Malc said: "Hey, what are we going to do tomorrow? What about Zero – we've never done it?"

"Okay, but you'll have to lead. I'm not fit enough."

"Fine. We'd better get some kip then."

He lay in one of the top bunks behind the door into the inner sanctum of the hut, unable to sleep. At one point he thought that he heard the outer door open and someone quietly arrive but it could have been one of the residents getting up for a pee. He thought about Zero – it was nice a round number but did it mean anything? A mood of oppression came over him which was still there in the morning.

He had thought that life was movement up a slope, maybe not steady but surely, continuous, like climbing itself, where one route always led to another. There always had to be one more step. Now that was wrong. He was over the top and making his tired way down the other side only to be trapped above a dripping, slimy cliff, wounded bodies at its base. They weren't climbers but the images from war – it didn't matter where…the Somme, Auschwitz, Kosovo, Iraq…haunted eyes beseeching him for the help that he was powerless to give…all the screams of pain ever uttered by the innocent and blended together, a terrible, piercing shriek carried on the wind forever, a rising crescendo of…

WHOOOMPH!

a hurtling silhouette framed within the walls of the gully flashed past him. He barely had time to see it but, as the body whirred past, there was a distinct change in the pitch of the scream, accompanied by a thrumming from the trailing flaps of clothing. He waited – the almighty wrench that would follow as Malc's ropes ripped through his gloves, twisted him round, ripped out the pathetic ice-screw belays, plucked him into the abyss…

…but it didn't come. Instead, the ropes continued to lead out at a slow rate. He knew what had happened yet couldn't believe it.

He had been shivering on the icy stance no wider than the superfluous guidebook which had twisted in his jacket-pocket and which, like a recriminating finger, was poking him uncomfortably in the ribs, when a solo climber had appeared at his feet. He had seemed confident when they exchanged a few words.

"Alright." Was it a question or a statement?

The stranger, a young Glaswegian lad he guessed, had asked for permission before climbing through, which he had reluctantly given. As the spindrift swept down and covered them both it had been difficult to see much of his face but his eyes seemed familiar. The climber had moved confidently up, and he caught the faint vibrations of a tune that the lad had been whistling to himself. He had started to hum the same tune and recall some distant words…

and what did you see, my blue-eyed son?
what did you see, my darling young one?
I heard the sound of thunder that roared out a warning
heard the…

"ALRIGHT." The explosive ferocity shocked him and echoed round and down as splinters of ice flew in alarm. This was neither a question or a statement. It was a demand. He tried to shout back but could only manage a dry whisper. He felt sick. A few moments ago the person had been warm and responsive, now his body would be just shattered bone and torn flesh, blood oozing into the snow. What a waste. Why was he on his own anyway?

The ropes pulled him, urging him to move. He fumbled with the knots, dropping a karabiner before he started to go into auto-mode. His temples throbbed as blood pounded…pounded… pounded…*it's a hard rain's a gonna fall*…THUMP…*I saw a black branch with blood that kept drippin'*…THUMP…*I saw a room full of men with their hammers a bleedin'*…THUMP…*a white ladder all covered with water*…THUMP…

"Steady," as he nearly smashed an ice-axe into one of Malc's plastic boots.

"What?…Sorry." He slumped over, gasping for breath.

"How did you get up there so quickly – hey, what's wrong?" Gulping great lungfuls of powder-laden air, he asked: "What the hell happened Malc?"

"What are you on about. Nothing's happened. Hey, we've just about climbed Zero. Didn't you hear me shouting?"

"No, no – the guy who came up past me – didn't you see him?" he urged.

"I haven't seen anything, just a load of spindrift. The weather's getting worse. Come on, let's get the hell out of here while we still can. It'll be dark soon."

"I tell you, someone came up. He's fallen, nearly hit me…I know him…" Malc looked at him. Could it be true?

"Look, c'mon. We've got to move. There's nothing we can do now. We'll report it to the police when we get back to the hut."

The road twisted up past the Meeting of the Three Waters and he glanced up to his left, towards Am Bodach where it had all started. Zero…yes, it did mean something…full circle and he was back at the beginning and had the chance to start afresh. The piece of paper was still in his pocket. In the sky beyond Sron Gharbh he thought he caught a glimpse of blue as the clouds parted for an instant. At that very moment too, by some quirk of reception, the radio crackled into life halfway through Bryan Ferry's thumping version of Dylan…

…where black is the colour, where none is the number
and I'll tell it and think it and speak it and breathe it
and reflect it from the mountains so all souls can see it…
…and it's a hard rain's a-gonna fall.

THE PSYCHOLOGY OF CLIMBING

By Malcolm Slesser

WITHOUT the force of gravity climbing would be both pointless and boring. There would be no physical danger and, in the absence of risk, the mind is not engaged. What makes climbing so satisfying to its adherents is the intellectual component of an apparently purely physical activity, namely the will to pit your skill against the mountain, not as your adversary, but as a sparring partner. Added to this is the aesthetic reward of reaching wild and lonely places. It turns climbing into a way of life. Furthermore, to caress the rock above you in search of holds is as sexy as stroking the Venus de Milo.

Due to the acceleration of gravity a falling body on our planet Earth, and here I use the term in its scientific context, drops 16ft. in the first second, a farther 48 in the second and an additional 80 in the third by which time its velocity is more than 90ft. per second or 60mph. If the unprotected human body hits *terra firma* at that speed, damage is intense and survival unlikely. So why do we do it?

There is, of course, the purely athletic pleasure of exercising one's muscles in unusual ways. Indeed this is such a delight that climbing walls have sprung up all over the world where, secured from the risk of a fall by an overhead rope, one can test one's athleticism. This is fun, and good training, but it's not the real thing that gets the adrenaline going. Climbing is the solution to a very personal equation. It is the potential consequence of a fall that renders the act of climbing such an intense experience. No-one obliges you to tackle something that may be exhausting or life threatening. The choice is purely yours. Yet the harder the climb the more we relish it, seeking ever-greater challenges until each of us reaches the point where the difficulty either exceeds our technical ability or our mind rebels.

Technology has advanced, and the climber these days has a safety belt of sorts. Risk can be diminished by placing runners, in the old days it was a piton. With such precautions taken, say, every 20ft., the climber's fall velocity is limited to 20mph. While the kinetic energy of the falling body is absorbed by a longer length of rope. Climbs can be stitched up with so many *runners* that a fall is no big deal. Thus assured, the modern climber exploring new routes can push out the envelope of endeavour with less risk than Whymper experienced on his first ascent of the Matterhorn, by what would today be considered the easy route. But there are also places where such precautions cannot be taken for lack of an obliging rock surface. One such example is the technically easy staircase up the Inaccessible Pinnacle with 200ft. of space to one side. What is formidable is the sense

Sron Ulladale, West Face. Photo: Alastair Matthewson.
Al Matthewson enjoying one of many airy jumars on Pitch 4 of The Scoop. Photo: Jamie Andrew.

of exposure to the void below, and its effect upon the mind of the climber, even one roped from above.

So, do climbers attain their goals by shutting their minds to the consequences of a fall? Many do. Up to the age of 21, when I had been rockclimbing for about five years, I believed I was immortal. It couldn't happen to me, could it? Then I fell off. It was on small crag and I suffered little more than an injured ankle and dented pride. Looking back, I realise how lucky I was, for it changed my attitude. Marriage and children alter the balance of risk. Many are induced by their wives to give up. I was one of the lucky ones permitted to continue and even extend my experiences to my children.

The risks associated with climbing are not like the dangers of battle. We are our own commanders. Nonetheless, some overplay their hand, some are careless. Some die. But these are subjective risks, where the mind is, or should be, in charge of events. In a quite different category are the objective risks, things we cannot control, such as stonefall from above, avalanches or a deterioration in the weather. In 1966 five of us were attempting to climb the third highest peak in the Americas, Yerupaja in the Peruvian Andes. To gain the south-east ridge we had first to climb a rock wall. But one look at the glacier surface gave us pause for thought. It was graveyard for the thousands of rocks that were continually falling from the cliffs above. Yet this was the only route possible. Placing our rucksacks on our heads we dashed unscathed through the danger zone with all the speed our breathless lungs could muster at 17,000ft.

If you drive long enough you will eventually come face to face with an accident, so in climbing. For many that is the time to retreat to the climbing wall. For others it is a wake-up call. My first experience of an accident was in 1944 in Skye. My companion and I were striding up the whaleback of Sgurr Dearg heading for the Inaccessible Pinnacle. At a step in the ridge, instead of walking round it, he stretched up and grasped a large detached block to pull himself up. It probably weighed quarter of ton. It slid down and crushed his thigh. It happened during a meet of the Edinburgh University Mountaineering Club, and much as we were distressed at the death of our friend, none of us gave up climbing, for we saw it as an error of judgment that with a greater sense of awareness would not, should not, have happened. The mind is the safety net, not signs, rules or balustrades.

Shortly after this incident I was attempting a first winter ascent of a summer rock climb on Ben Nevis. A gale was blowing powder snow off the summit into a plume that shot 100ft. into space before gently parachuting onto our cliff. Mini-avalanches were constantly cascading down. I was just a few feet from the end of the technical difficulties, and knew from summer explorations that beyond rose an easy snow slope to the summit plateau, capped no doubt by a vast cornice. This in itself presented no problem. One could tunnel through it. But was the slope safe? Each time I stepped up, my intuition told me to step back down. Each time I did so a voice within me said: "Wimp," and I stepped up again. This cycle was repeated several times. The spindrift grew more violent. I decided to retreat, and was just above my companion, Norman Tennent, when I was embraced by a mass of snow, and pulled off my feet. Norman held me. The avalanche continued for what seemed like minutes but was probably just a few seconds – it was big. Most of it shot over our heads. Now is there a moral to this tale? Had I overcome my timidity, I would have been swept off and my companion would have been plucked after me like a puppet on a string. I had exactly the same experience in the Peruvian Andes many years later. Such events highlight a fascinating issue in climbing, that becomes ever more relevant the bigger and the higher the mountain, that in Iain Smart's immortal words: "Where is the boundary between constructive boldness and destructive folly?"

Being scared is quite an important component in staying alive. It sharpens the senses. One of the qualities that allows one climber of comparable ability to go farther than another is the control of that fear. It can get one out of a tricky situation. Four of us, two of whom were inexperienced, were making an ascent of the famous Wolf's Head arête in the Wind River mountains of Wyoming. This 10,000ft. blade of impeccable granite thrusts more than 1000ft. above the meadow below. Somewhat slowed by our less-experienced companions, it was an hour to dusk when we reached the final move onto the summit block. It required one to shuffle along a horizontal crack barely an inch deep sustained by handholds above. Halfway along these petered out and that last 10ft. depended entirely on keeping one's balance on a near vertical wall. It was a breath-taking move given the 1000ft. drop below, and led with great aplomb by Bill Wallace. Two of the party were quite terrified, yet they admirably controlled their fear. For one, however, it was one emotional stress too many. It was time to hang up her boots. Now how do you explain this sort of fun to people who don't climb mountains?

TWO THOUSAND YARD STARES

By Al Scott

THE term 'Thousand Yard Stare' is one I've come across several times in a few different contexts. For me, it has two very different connotations. Firstly, it describes very well the despair and subsequent depression I suffered after the loss of a close friend in a climbing accident, and the emotions I felt the first time I returned to the scene. Secondly, it much more light-heartedly conjures up the determination required to compleat one's Munros…

Part One:

> Hand me a bottle to drink away my sorrow,
> Cause I don't want to go back there tomorrow,
> But I will, oh I will,
> Tho dread does my heart fill.
> I go there every day,
> Tho God knows I try not to in every way.
> For sometimes life is hard to bear
> At the end of my Thousand Yard Stare!
> (Gary Jacobson, Vietnam War poet)

I write this as I approach the Fifth Anniversary of the death of my good friend, Grant Scotland, in a climbing accident. It is something of a catharsis for me as I have bottled up the feelings and emotions of that desperate and traumatic day for too long.

Grant and I were work colleagues as well as friends, near neighbours, training partners and drinking buddies. He was a keen mountain biker and weight trainer, and developed an interest in climbing through me and we went regularly to the Ibrox climbing wall for a couple of years. We had had a couple of days out on the crag doing Agag's Groove and had been up to the Etive Slabs to do Spartan Slab. Both of these trips had been wonderful days and Grant had thoroughly enjoyed them. He wasn't a naturally gifted climber but was fit, strong and incredibly determined.

We had been out for our usual Friday night pint after work and had arranged to go climbing on the Sunday of that holiday weekend. We didn't have any concrete plans of where to climb, I would just decide on the day depending on the weather. On the morning of that fateful day in September 1998, I left home at around 8am with a rack of Guidebooks – Southern Highlands, Glencoe and Glen Etive, Central Outcrops, still undecided where to go.

We drove north in my car, up the Loch Lomond road where it was wet, so I decided that the Cobbler wasn't really an option. Farther up towards Crianlarich it brightened up, but as I didn't fancy another visit to the bolted routes by Aberfeldy I decided on the Etive Slabs again.

We got down to the road end by about 10.30am and there were only a couple of cars. This was reassuring, as I knew how busy this place could get – especially on holiday weekends. We packed our sacks and headed up to the crag. I had a notion to do either Hammer or Swastika, depending on who else was up there, and which route was free. When we got to the Coffin Stone, there were some parties on Hammer, The Pause and Spartan – so Swastika it was then. Decision made.

I had done Swastika before – many years before, on a GUMC trip back in the early Eighties and I was keen to see if I could free the top pitch. Big Grant was just 'keen' as usual. He was happy to second me on all the pitches as he hadn't led anything outdoors up to that point. It was only his third outdoor rock climb and I wanted him to see what went on with the runner placements, ropework, belays etc.

Things went very well right up to the wee overhang on the section below the final headwall – it was sopping wet. I had to use aid to get up that and Grant had a hard time following it. It was the same story on the final pitch – lots of aid had to be used and I set up belay on a couple of small trees in a bay at the top of the crag.

Grant struggled up the pitch and joined me on the belay. He was totally elated at having done the route, by far his hardest to date, and we stopped a while to admire the views and take in the surroundings. All that was left to do was a short scramble up some heathery terraces to the descent path at the top. Grant had all the gear on his harness and said he would just go on up to the top. As it looked pretty easy, I gave him the nod and said: "OK Grant. Up you go."

It was that single moments decision, more than all the others that I had made that day, that was to prove to be the worst and most devastating of my whole life.

I made that decision. *I gave him the nod. I said: "OK Grant. Up you go."*

He set off up the scrambly heather, a rising rightward traverse up to the path, the rope snaking behind him. He ran out about 50ft.-60ft. It was easy ground. No bother. There was a wee rocky step, no more than a few feet. I can picture it to this day. Grant shouted down that it was a bit wet. I craned my neck to get a better view, just as Grant's foot slipped and he seemed to slither down a couple feet…he stopped for a second then seemed to overbalance backwards…he did that almost comical kind of swimming motion with his arms but his momentum took him back. There wasn't a sound. He tumbled over…and over again. The rope seemed to snake towards me…oh f o r f-u-c-k s-a-k-e G R A N T ……..**NO**………

NO…………NO!

In a split second the enjoyment of the moment with my big buddy on the crag was shattered with gut-wrenching intensity. The almost idyllic beauty of the place and the sense of accomplishment were exploded in an immediate paroxysm of dread. An enormously powerful force pulled me with a massive jerk as Grant's weight came on to the rope. How the hell the belay held I will never know. I was pulled all over the place and Grant's weight was hampering me from getting into a position to see what had happened. All the while I was screaming Grant's name, over and over, completely panic-stricken.

After a few moments, I somehow managed to tie off the load-bearing rope and lowered myself down a few feet to the edge of the crag. What I saw below was to hammer home the sickening enormity of what had happened. It was a sight that shall remain etched into my mind forever. I knew in my heart that Grant was dead – and yet just a few minutes beforehand we were on top of the world. I couldn't understand it.

I wept uncontrollably, trying to come to terms with this horrific event. I remember thinking of what the hell I was going to say to Grant's wife, Donna. What *DO* you say? I kept screaming Grant's name…willing him to come back…willing this nightmare to finish. The other climbers on the crag had seen and heard what was going on and had alerted the rescue. I really have no idea of time scale at this point. One of the other climbers lowered down to my position to help out in any way they could.

I remember the rescue helicopter hovering overhead, the powerful blast from the rotors buffeting me. I remember the rescue guy lowering down to my position and the look on his face when he went down to Grant. I remember being shepherded down the descent path by the two climbers who came over to help (and if you ever read this, I am indebted to you). I remember the way the rescue guys lowered Grant's body down the crag. I remember having to identify Grant's body in the helicopter and not understanding why I had to. And I remember being left alone and having to drive home when everyone else had gone. I also remember going to see Grant's wife later that night.

A very difficult year followed, with feelings of guilt dragging me into an abyss of despair and depression. I blamed myself for Grant's death that day, having made all the decisions that led up to it. But, ultimately it was Grant's own decision to be there with me and to set out from that last belay and I do finally, almost, accept that.

On the First Anniversary of the accident I went back up to Glen Etive and with permission from the estate manager, placed a small plaque on the path by the loch side in memory of the Big Man, and I'd like to thank some special friends, particularly in the Rannoch, for helping me with that. On the Second Anniversary I went all the way up to the crag, sat on the oh-so-aptly named Coffin Stone and just thought things through. I've been back to Glen Etive on the Anniversary every year since. Somehow it just helps.

This year I went up again. The plaque was gone. Removed. At the time I was devastated, who could do such a thing? But after a lot of thought I accepted that maybe it wasn't such a bad thing and it was a chance for me to move on. Not forget – just move on.

The whole episode brings home to me just how *good* climbing can be – and just how *very bad* climbing can be. But we still do it because we love it. I thought long and hard about packing it all in, but in the end I just couldn't.

Part Two:

> "Sir, I salute your strength,
> your courage, your indefatigable air
> but why did ye have to
> make that List?
> cos now I've got a Thousand Yard Stare"
> [Big Al to Saddman T. Munro in Baggedhad]

Thousand Yard Stare *n* (from: Brewing Dictionary of Feeble Phrase) – A determined, resolute, single-minded, stubborn and unflagging decision to get up off one's arse and pull out all the stops to get the feckers in the bag once and for all.

…because, Jeezoman it's 26 years since I started doing the stupid things.

…but even before that, by way of a hill education in my pre-pubescent yoof in the late Sixties and early Seventies, three of us schoolmates would take Shanks's Pony from Drumchapel up into the wilderness of the Kilpatrick Hills. We had many enjoyable hours of fresh air, superlager, peat bogs, strong cider, cowpats, and solitude. Until that is, the Clydebank Shamrock, our arch-enemies, sent out hunting parties and we got involved in running battles with sickening savagery on the bloody slopes of Duncolm, (mostly running it has to be said). The hills certainly offered us young lads an escape from the gangs and grim reality of 'scheme' life.

Yes, 26 years after my first Munro expedition in 1977. Ah yes, the memories…catching the bus from 'The Drum' kitted-out with those big orange aluminium-frame rucksacks; Doc Marten boots; Coopers Fine Fare plastic bags for gaiters; spit-through parka-cagoule-anorak type things; and of course, some bevvy for the journey to Glencoe. Then the interminable walk all the way down Glen Etive and camping halfway up Stob Coir'an Albannaich in a midge-storm…the searing heat, the warm lager, the dust, the flies. Oh yes – it was hell back in those days.

Since then, there have been countless good days on the hill with the Rannoch Club, into which I had been invited by that great old Rannoch luminary B. E H. 'Ted' Maden. The good-fellowship; the convivial bonhomie; the brotherly badinage; the support and succour of ones like-minded mountain loving friends...

.......**NOT**

...more like 'Death Race' with trekking poles. Blood, sweat and beers. Last up the hill is a diddy. Lung-bursters interspersed with cruel jibes. Personal taunts. Vicious one-liners and putting the metaphorical boot 'intae yer mates'. I wouldn't have it any other way!

Oh yes, back to the Munros, and some Munro-bagging memories...

During a week away hillwalking in July 1978, doing the Grey Corries, Aonachs and Ben Nevis stuff. There was a heatwave and we seemed to spend the whole time walking around in a 'halo of flies'. Nothing to do with all of us being heavy metal freaks and big Alice Cooper fans, but for the duration of our trip we had an incessant plague of flies buzzing round our heads. Total insanity ensued.

Also, in that same year, this time in winter, we were doing the Bidean-Sgreamhach-Beinn Fhada ridge in deep snow and white-out conditions. Our navigation skills were in their infancy, to say the least, and we took a bearing from Sgreamhach to Beinn Fhada and set out, compass outheld, heads down. Half-an-hour later, we ended up exactly where we started! Very spooky and I still cannot to this day explain what happened.

There was fun and games on Ben Lawers in January 1981, when it became so windy on the hill that we had to lie on the ground clinging onto boulders for dear life, with legs flapping around worryingly and the rucksacks being ripped off our very backs. Very, very scary.

July 1982, a simply idyllic evening on Cairn Bannoch and Broad Cairn after a superb day's climbing on Creag an Dubh Loch. Rock routes, Cougar and Giant if I remember correctly. All followed by superlager and voddie cocktails – but I can't remember correctly.

An unusual day in September 1989. Camped by the roadside near Ben Klibreck, we were rudely awakened by quite possibly the worst clouds of midges I had ever seen. We fled the campsite and skedaddled up Ben Klibreck just to escape the wee biting basturts and were back down from the hill by 8.30am! After a leisurely breakfast in the improved conditions we visited the Falls of Shin to watch the salmon leaping. I'll always remember one of the party (who shall remain nameless) looking *UPSTREAM*, expecting the salmon to be leaping *DOWN* the way! D'uh! After lunch we got bored and went off to do Seana Braigh. A stunning hill, and an utterly brilliant day. Unplanned. Unexpected. Unbeatable.

Coulags Bothy. Nov 1989 saw the first rendition of the Rannoch Club song (*see www.climbrannoch.com/BigAlWrites*) during a raucous evening, and the sight of Bunny and Mick the Fish engaged in pugilistics over a woman! A classic night. Followed the next morning by my one memory of beating JD up the hill, *mano-a-mano* on Maol Chean-dearg. On the way up the hill I deliberately dropped a five pence piece, knowing what JD's reaction would be. It hit him on the back of the head! He's like that, and as he scrabbled in the dirt to pocket it, it gave me the valuable time I required to put distance between us and bag the hill first. I admit it, a shocking piece of bastardmanship. But, hey, anything goes on the hill, it's dog-eat-dog out there!

December 1991. Slioch. It's supposed to have an easy bridge crossing – but we missed it and an epic river crossing in spate conditions ensued.

Myself, my wife Maureen and Wee Al had missed the bridge on the way up Slioch, (cue jokes about 'Nam and the Gooks having blown it up etc). We followed the river up the hill until the point where we thought we could get across. It is a raging torrent but not too deep. Me and Mo did the sensible thing and removed our boots and tied them on to our sacks then struggled across the flow together. Wee Al? Oh No. No. No. He took his boots off and tossed one of them across the stream, it landed safely. Phew! He chucked the other one. It landed on the other side then starts to r-o-l-l s-l-o-w-l-y down a wee slope and into the torrent and starts to float downstream.

Oh SHHHHHHEEEEEIIIIIIIIIT!

Just picture it. Wee Al scrabbling barefoot and panic-stricken across the icy boulder-strewn water as his boot (right one I think) floated merrily away, bobbing about playfully, almost in slow motion, taunting him. With a desperate last-minute belly-flopping lunge he snatched the laces just before the boot went 'doon the watter' and into Loch Maree. If there had been a panel of comedy judges set up on the banks of the river that day, they would have shown 6.0 6.0 6.0 6.0 6.0 6.0 6.0s all the way. TOP TOSSING!

Wee Al deservedly got the Rannoch 'Mug of the Year' award, indeed, I think it was his third year in a row – so he got to keep it.

It's a shocker to admit that between 1994 and 2002 I didn't do a single new Munro, and it has to be said, not much rockclimbing either, apart from Rannoch Hot Rocking that is. I guess it must've been something to do with the kids arriving on the scene, followed by my involvement in the aforementioned fatal accident. However, things got rekindled again at the 2002 Rannoch Dinner Meet when I *really* acquired the 'Thousand Yard Stare' after bagging nine of the 11 Skye Ridge Munros, leaving me just 10 to do.

Then in Spring 2003, the usual Rannoch Hotrock Spanish trip had to be cancelled due to irreconcilable wotsit personality thingummies. There was a split. Colin and JD headed north on an ill-fated 'Back to Basics'

Scotrock Tour. Myself, Iain and Chris decided to have a week in the Highlands bagging nine of my remaining 10 thus leaving Beinn Ime for compleation in the autumn.

Primary targets were four of the Fisherfields, Lurg Mhor and Cheesecake, Sgurr nan Gillean and Am Basteir and Meall Buidhe (Knoydart). A piece of piss then.

In preparation, I had purchased a pair of 'Superfeet' insoles in an attempt to avoid blisters with my troublesome old canvas/goretex padding boots. So when we set out for the walk over to Shenavall Bothy on Saturday, May 3, I was confident that my feet would be in good nick for the padding week ahead. How wrong can you be! Within half-an-hour I knew there was trouble afoot, and by the time we reached the bothy in the pouring rain my heels were shredded.

The bothy was busy, with around 20 people in residence and a few tents outside. But with a bit of brass neck and luck we muscled into the main room with the log fire, sorted out some floor space, and milled around drinking beer and chatting. It was around 9.30pm and there had obviously been a lot of bevvy consumed and the banter was raucous to say the least. One of the wimmin in the company remarked that she had drunk rather a lot and expected to wake up with 'a big thumper'. I felt I had to clarify the situation by pointing out that it was only blokes that woke up with 'big thumpers', and that seemed to set the tone for the evening.

The following morning, we awoke to a bright day but one with the obvious threat of rain. I put on an extra pair of socks and got 'compeeded-up' in an attempt to avoid worsening my blisters, but to no avail. We waded the rivers to get on to the stalker's track leading over to Carnmore, and followed this up to the col between A'Mhaigdean and Ruadh Stac Mor. The weather really crapped out big time here and there was a very heavy and prolonged hailstorm.

We continued round my remaining Fisherfield hills, and back to the bothy extremely wet and cold. My feet were in a truly shocking state. It had been a long 10-hour+ day. However, I had some canned anaesthetic with me and we had another great night in the bothy. Particularly good fun, were Gordon and Fiona from the Kyle Mountain Club who were terrific company. Much credit goes to Fiona especially, for doing all six hills in appalling conditions, a really tough 12-hour day. I think she had her own 'thousand yard stare'.

Our plan for Monday was to have an easy walk out from the bothy and not a lot else. However, the state my feet were in led to it being a dreadful ordeal. We decided to walk out via the Strath na Sealga, a bit longer but with supposedly easier walking.

…..plod….**ooyah!**….plod….**ooyah!**

…multiplied by about 10,543 approximately, but who's counting? I was sure I'd have to visit my dentist as I was gritting my teeth so much and I was nearly heaving with the pain. Not an enjoyable experience. Mr Simpson, I doff my cap to you sir, I know how you felt. I was touching the cloth.

On Monday night we dossed at the Kinlochewe Bunkhouse, and had a few beers with JD and Colin who had just arrived for their Wetrock Tour 2003. Poor guys – it was wet, wet, wet.

Tuesday was our big cycling day – from Attadale into Bendronaig Lodge at the foot of Lurg Mhor and Cheesecake. It's at times like these that I realise that I am just so NOT a mountain biker. The uphill bits are desperate and you end up pushing the fecking bike and when you do get a downhill bit you get shaken and rattled to buggery. My brakes were 'beagling', my arms and hands were 'screaming' and my legs were 'howling'. What a racket! The hills, however, were surprisingly straight-forward from this side. We got a soaking in some very heavy showers but there was the occasional view to make up for it.

'Stare' still on and going to plan.

Wednesday was our rest day. We drove round to Kyle of Lochalsh, then over on to Skye and the Sligachan Inn, where we booked in to the Bunkhouse. A good pool and beer session ensued. All the while the weather had been poor but it was nothing to what was to come overnight! In all my years I have never seen weather like we had that night on Skye, it was monsoonmungous!

Thursday dawned and it was still really crap. We thought there was no way in the world we'd get on to the hill that day. So we had a Portree shopping trip instead. Iain was looking for something for his chafed hips and arse. I suggested Pampers, but he wasn't impressed. We went to the Outdoor shop where Iain asked the rather attractive sales assistant: "What have you got in the way of underwear?"

I quickly interjected before Iain got a slap.

"He means what you're selling, not what you're wearing."

The lass took it well, because we got a complimentary coffee and the obligatory small talk. By the time we got back to Slig for what we thought was sure to be another pool and beer sesh, there was just a hint of a break in the weather.

We hurriedly got the gear together and Iain had a chance to try out his new anti-chafe undershorts. With the constant threat of the weather changing we really shifted, and were on the top of Am Basteir in two hours from the bunkhouse. Then up and over Sgurr nan Gillean in a bit of a hail storm which added to the excitement. We had snatched these hills from the jaws of defeat, and it was magic! On a sour note though, I went over on my ankle several times on the way down the hill. The footwear I was using were little more than trainers with no ankle support and I was paying for it.

Incredibly, we had done everything in our itinerary according to plan. Amazing when you consider the weather, but the Friday was going to be a hard last day. We had an early start to drive down to Armadale for the 9.15 ferry to Mallaig. That got us there in time for the 10.15 ferry to Inverie. We then had exactly fours hours to do the Meall Buidhe round trip, and we felt confident enough that we could do it. We were now pretty fit, but in retrospect I think we had underestimated this hill. It's funny what a 'Thousand Yard Stare' can do to you. It's a 21km round trip with 960m of ascent, and even with cycling the first 3km and going at what Iain called 'panic pace' there was just too little time to do the hill and get back for the 15.00 ferry. The weather was appalling, lashing rain and hail, gale force winds and very very cold. Oh Yes! This is May in Scotland all right. The path up the Mam Meadail was a stream and with a dodgy strapped-up ankle it was just never going to be. I was staring defeat in the face. We got to the col at 550m then had to turn back, and even then only got back just in time for a swift pint before the ferry arrived.

If the Skye hills had been snatched from defeat, then Meall Buidhe was a bit of a kick in the baws. Very, very disappointing…a Meall too far…an unfinished Meall…one for the doggy bag to be finished later.

In fact, I would say Friday, May 9, was in my top three of memorable days on the hill, for the wrong reasons.

In third place Meall Buidhe, Knoydart – pishing wet, freezing, sore feet bollocks, so close to being my penultimate Munro, yet so fecking far away.

In second place An Sgarsoch and Carn an Fhidleir from Glen Feshie on a Rannoch Bothy Meet. Nine hours in deep snow in a whiteout only to return to a bothy full of Embra' Yoonie tossers – truly shocking.

The worst/best day on the hill ever is reserved for those countless days (and many still to come hopefully) on the hill with JD and the Rannoch team and the blood-sweating toil of trying to keep up with the sods. Hell. Marvellous.

I did get Meall Buidhe in the bag a few weeks' later at the end of May. A cracking weekend at Barrisdale Bothy. I was then staring my Last Munro in the face – Beinn Ime. It's you and me. In fact, therein lies a strange tale. I had been on Beinn Ime before, way back in the late Seventies. We had reached what we thought was the summit cairn in appalling weather and went down immediately. The following weekend we were up on a neighbouring hill, and we could see clearly the twin summits on Beinn Ime and realised that we hadn't been to the true summit. From that day I decided to leave it for my last.

September 2003, 13 – Beinn Ime. My 'Stare Way to Heaven' was from the Butterbridge side and my rather romantic idea was for it to be my two sons Calum and Craig's first Munro as well.

I loved the day, but believe it or not was totally stressed out about how it was all going to turn out. Invitations had been sent out but who would come? Who wouldn't? The weather? The route? How would my boys do? What was the hall for the celebrations afterwards like? Have I got enough food? Drink? Would people have a good time? Will folk stay over? Worry-worry-worry. Fret-fret-fret.

Of course, in the end it was fantastic, 30 great friends on the hill, albeit on a cool and misty, but thankfully dry day. Eight-year-old Calum's first Munro. The only slight disappointment was that my wee Craig (six-years-old) and hence Her Wifiness Maureen couldn't quite make it.

The Bubbly, the Stella, the malts, the handshakes, the hugs, the gags, the one-liners, the photies. Then back to the excellent Cairndow Village Hall for a superb night. Naff speeches, great company, superb chilli, bevvy galore, music, dancing, ping-pong and so much more.

And afterwards, the strange sense of Compleat Emptiness or is it Empty Compleation? I can't decide. It is really very difficult to explain, so I won't even bother to try, but, there remains…what now?…Corbetts? Grahams? Donalds? Marilyns? Messners? Buhl!

Aye right!

…stares into the distance.

CLIMBING AND WRITING: THE VICTORIAN WAY

By Robin N. Campbell

I SHOULD like to begin with a confession. Since my taste in literature is irredeemably low-brow, I address my chosen topic as an imposter. My idea of a really good book is one written by Arthur Conan Doyle, Rex Stout or P. G. Wodehouse. If, preparing to bivouac, I were to discover the work of a Booker prize-winner included by some mischance in my rucksack, I should not read it, but instead use it as a prophylactic for piles. So far as poetry is concerned, I share Wodehouse's opinion, epitomized in his golf story, *Rodney has a Relapse:*[1]

"I have generally found, as I have gone through the world, that people are tolerant and ready to forgive, and in our little community it was never held against Rodney Spelvin that he had once been a poet, and a very virulent one, too; the sort of man who would produce a slim volume bound in squashy mauve leather at the drop of a hat, on the subject of sunsets or pixies...it was golf and the love of a good woman that saved Rodney Spelvin."

For Wodehouse, as for me, the poetic impulse is the product of a debilitating condition, in its effects resembling malaria, which seizes hold of its victims at moments of weakness and reduces them to gibbering wrecks.

Rodney Spelvin was a poet redeemed by golf. Could a poet be redeemed by mountaineering? Perhaps Andrew Greig would count as such a case. However, there are many counter-examples of mountaineers who, most regrettably, have succumbed to poetry, usually with dire results. The official Songs of our older Clubs (except for our own) bear ample testimony to this embarrassing tendency. The Song of the Yorkshire Ramblers, composed by three mountaineers, whom I will forbear to name, provides a grim example:

> Forty in round numbers are
> England's counties great and small
> And of these shall ever stand
> Yorkshire, greatest of them all;
> Shouldering the stalwart North,
> Buttress staunch and true is she;
> Is there county can compare
> *With her of the Ridings three?*

Of course, the problem with mountaineering as a cure for poetry is that it offers too many subjects apparently fit for poetic treatment. That is, there are plenty of non-mountaineering mountain poets, whereas there are no golf poets – golfing or otherwise, since golf is gratifyingly barren of topics suited for poetry. So golf, darts or snooker are much more promising antidotes than mountaineering.

These prejudices declared, it will be obvious that my own interest in the writings of Victorian Scottish mountaineers is not by any means a literary one: rather, it has been historical. I first became involved with their writings in the late 1960s when I served as apprentice to Geoff Dutton, who was at that time Editor of our Journal. Its first 10 volumes – up to 1909 – are a wonderful evocation of climbing when everything was new, unspoiled and innocent – hills, crags and climbers alike. Editors – even sub-editors – enjoyed a Club copy of the entire run of Journals as a perquisite of office, so I was able to comb through this early material thoroughly. I began this reading with the usual set of derogatory opinions: that the early climbers were technically incompetent; that they were old and portly; that they were hampered by great difficulties of travel and of access, etc. As I continued to read, I abandoned these attitudes one by one and came instead to the view that mountaineering in the 1890s was much the same as mountaineering in the 1960s and 1970s, but much more amusing, since so few were doing it, and since so little had been done.

Behind the beards and moustaches, below the glengarries and deerstalkers, there were extremely fit men in their twenties and early thirties. They reached their mountains using efficient and regular trains supplemented by bicycles and a plentiful supply of ponies and carriages: indeed, many hills could be reached more easily then than today. The absence of huts was no hindrance, since every Highland glen was populated, providing food and shelter near to every mountain.[2] And I was able to show that technical standards – particularly on ice climbs and mixed routes – reached a level in the 1890s that they did not regain until the 1950s. Harold Raeburn's winter ascents of Crowberry Gully (Buachaille) and Green Gully (Ben Nevis) and William Naismith's winter ascent of the North-east Buttress (Ben Nevis) were ignored or forgotten by the next generations of climbers.[3] No doubt they held the same prejudiced views as I did, and never thought to consult the record. Nor was this Victorian competence confined to 'stars' like Naismith and Raeburn. At the Club's Easter Meet at Fort William in 1896 all the great ridges of Ben Nevis were climbed, and the Tower Ridge was ascended by five separate parties.

The rockclimbers of the 1890s, although perhaps less enterprising, expressed surprisingly modern views and interests. For example, the Club's founder Naismith zealously explored many low-level crags and quarries. His friend Gilbert Thomson wrote in 1892 that:

"Saturday afternoons and summer evenings (or mornings, sometimes) might be well spent, not in roaming over roads or moorland, but in hunting up dainty bits of rockclimbing and the like where there was sufficient difficulty to keep the faculties up to the mark. A precipice 20ft. high does not sound very serious, but there may be more fun and real climbing in getting up and down such a place than there is in ascending the 4406ft. of Ben Nevis."[4]

In this after-hours fashion Naismith and Thomson explored the Whangie and Loudon Hill and other small crags within easy reach of Glasgow. Later, in Edinburgh, Raeburn and William Inglis Clark made illegal ascents of the fine little routes in the quarried faces of Salisbury Crags. Enthusiasm for small crags was not confined to these fanatics: a post Annual Dinner Meet held late in 1892 at the Whangie and attended by Horace Walker, Alpine Club President, was described by Thomson:

"The whole hill and moor was covered with a coating of soft snow, and the rocks themselves presented a very wintry appearance, which the sense of touch fully confirmed. The crevices were filled with snow and ice, many parts were festooned with icicles and the difficulty of scrambling was considerably increased. An hour or two, however, was very enjoyably spent in various pieces of fancy climbing, the concluding part being done to the accompaniment of a fierce snowstorm, which pelted us well as we made our way back across the moor."

Four years later the Journal carried an article by another friend of Naismith's – Fraser Campbell – about 'bouldering'[5]. It proposed the formation of a Boulder Society and was illustrated by minutely tedious drawings of boulders – this at a time when the Highlands were largely unexplored and large virgin buttresses and faces lay conveniently to hand! Campbell had the decency to allow that "it must be admitted that the exercise of boulder climbing is almost purely athletic, but the training to nerve and muscle may stand the climber in good stead upon some more important occasion".

Perhaps the clearest expression of this early interest in climbing for climbing's sake came from John Hart Bell, who 100 years ago wrote a short piece for the Journal entitled *A Purely Climbing Ideal* [6]. Bell was a fine climber who made many good routes throughout Scotland. Perhaps his best-known efforts were ascents of the Sannox face of Cîr Mhór in 1895, of the Church Door Buttress of Bidean in 1898, and a second ascent of the Waterpipe Gully (Skye) in 1896. He had the misfortune to share the same name and a middle initial with a much later Bell – James Horst Brunneman Bell – who became very well known. As a consequence, many of John Bell's climbs were credited in our guidebooks to James Bell, conferring unparalleled longevity and potency on the later Bell. John Bell's short article attempted to describe what constituted an ideal climb:

"In my opinion, chiefly four things [make a climb ideal]. It should be *new*. It should be *continuous*. It should be *difficult*, yet, once started, it should be the *easiest available*." [my emphases].

I doubt whether a modern climber would answer Bell's question differently. Perhaps more salient than the points that he includes are those that he omits. For example, there is no mention of length of route, of a mountain setting or of the quality of rock. And these, I am sure, would have figured in definitions offered by climbers from the Twenties through the Seventies.

Bell goes on to remark that:

"When a man needs all the mountain knowledge that he has, and all his skill and muscle to take him up the next few feet, he is not likely at that moment to pay much attention, even although the sun may be setting in a flood of red and gold over the sea within his view. If at the last hole in a game of golf a man is putting for a half, he won't at that moment think of the ever-changing sounds and sights of the sea, or of the cloud shadow moving across the hill."

So a romantic mountain ambience is not at all an essential ingredient of Bell's ideal climb. Wodehouse would ,of course, have been greatly warmed by these vigorous anti-poetic sentiments of Bell's and by his sound understanding of the golfing priorities!

To summarize the tendency of these remarks, the Victorian Scottish mountaineer may, without much difficulty, be seen as the next worst thing to a sport climber. He did not care whether he was on a high crag or on some miserable lowland escarpment or roadside boulder. The climb was the thing: not where it was, nor how long it was and certainly not whether you might watch the sunset from it!

Despite my opening remarks, I will now attempt to make a few observations on the qualities of writing desired and achieved by these mountaineers. Naturally, the general standard of writing was high. In those days – before photography, film, and radio began to compete – the principal amusement was reading and the only forms of record were writing and drawing. So every educated person drew well and wrote well, since comfortable employment depended absolutely on these skills. They also wrote copiously. The early SMC numbered only 100 or so, yet they produced material enough for three Journals a year, each efficiently produced in six weeks from handwritten edited copy to printed product. In more recent times, working with material type-written or in electronic form, we manage only one issue a year, take about three months to get it published, and much of it is not worth reading. Were we to produce three issues, it is doubtful whether the members would take the trouble to read them.

Much of Victorian writing is nevertheless somewhat dull. Perhaps the worst case is Hugh Munro. Munro contributed 85 articles and notes over a period of more than 20 years. As a historical record of events and facts they are exemplary: dates are always given, his companions are fully identified, the weather, mountain conditions and events of the day are accurately described. But there is almost no humour, very little account of his thoughts, hopes or fears, and little or no evocation of the mountain scene beyond an occasional estate agent's catalogue of distant summits visible from the summit reached. And this is a considerable shame, since Munro's climbing was certainly interesting. Much of it was done alone and in winter: alone since he was not much liked – perhaps due to his habit of talking incessantly – and in winter because, being a landowner himself, he was reluctant to climb in summer where the owner might take his trespassing amiss. In his declining years, when he was struggling to complete the ascent of the 538 Tops of his famous Tables while suffering from worsening rheumatism, he adopted the compromise method of climbing through summer nights – a practice which sometimes resulted in severe confusion and error.[7]

While most of our Victorian mountaineers wrote in the same stuffy style as Munro, describing their climbs in military manner, there were some exceptions. I will draw attention here only to Norman Collie and to Joseph Stott, our first Editor, who initiated 114 years of continuous publication in 37 fat volumes with the hapless admonition: "Let thy words be few!"

Collie's colourful account of his winter ascent of Tower Ridge in 1894 is well-known. It was entitled *Divine Mysteries of the Oromaniacal Quest* and signed 'Orlamon Linecus', an anagram of his name with added Latin masculine suffix – *us*.[8] It was written in the manner of Bunyan's *Pilgrim's Progress* as a religious tract, but with intrusions modelled on alchemical or Rosicrucian writings. The two excerpts that follow describe the approach to the Ridge and the conquest of the Great Tower and give the flavour well:

"[They saw] the great Mountain, the Immensity of Greatness, the majestic Silence, the prodigious Dampness, the Height, the Depth, in shape like a great Dome, whereof the base is in the floods and the waters, whence issueth forth delectable springs, welling up for ever, continually ascending, yet ever flowing downwards… Then behold before them rose hugeous rocks and bulky stones standing on end facing to the north, where the ice and snow tarry from one winter even until the following, for in those places the sun shines not, neither are found the comfortable soft and juicy breezes of the south; there the brood of the black Crow and the white vapours and comprehensive congelations of the Mistus Scotorum are produced. So were the three Brethren sore amazed but as yet could see not even the first matter of the work.

'But presently came they to a great rock, a majestic tower; here were they perforce compelled to depart to the right hand, placing themselves in steep and perilous positions on slopes of ice, which downwards seemed to end in the empty air, even in the great void …Still all things have an end at last, – good Wine, Pinnacles, Spires, cabalistic Emblems, and oromaniacal Wanderings, even the green Sauce of the philosophers and the pythagoric Mustard of the Great Master himself, spoken of by Alcofribas Nasier in his merrie work. So did the Three find the perilous passage across the headlong steep finish. Then did they pass onwards to the Labyrinth, the rocky Chaos, and greatly did they marvel at the exceeding steepness thereof; so that only by great perseverance, turning now to right and now to left, were they able to break themselves free from the bonds and entanglements, and climb sagaciously upwards to the summit of the great tower."

While there is a self-indulgent immaturity about the 'Quest', Collie's handling of this bizarre style is assured and its application to mountain narrative is certainly innovative and tolerably successful. A later piece by Collie which also exhibits unusual qualities of style is *A Reverie*.[9] The latter part of this is a fairly straightforward account of exploration of the Central Gully and Buttress of Coire Mhic Fhearchair on Beinn Eighe. But the first part consists of several pages of a 'stream of consciousness' report of an evening spent alone with his pipe in his Campden Grove rooms, mulling over future plans, past deeds and present duties. Here is a brief example:

"By this time my pipe is out. Where are these matches? I know the last time I saw them they were on the corner of the table. I shall look for them presently. In the meantime, my thoughts have taken a fresh plunge, and I follow them with a feeling of languid interest. Where on earth are they going? I see the head political officer of the Gilgit district playing golf on the Maidan above Astor, amongst the stately pines on the Himalayan mountains, whilst ranged round me are the snow-peaks and the glaciers. Those wonderful mountains! What magnificent outlines, what grandeur, what mystery, what! … Stop! Can I be growing sentimental? It must have been the Stilton or the sardines that have produced this particular physiological sensation. Yes, without doubt, the sardines, for now do I remember having read long ago, in a goodly book of right pleasant and entertaining anecdotes, a story, a most sentimental story, all about two Sardines, who lived and loved amongst the purple waves of the roaring Adriatic. But that is another story."

This style may not be particularly interesting nor very successful, but it shows that Collie had a taste for experimental writing and is a tribute to the taste and tolerance of his editor, William Douglas. In the second part of the *Reverie* Collie concludes his account of the climb with a sarcastic rejection of the poetic impulse (already trivialized in the preceding excerpt as a mere by-product of over-indulgence in sardines):

"It is now evening, and I ought, if orthodox, here to insert a description of the sunset, to become suddenly poetical, to talk about 'The sun-god once more plunges into the baths of ocean'. The sea too is always useful at such moments. 'Banks of sullen mist, brooding like a purple curtain,' &c., sounds well; and one must not forget 'the shadows of approaching night,' they form a fitting background for the gloomy and introspective spirit which ought to seize upon one at this particular psychological moment. 'The tumbled fragments of the hills, hoary with memories of forgotten years,' come next, with a vague suggestion of solitude, which should be further emphasised by allusions to 'the present fading away, and being lost in the vast ocean of time, a lifetime being merely a shadow in the presence of these changeless hills.' Then, to end up, mass the whole together, and call it an 'inscrutable pageant'; pile on the shadows, which must grow blacker and blacker, till 'naught remains but the mists of the coming night and darkness'; and if you have an appropriate quotation, good, put it in! What the party really did was to hurry down into Allt a' Choire Dhuibh Mhor, and hasten with more or less empty insides to the 'machine' and dinner."

The first Editor, Joseph Stott, did not much care for this sort of bathos. In a letter to Douglas,[10] he complained that "the Oromaniacal Quest is amusing, but so damnably vague that, but for the note in *Notes and Queries*, you would not know what they'd been up to on Ben Nevis". Stott had firm views about how mountaineering should be described but he was generally scathing about the lifeless narratives usually produced. In another letter to Douglas[11] he complained bitterly that his beloved Journal had become full of "miles, feet and minutes, and endless dissections of the unhappy points of the compass. To me these are really little more interesting than an architect's specification for building a stane dyke!" Instead what Stott required was "something in which I can hear the roaring of the torrent, and see the snows, and the brown heather, and the clouds and scud flying athwart the blue above the rocky peaks…something which will set my pulses beating, and conjure up dear old Scotland!"

Naturally, we should expect to find evocative descriptions of this sort in Stott's own writings, and indeed we do. However, they are usually over-written and sometimes nauseatingly sentimental – the very style that Collie found so uncongenial.[12]

We have, I think managed to improve a lot on the efforts of the Victorians. We know now that humour is indispensable in mountain narratives, that some account of the thoughts of climbers adds life and colour, and that dialogue – wholly avoided by the Victorians – helps as a vehicle for humour, gives the characters in our narratives the semblance of independent life and draws the reader into the scene more intimately. There is occasional deployment of all three ingredients in earlier writings (Mary Mummery's account of the Teufelsgrat is an outstanding example,[13] as are many of Dorothy Thompson's narratives[14]), but it was perhaps not until Tom Patey and Allan Austin that the most compelling evidence favouring the use of this mixture was provided.

Other ingredients are desirable, too: fine writing, of course, and, although he did not have the trick of it himself, the missing ingredient that Stott complained about – evocation of the mountain scene. There is great drama in the scenes of mountaineering and I do not think that modern writers convey that drama any more successfully than did the Victorians. Certainly Patey and Austin did not do so. Perhaps this is because, as John Bell observed, the activity of climbing is so engrossing that the dramatic aspect of the scene escapes us. Indeed, it may be indispensable in technical climbing to keep the imagination under wraps. "This hold is OK," we say, "and this one too. So I might as well be lounging on a street corner. No problem here. Up I go." and never think about the difficulties ahead or of the clutching void below.

If there is a weakness in modern mountain writing, then I would locate it here. As a cure we might study writers of the period between the Victorian era and the Sixties, such as Claude Schuster and Bill Murray, who both knew well how to evoke, with a light touch, the drama of the mountain scene. Here my taste in reading, announced at the start, makes its point, for Stout and Wodehouse were nonpareils in the use of wit and dialogue in first-person narratives, and the narratives of Conan Doyle, of course, were effectively film-scripts in which the drama of every scene was perfectly conveyed. Oddly enough, in view of his attitude towards poetic or sentimental display, Collie occasionally made the effort to capture in writing the strong impression which mountain scenery made on him. When he did so, he succeeded very well. Master of all types of climbing, Collie seemed determined to master all styles of writing, too. The closing paragraphs of his *A' Chuilionn*[15] are everything that poor exiled Stott would have wished for. Although there is too much of the prose-poem about these descriptions for modern tastes (and certainly for mine), those who know the Cuillin well will recognise the mysterious mountain essences which Collie strives to characterize here.

"The individuality of the Coolin is not seen in their summits, which are often almost ugly, but in the colour of the rocks, the atmospheric effects, the relative largeness and harmony of the details compared with the actual size of the mountains, and most of all in the mountain mystery that wraps them round: not the mystery of clearness, such as is seen in the Alps and Himalayas, where range after range recedes into the infinite distance till the white snow peaks cannot be distinguished from the clouds, but in the obscure and secret beauty born of the mists, the rain, and the sunshine in a quiet and untroubled land, no longer vexed by the more rude and violent manifestations of the active powers of nature. Once there was a time when these peaks were the centre of a great cataclysm; they are the shattered remains of a vast volcano that ages since poured its lavas in mighty flood far and wide over the land; since then the glaciers in prehistoric time have polished and worn down the corries and the valley floors, leaving scars and wounds everywhere as a testimony of their power; but now the fire age and the ice age are past, the still clear waters of Coruisk ripple in the breeze, by the lochside lie the fallen masses of the hills, and the shattered debris left by the ice, these harbour the dwarf hazel, the purple heather, and the wild flowers, whilst corrie, glen, and mountain-side bask in the summer sunlight.

"But when the wild Atlantic storms sweep across the mountains; when the streams gather in volume, and the bare rock faces are streaked with the foam of a thousand waterfalls; when the wind shrieks amongst the rock pinnacles, and sky, loch, and hill-side is one dull grey, the Coolin can be savage and dreary indeed; perhaps, though, the clouds towards the evening may break, then the torn masses of vapour, tearing in mad hunt along the ridges, will be lit up by the rays of the sun slowly descending into the western sea, robing the gloom with a vesture of diverse colours, of which the threads are purple and scarlet, and the embroideries flame; and as the light flashes from the black rocks, and the shadows deepen in the corries, the superb beauty, the melancholy, the mystery of these mountains of the Isle of Mist will be revealed. But the golden glory of the sunset will melt from off the mountains, the light that silvered the great slabs will slowly fail, from out the corries darkness heralding the black night will creep with stealthy tread hiding all in gloom; and last of all, behind the darkly luminous, jagged, and fantastic outline of the Coolins the glittering stars will flash out from the clear sky, no wind will stir the great quiet, only the far-off sound, born of the rhythmic murmur of the sea waves beating on the rock-bound shore of lonely Scavaig, remains as a memory of the storm."

[1] In *Nothing Serious*. Herbert Jenkins, 1950.

[2] See 'Transports of Delight' in Peter Drummond and Ian Mitchell's *The First Munroist*, Ernest Press, 1993.

[3] 'The First Scottish Ice Climbers'. *SMCJ*, 1972, 30, 48-57.

[4] 'Practice Scrambles'. *SMCJ*, 1892, 2, 8-12.

[5] 'On Bouldering'. *SMCJ*, 1896, 4, 52-56.

[6] *SMCJ*, 1904, 8, 1-3.

[7] E.g. the well-known debacle on An Scarsoch, *SMCJ*, 1909, 10, 230, repeated in *SMCJ*, 1989, 34, 219-227.

[8] *SMCJ*, 1894, 3, 151-157.

[9] *SMCJ*, 1898, 5, 93-102.

[10] Headed 'Wellington, 22/10/94'. This letter and others identified below were preserved by Douglas and are deposited in the National Library. The Stott letters are reproduced in my 'Dear Douglas'. *SMCJ*, 1990, 34, 388-399.

[11] Headed 'Wellington, 7/2/95'.

[12] See my 'Stott's Mountaineering Club', *SMCJ*, 1974, 30, 257-263 for numerous grotesque examples.

[13] In A. F. Mummery. *My Climbs in the Alps and the Caucasus*. Fisher Unwin, 1895.

[14] See *Climbing with Joseph Georges*. Titus Wilson, 1962.

[15] *SMCJ*, 1897, 4, 259-266.

SKYE IS THE LIMIT

By Julian Lines

TROPHY CRACK was one of those routes that had been playing on my subconscious for well over a decade. Did I have the audacity to solo it? It felt really tempting and on completion would leave me with a reckless sense of pleasure and an eternal memory.

April 2003, and it was time for my trip to Skye, the forecast of two sunny days and no midges to contend with was a real opportunity and one not to be missed.

On arriving in Glen Brittle, I had little incentive as the mist was down over the Cuillin and darkness was imminent. However, after a brief spell of procrastinating, I made my way through the gathering gloom up to my usual haunt in Coire Lagan. During daylight, it is a beautiful spot, a clear blue lochan idling in secrecy among the dark chocolate coloured spires. The lochan only allocates you a small shale/mud beach to pitch a tent on, in close proximity to a plethora of dreamy boulders. These boulders lure you on to try the beautiful moves they have to offer, but, like the 'Sirens', there is malice here. It's akin to playing catch with an angle grinder and, in return for graceful movement, bloodied fingertips are your reward. Gritstone is soap in comparison to this stuff!

I arrived in the dark and started walking through the lochan in the mist. Within minutes the tent was up and I was cocooned in my bag, staring at the walls wondering what the morning would bring. Deep into the night the patter of rain tinkling on the fly sunk my hopes a little. Tents always amplify sound I assured myself, while hoping the whole trip was not going to be a total waste of time.

Morning light, visibility is down to 100ft. and, cursing lamely, I curl back up into the embryo position. Some time later, lying on my back and carefully studying the guide, a direct ray of the sun's energy makes contact with the tent and, like a cold-blooded reptile, I mentally and physically metamorphose in a split second, springing out of my nylon tomb and into the awaiting world. The mist still embraced those dark menacing summits but the higher cloud dispersed gradually to produce those lovely azure patches bringing heat and hope.

The only crag to have the mid-morning sun in April was on the south buttress of Sgurr Dearg. I remembered eyeing an unclimbed central slabby arête up there some years before and, as I looked up, there it was winking at me. A beautiful edge of perfect gabbro basking in the sun and casting its shadow onto the wall behind, making it even more appealing. Once again, could this be mythology repeating itself? The edge peering down on me like 'Circe', trying to lure me on and kill me in cold blood. Am I the suitor she is looking for? Will I fall victim to such atrocities? I consider myself typically humble, a Hobo! Not a warrior, I have no hardware, just two slabs of sticky rubber and some white powder and quite possibly the wrong white powder for the unknown mission ahead.

After 20 minutes I arrive at a small oasis beneath this foreboding edge, where a burbling spring emerges out of the base of the cliff producing this small area of pure green, springy moss. The adjacent route is aptly named *Styx* (HVS), another omen, was I going to hell? A perfect wall of gabbro is bounded on the left by this arête and, with the sun's energy on my back, this seemed light years from hell. I started with caution up a thin basalt dyke to a resting point. Then I had to make a decision, the flake on the right or the arête on the left, I decided to thinly move out to the jug on the arête. Committed now, the Gods seemed to smile kindly on me as huge ladder holds just kept emerging all the way to a comfortable ledge at 25m. The remainder looked easier and it was. Pleasant climbing up cracks and slabs on warm rough rock.

The pitiless *Hobo* (E3) was born.

Soon I was back down at the lochan, the sky had ripened and flourished into a deep shade of blue but, disappointingly, a certain keenness to the April wind that stopped me spiralling into total lethargy.

It was time for *Trophy Crack*. From the lochan there is a dyke like path, which cuts across the base of the west face of Sgurr Sgumain, a scramble in parts, it provides quick access to Sron Na Ciche. The sun was arcing across the sky, but not yet enough to touch the high, looming face above. When it does, the face portrays its age, the shadows of the routes are like wrinkles. *Cioch Direct* (1907) being the first wrinkle to appear. Fifty years on and *Trophy Crack* (1956) adds another. Others will form, the face is immortal. More wrinkles, more wisdom and more worshippers. But I still haven't calculated how a Cioch grows out of a face!

Scrutinising the face above, I found a patch of grass out of the wind and buckled down to some serious sun bathing to speed up the rate of my own wrinkle growth. The earth's rotation is slow and I was becoming impatient watching the huge shadow diminish all too slowly. The rays of sun gradually caressed the tip of the Cioch, alas, the sun's best notions did not make it grow, it remained sombre and motionless.

Cioch Grooves (HVS), first climbed in 1957, seemed like the logical start on this 900ft. bastion of impeccable gabbro. Although the first pitch was rather wet in places, it was fun on immaculate rock, up slabs and cracks. The wall at the start of the second pitch was rather scary, but when I arrived at the crux thin traverse, it was all quite readable and positive. The next pitch gave immaculate jamming leading to the terrace.

ArrowRroute (VD) was next on the agenda. I bet this puts the fear of God into most V.Diff. leaders, an absolutely amazing piece of low angled rock, perfect and near protectionless. Sixteen years before, at the tender age of 18 I had climbed *Slab Corner* (D). I remember feeling safe in the

Malcolm McMahon on the traverse, pitch 3 of Labyrinth, Arran. Photo: Alastair Matthewson.

corner and just looking out across the exposed *Arrow Route* scared the shit out of me! I now savoured the next five minutes of fine high-quality climbing making my own path up its dimples and contours. Moreover, what could be better than sun on top of the Cioch where I stretched out and took a short catnap.

Trophy Crack (E1) was not, however, revelling in the sun and I thought it was rather unjust to have to climb in the shade. It was chilly and a low level of anxiety was pumping round my veins. A pleasant little grass platform lies at the base of this route, and weirdly, it gives peace of mind to a soloist, a haven among hostilities. The start was steep and powerful and, after 15m of brilliant sustained climbing, I came to realise that it was not as slabby as I thought it would be. I smiled to myself as I recounted this being a Pat Walsh route.

I met Pat once at a party, a jovial sort, short with grey hair, even at 70 he looked bloody strong. He seemed the sort that if you asked him for an arm wrestle there would be a broken ulna splattered over the table, and you would be knocked unconscious from the fumes of pure malt (quite possibly a Talisker) to ease the pain! What a legend, and, if I had had more time to listen, I'm sure the sagas would have burbled out of him. This route seemed to typify him, being constantly sustained and somewhat traditionally powerful.

A piece of white tat hung out a few feet below the belay so I assumed this was the crux but it turned out okay. I remember looking down and placing my feet on some dimples and the glare reflecting back in my face off the *Arrow Route* slab which was now basking in the sun 50m below. I savoured the moment and the atmosphere then leisurely cruised up the perfect second pitch.

My inner happiness on completion was cut extremely short by an icy persistent wind. I had to keep moving. The sun was still high in the sky and I realised that the west face of Sgurr Sgumain would be in the sun. I had read there was a recommended classic there called *The Klondyker* (HVS) which sounded like it needed to be searched out. I had pre-written the description down on a piece of paper which I had slipped down my pants hoping it would catch in the elastic at the waist.

Another impeccable piece of climbing as I reached the ledge halfway up the second pitch. This is where things all went slightly wrong. An obvious crack went diagonally left and there was a direct line, which looked improbable. About this time there were about five people at the lochan on their way down from the summits, they saw me and, as I didn't want to give them cause for concern and scare them shitless, I sat down in this niche and meditated. Staring out over the Isle to the sea and infinity, no finer country in the world than Scotland when the weather is good, I mused.

Back to reality, back to being between a rock and a hard place. The holds dictated my movement straight up but I had lost my rhythm and

Neist – Neil Smith high on Bad Dream E3, with Roger Lupton. Photo: Colin Moody.

became a little ruffled. The roof seemed hard for the grade, a poor jam in the lip but the feet were good. One move at a time then big laybacks. On up to the terrace where I pull out my description, memorise the last three pitches and climb them in little time. I remember the 4c pitch being space-walking on buckets, one of the most exposed and out there VS pitches I had ever done.

My feet were aching and swimming inside my boots and I thought that was enough for one day, but there was still about three hours of sun above the horizon. It was a perfect day and they do not come too often in Scotland. I knew exactly what was nagging at my subconscious, it was the words, Vulcan Wall. The sun had arced sufficiently to soak the wall in glittering light and access was little more than five minutes from the top of *The Klondyker* across scree. I knew I would kick myself if I didn't.

Within 15 minutes, I had just completed the most enjoyable and perfect 70m of HVS climbing in Scotland, if not the UK. Now was a good time to call it a day and prepare my itinerary for tomorrow's play. At least if the weather turned foul this was not a wasted trip.

Cheese, oatcakes, beetroot and tuna was the gourmet meal, which awaited me. On these short trips I tend not to bother with cutlery or stoves and anyway, it's a good way to detoxify for a few days and feel healthy.

It was another restless night with little sleep, my thermarest did not hold the air in a uniform manner and was more akin to a waterbed tossing me in all directions. I had melted it in Spain (on a deep-water soloing festival) while trying to sleep over a high wattage light, set into the pavement in a harbour area. The light was so strong that I decided to sleep over it to curb the brightness but I was burned for my chivalry. I lay with the tent open just staring up and gazing at the stars, Ursa Major, Ursa Minor...Ursula Andress that was about my limit. The wind picked up, buffeted the tent and rendered me sleepless.

At last, the light was dawning and it was time to get up and head over the ridge to the Coireachan Ruada face. The descent route *Rotten Gully* lived up to its name, but it was really sheltered over on the east face. I stood awestruck at the size of the cliffs and the blatantly obvious unclimbed lines. It was like the cliff that time forgot. Moving round to the foot of *King Cobra* (E1) and *Dawn Grooves* (VS) the face loomed menacingly and far bigger than I had ever anticipated. I had decided only to do one route because the access was difficult and time consuming so *King Cobra* it was to be. The sun was a sulky orange behind some thin cloud and only about 5° above the horizon. Shit, it can't have been much past six in the morning (I never wear a watch), was I properly awake? My legs felt rather tired.

With a written description shoved down my pants again, I ventured up into unlikely looking and hostile territory. 45m. of scrambling on dark and shattered basalt began to fray my soul. I felt like a soldier on the front line told to go out and fight an unseen enemy with no weapons. If I had any intelligence I should be running for cover, but, oh no: "It's bound to get better it's a classic!" I thought to myself. Soon the line took shape, a sort of corner with large holds. The enormity of the cliff and its remoteness was making me rather anxious which in turn ran a low level of adrenaline through my body making me tremble slightly and lurch for holds. The whole scene was all rather pathetic and it was about to get significantly worse.

Having passed a rusty peg I swung right to the base of the bottomless crux groove where I stood on this ledge about 18ins. long and 6ins. wide visibly shaking with more than 60m. of space beneath my feet. This so-called ledge was written up in Tom Patey's *One Man's Mountains* as being a "sloping foothold, large enough for a roosting seagull".

I was now standing there shaking and trying to work out how to do this almost holdless groove and thinking what a good effort by Bonington. Two rusty stains in the crack in the back of the groove were no doubt from the first ascent. My mind wandered as I built this picture in my head of the two stalwarts hammering in these long lost relics and doing battle with the groove back in 1960.

Hey, snap out of the reverie you bloody fool! The reality was I had to negotiate a blank groove more than 200ft. up with no ropes and a body akin to a sapling blowing in a Force 8 gale, just marvellous!

I carefully studied the groove and worked out all the options discarding certain holds and searching for anything useful. All I had was a shallow fingerlock for the right hand and a good hold on the right wall that was too low for the hand and too high for the foot. The left hand was a poor layaway, but there seemed to be better holds higher up. They were red herrings. The feet were just on smears on either side of the groove. In a short time, my feet were swimming in my boots so I had to down climb 15ft. to a ledge, tighten my boots and try to relax. Try doing yoga when you are frightened – it is impossible.

Soon I was back up at the groove, I bridged across to a smear, this was unbearably frightening – the exposure gripped me something akin to a rabbit being frozen in the headlights of a 10-ton truck. Movement seemed to be in slow motion, right foot up to toe smear in the groove: "Wow I am still sticking." I thought to myself, now I will just step down have a wee breather and then commit next go. But then it all went horribly wrong. I tried to put my foot back down but could not bring myself to re-weight the right foot in case I slipped. In that split second my unconscious and conscious minds went into a state of combustion. For once, there was no indecision between them, preserve life no matter what. The adrenalin surged and my soul had changed from being frightened and frozen to a "Give it everything you've got and climb for your life" scenario. I slapped to a reverse layaway then to a good lock and then out to a bridge, the holds were better now and I started really enjoying the pitch and the exposure in this smooth groove. It seemed to be all over to soon.

Above, the climbing went back to the shattered basalt type, but the holds were reasonable, not a place to be soloing on though. No one had warned me of this route but then again, I didn't know of anyone who had done it, possibly because I never asked. The word 'classic' certainly took on a new meaning that day.

A huge overhang loomed above me and two spikes stuck out of the ledge I occupied, just like two fangs. Maybe that is where they got the name *King Cobra*. Before I embarked on the next pitch, I studied my surroundings trying to take it all in and relax. The car-sized boulders at the base now took on the form of a shingle beach. I knew deep down I didn't want to be here, the rock was far from perfect and this worried me. I made doubly sure of every hold as I meandered my way up another 300ft. of interesting climbing, a jammed friend being the only sign of modern passage.

Thankfully, the ordeal was soon at an end atop the ridge in a refreshing wind. The descent, however, was arduous as I threaded my way down the east face from the notch on the ridge.

Back at the base of the cliff I glared up at the face the sheer size overwhelming me. The only words I could think of were: "Bloody idiot!." There's no way I would of soloed that had I first seen it, as it now was, in the full light of day.

I decided to scramble round by the Thearlaich Dubh gap and try *The Asp* (E2) and *Cons Cleft* (HVS). The sun was moving round and, being south-facing, both climbs would be in its light and not so sombre as the previous route. I dug out a semi-comfortable patch beneath the crag for some sun bathing and a snooze. Voices could be heard reverberating around the corrie. I tried to pick them out but could not until some ravens, obviously looking for food, hovered beside them and gave away their position.

I decided I was only going to do one route and I went for *The Asp*, a splitter chimney-cum wide crack line. Beautiful jams and thrutchy body positions led on upwards until my fleece caught on a huge needle of rock on the back wall and pulled it up out of its lodgement. After throwing it down, I went to jelly and wobbled my way back to terra firma.

"That's enough for one morning!"

With tail between my legs, I sloped off down to my tent in Coire Lagan for a siesta. I spent most of my relaxation time bubbling with anxiety for what lay ahead. At least, I knew this route was not to be as loose as *King Cobra,* albeit technically harder. When the sun was about 40° above the horizon in the western skies and hovering over the Minch, I realised it was time to release the tension and go. And so, with chalk bag strung round my waist and rock boots shoved down my jacket front like a huge pair of breasts, I made tracks for Eastern Buttress.

Climbing parties were strung out over Sron Na Ciche indulging in classics such as *Cioch West* (S) and *Wallworks Route* (VD). The face shone boldly in the evening light and soon I was standing at the base of Vulcan Wall. This time I had brought my newer boots, the first time I had used them on this trip. As usual with big solos, I tend to tie and re-tie my boots at least twice before an ascent, a weird subconscious kind of karma. If I was seconding the route I would not bother to tie the laces.

There is very little niggling psychology with soloing mountain routes. Once above 15m. you really are in the death zone anyway and it is just a case of do not fall. On gritstone, the routes rarely reach 15m, and sometimes soloing an E5 with a good landing has so much more 'peace of mind' than an E2 with a real bone-chewing landing.

The real beauty of soloing *Spock* (E3) was that the steep thuggish start really gets the blood flowing and leads you perfectly into the more delicate climbing above, the holds are always there and the rock is totally impeccable. It was like climbing in a trance enjoying the exposure and brilliance of the route. A few metres below the roof I climbed a move rather badly. There was 35m. of space below my feet and I knew at that point, while committing to a rockover, that if I slipped then…game over. In a strange way I was smiling through my inner being, with no state of anxiety or fear, my mind was playing out a version of me freefalling in slow motion and then nothing but happiness. Maybe this is due to the animal instincts from evolution, an inbuilt sense that all creatures have, but one that humans are losing in a civilised society. For instance, a gazelle in the clutches of a lion will do anything to escape its predator, but somehow, when the odds are stacked against it and it's caught between two huge paws it accepts its predicament and dies gracefully. It's all part of the evolutionary cycle. Humans have no predators and so, to acquire this natural fear, solo climbers position themselves between a rock and a hard place, add a sprinkling of gravity and…Hey Presto…but I don't fancy that opportunist raven up there pecking my eyes out. The higher I went the slower I moved, the holds were friendlier and I just took my time savouring every moment of the route's perfection.

On the way down, I tried to think quickly of anything else I could do in the allocated time between now and when the golden orb of the sun disappeared over the horizon. Deciding however, that I wanted to savour one of my most memorable solos ever, I went back to the tent and juggled with the some angle grinders until dusk had settled. After another *Cordon Bleu* meal I was lying face up in my tent peering out over to Sron Na Ciche and watching a climber on *Slab Corner*. It was rather bizarre to watch someone climbing upside down in near darkness.

GUIDEBOOK ODYSSEY

By Ted Maden

AUTHORS were being sought for the new edition of *The North-west Highlands District Guidebook.* Donald Bennet and Tom Strang were stepping down, having given long service as authors of recent editions of *The Western Highlands* and *The Northern Highlands* and then the first edition of *The North-west Highlands.* Dave Broadhead was in on the new edition from the beginning, I joined soon afterwards, and Alec Keith completed the group. Rob Milne succeeded Donald Bennet as series editor, and soon his e-mail transmissions were humming with messages commencing: "Hi, team." Nevertheless, it was clear to all of us from the outset that the size of the area to be covered demanded division of labour, especially for the fieldwork.

My assignment was the Northern part of the Western Highlands, from Glen Shiel and Glenelg to Glen Carron. This region is 'relatively' compact, but is larger than the English Lake District, for which Wainwright wrote his famous set of seven hillwalking guidebooks. Moreover, Glen Shiel and Kintail contain a high concentration of Munros, aptly dubbed 'Munropolis' by Dave Hewitt in *Walking The Watershed.*

I had compleated the Munros a few years previously, but not all of them by the best routes for the purposes of guidebook descriptions. I had done only a couple of the many Corbetts in the region. Therefore my aim for the region was to repeat all the Munros and do all the Corbetts. My journeys would be from Liverpool, following a precedent established by Graham McPhee long before the motorway era, when he worked on his Climbers Guide to Ben Nevis. I anticipated a few trips of about a week each and a few shorter ones. The reality was very different, but my long-distance commuting gave me a sense of identity with the many potential readers who would also travel long distances to the area. Here, then, is an account of my guidebook fieldwork odyssey.

The first short trip was in March 1997. Beinn Sgritheall seemed an attractive initial proposition. During the drive down Glen Shiel there were hints of the Kintail Curtain ahead, but I persevered over the Bealach Ratagain hoping for sunshine on the other side. I was met by low cloud and drenching drizzle. Lesson learned! Back to Cluanie, where the cloud base was now above Corbett level. Am Bathach was 'on'. My wife had given me a miniature tape-recorder for recording impressions during the fieldwork. This piece of technology served admirably throughout the campaign, except on this first hill, when, as I discovered that evening, I had failed to master the controls. The next day I ascended Meall Fuar-mhonaidh. This fine eminence overlooking Loch Ness is of less than

Corbett height and was not in the first edition of the Guidebook, but its merits were recognised by honorary inclusion in the Corbetts Guide. The cloud level was higher than yesterday. Clear air with occasional shafts of sunshine made for memorable views along the Great Glen and to the big peaks to the North-west. I was satisfied that my fieldwork had started. But there it stuck for six months, during which time no opportunity arose for a week-long visit.

Little white mice of panic:

By September further progress was becoming a matter of urgency. I opted for another short trip and drove to a B&B by Loch Lochy. During conversation over evening tea and cakes I mentioned the purpose of my visit. A Canadian guest quizzed me as to the possible hazards of solo hillwalking. I assured him that all was well if one took care.

Next morning I set off from the road head car park in Glen Affric. Mist filled the glen, but as I climbed Glen Affric's Sgurr na Lapaich the promise of blue sky above materialised. Mam Sodhail gave wonderful, far-reaching views. As I descended to the north the sun's rays were touching the slope exactly at grazing angle. This prompted some trivial pursuits-style mental arithmetic: at the equinox the sun was over the equator, at the solar noon the sun was at its highest in the sky, I was at 57° north, so the slope was 33°. I continued to Carn Eighe and then to the fine promontory of Beinn Fhionnlaidh. On the way to the latter I heard a distinctive clanking, which turned out to be emanating from a walker with a metal leg. We exchanged greetings. He had come up from Loch Mullardoch and was heading to Glen Affric. I did not think to inquire as to his starting point; most likely he had been ferried to the head of the Loch by boat. He was the only person I encountered all day.

Regaining Carn Eighe, I made good pace over Tom a' Choinich to Toll Creagach, where I arrived just after 6.30pm with sufficient daylight in hand for the descent. Afterwards an easy walk on a track and the road would take me back to the car. I paused briefly to take in the wild prospect. Benign cotton wool clouds had been building up over Loch Mullardoch, and one of these stealthily enveloped the summit. I set off down, resolving to check the compass soon. I had used it in the morning mist, and it had been transferred from its usual place in the top pocket of my rucksack to an anorak pocket, and the anorak was now at the bottom of the rucksack.

I emerged below the mist onto some level ground, decided I had come down too far left and traversed rightwards a bit. The lie of the land was not easy to reconcile with my expectations. I rationalised that the large loch below must be Loch Beinn a' Mheadhoinn. Soon I should see the road. I gained an uninterrupted view down to the loch shore. No road! Simultaneously, all sorts of things were not making sense. What were those big hills across the loch? Why was the sun's afterglow illuminating clouds in the east and not in the west? I retrieved the compass, hoping it would provide a reassuring explanation. Its message was brutally unambiguous. I was looking north. The loch below was Loch Mullardoch. I was halfway down a remote hillside, in fading light, the Mullardoch dam far away to the right, the intervening ground notorious for its deep, untracked heather. I was utterly alone. A phrase from Robin Smith's *Goofy's Last Climb* described my state: "...little white mice of panic whispered round the walls of the brain...".

What to do? Retrace my steps to the summit, arrive in moonless darkness and mist and seek the right descent? I was tired and this would be folly. The line of least resistance was to keep traversing, but the level ground soon ended and I met the first of the deep heather, on a steep hillside, with hidden holes. I was beginning to sweat profusely. Moreover, I was in fell-running shoes. I *had* to take care. I accepted the inevitable: I would have to descend. The ground got worse. After losing height I even considered bivouacking in the heather till daybreak, but I had made arrangements whereby I would be missed if I did not get back to civilization by about 10.00 pm. Down off the slope the heather was waist-deep on an ankle-twisting, knee-wrenching base and the last twilight was fading. I decided the loch shore might give easier progress. The water level was low, and fortunately, I had a head torch. After about an hour-and-a-half of slow, careful going I reached the dam.

There is no way across the top of the Mullardoch dam due to an impassable central tower. I already knew this, but I went to check anyway. In the darkness, and with my analytical faculties not at their best, it did not occur to me that there would be a road down from the south side of the dam. So after yet more thrashing around in heather and across two dry riverbeds beneath the dam I reached the road on the north side. Soon I was lucky. The first of the few buildings in the glen was a hostel housing some Danes on a deer-stalking holiday. They gave me beer and drove me down to Cannich, where the hotel I had booked into was still open. Next morning, some hillwalking guests gave me a lift up Glen Affric to my car. During the drive back to Liverpool my thoughts touched upon the question of whether, as a 60-something-year-old, I really should be doing this kind of project. I resolved to give it one more try.

Steady progress:

I made a two-day trip in a spell of good weather at the end of October after the stag stalking season had finished. Arriving soon after noon I did an enjoyable round of Meall Dubh and some of its secluded satellites, starting near the Loch Loyne dam. Access to this group has subsequently become more problematical due to new deer fencing and to parking restrictions near the dam. The next day I traversed Ben Killilan, Sguman Coinntich and Faochaig in superb, crisp conditions, with luminescent sunlight and deep autumnal shadows picking out the features of the Ling River basin and the Monar hills beyond, and in the middle of it all the solitary white speck of the Maol-bhuidhe cottage bothy. I walked down Glen Elchaig at nightfall beneath the dark mass of Carnan Cruithneachd and a starry sky. I was away from Killilan soon after 6pm and home in Liverpool before 2am.

A pattern was emerging. Short visits could be made between other commitments and to fit the weather. I had listed the hills into geographical zones and had a good idea of the various options: short versus long days, regional preferences to suit weather patterns. Visits lasting two or three days worked well. By making 'Alpine' starts from Liverpool I was able to do the motorway driving including the section through the Central Lowlands when the traffic was quiet and to make good use of daylight for the hills. Similar considerations led to relatively late departures at the end of the trips. I took adequate short rests in motorway service areas. I preferred midweek visits, particularly after my work in Liverpool changed to part-time. Given the somewhat strenuous nature of the visits including driving I favoured a Sybaritic mode of accommodation and cuisine, usually booking into B&Bs or hotels and dining at restaurants. Every intended hill day was productive, objectives often being chosen on the day to suit conditions.

Most of the walks were done solo, but early on I enjoyed two days on the Maoile Lunndaidhe to Lurg Mhor group of mountains with my former climbing mate Reg Pillinger, who was nearing his compleation of the Munros. Then Rob Milne, soon after taking over as editor, suggested that we meet up, which we did for the Cluanie Horseshoe. I was impressed by Rob's command of technology, which included phoning his office from the summit of A'Chralaig and checking the altitude with an aneroid contained in his wristwatch. Also I walked for various distances with people I met on some of the hills, sometimes mentioning the guidebook work, and, perhaps incautiously, the expected date of publication. Meanwhile, the project had been expanded by inclusion of the Grahams. These hills of seemingly modest height, which had recently been researched and written up by Andrew Dempster in his book *The Grahams*, offered attributes of remoteness, lack of footprints and, in some instances, a degree of seriousness that added interesting new features to the work.

From 2000 onwards the last of the fieldwork was being interspersed with the first drafts of writing. There was much healthy, even robust, mutual feedback, during the course of which my co-authors perceived that my grasp of historical matters was not especially strong. They were right; history had been my least favourite subject at school, and I had languished at the bottom of the class in that discipline. It now seemed timely to repair this deficiency, so one of my last field trips was devoted primarily to a remedial tour of brochs, castles, monuments and plaques. My attention to these objects was enhanced by the fact that the weather was unattractive for hillwalking, with low cloud and intermittent rain. However, I still had some unfulfilled hill objectives, among which were the remote Graham, An Cruachan, and the not quite so remote, Carn na Brebaig. These two hills can be accessed via Glen Elchaig, preferably by bicycle up the glen. During an evening diversion after the second day of history I discovered that I could hire a bicycle at Camas-luinie near the foot of the glen.

Next morning the weather remained unchanged, low cloud with a suggestion of rain, unattractive but not prohibitive. At 7.45am, in the car park of the Loch Duich Hotel where I had been staying, I placed the onus of decision upon a coin. Tails, I would turn left at the exit and drive home. It came heads. I turned right and drove to Camas-luinie and hired a bike. The first two miles of pedalling, to the start of the private road at Killilan, were flat. Then I narrowly avoided premature termination of the venture. I breasted a small hill, not expecting a descent on the other side. The brake handles were in an unfamiliar orientation and for a split second I could not locate them. A panicky grab brought them to hand and I thankfully regained control.

At the road head at Iron Lodge it was drizzling. I made heavy work of the walk up mist-clad Carn na Brebaig, perhaps due to a light breakfast and the unaccustomed effort of the cycle ride up the glen. A bite of lunch at Loch Mholcean reinvigorated me and I decided to press on past the head of the loch and look round the corner towards An Cruachan. The vantage point overlooked the Allt Coire nan Each tumbling down a wild V-shaped glen. The top of An Cruachan was truncated by cloud, which seemed to be lifting slightly. Tentatively at first, and then with a growing sense of purpose, I made my way along the overgrown right of way on the east flank of the glen, and thence up the hill. The summit is reputedly the most remote in Scotland from a public road. The cloud had now lifted, it was no longer raining and there were a few patches of sunlight. It was a magical place in the heart of wilderness, overlooking lochans, and ringed by higher mountains except to the west, where the Allt Coire nan Each becomes the Allt an Loin-fhiodha that passes lonely Maol-bhuidhe, then joining the Uisge Dubh to become the River Ling that flows to the sea at Loch Long. My return by way of Loch Mholcean to the bike at the road head at Iron Lodge, and a largely free-wheel ride down Glen Elchaig, were followed by the long, nocturnal drive home.

Last fling:

Meall Fuar-mhonaidh had been the first Graham of my campaign, though unwittingly so. An Cruachan was the final one. There remained seven Munros that I had climbed previously but had not managed to repeat during the guidebook work, and one Corbett that I had not done. By the summer of 2003 the writing had gone through multiple drafts, and for those few hills that I had still not visited during the campaign I had blended my own prior knowledge with available Scottish Mountaineering Trust descriptions. It was still possible to make small revisions to the text. At the end of June a short window of time for a trip coincided with a spell of good weather.

The Munros that I had not been able to revisit were those to the north of Loch Mullardoch and the Sgurr nan Ceathreamhnan group. Moreover, my strategy of short visits had not encouraged very long hill days; 12 hours had been my longest. In the text I had recommended the Mullardoch round as a possibility for fit and experienced hillwalkers, leaving open to individual preference the options of a single long day or an overnight camp, and the choice of how many of the 12 Munros to include. Alec had done the complete round in an impressive sub-12-hour time and had e-mailed me enthusiastically about it. I could not hope to emulate Alec's time, but I wanted to do the round in any shape or form. I decided to have a go.

I drove up one afternoon and evening in perfect conditions until reaching Inverness, where I was met by a haar. My plan was for a single big day with a very early start, requiring that I forgo the comforts of overnight accommodation. The gloomy haar persisted as I drove up Glen Cannich. I dossed down in the car at the road junction about a kilometre before the dam. After sleeping fitfully for about three hours I set off at 2am. Because of the cloud it was darker than I expected at this northern latitude and I carried a head torch. I was glad of this after the road ended just past the top of the dam, for the path soon became an abominable morass.

Despite my previous knowledge, and having described the way correctly for the book, I went wrong on the ascent of Carn nan Gobhar, taking a sketchy and energy sapping path up the east bank of the Allt Mullardoch instead of crossing the bridge and heading up the spur of Mullach na Maoile. The path faded out in a corrie. I was now between two layers of mist in improving light, but was navigating by compass from an imprecisely determined location. After some moderately steep ground in the second layer of mist I emerged onto a broad ridge, hoping I was to the east of and fairly near the summit of Carn nan Gobhar. This hope was dramatically realised by a parting of the clouds and a magical sunrise, the orange rays making a brilliant backdrop to tendrils of mist that continued to boil out of the corries, while the peaks all around became increasingly clear. I was prompted into a flurry of photography.

The Mullardoch Sgurr na Lapaich was swallowed up in cloud again before I reached the summit. I was in and out of cloud along An Riabhachan, but the sun was now gaining the upper hand, and the cloud dispersed as I descended the rocky ridge to the Bealach Bolla, giving a wonderfully clear prospect across the Monar basin. The ridge of the descent is in a supremely wild setting, and is also somewhat exposed and not a place to miscalculate, a point that I added in the final revision of the text.

Two walkers with big packs were descending from An Socach and we chatted at the bealach. They had walked along the shore of Loch Mullardoch the previous evening and had camped by the Allt Coire a' Mhaim. They were impressed by the amount of ground I had covered that morning. Nevertheless, I was off the pace for the full round, and on the summit of An Socach I felt the need for a rest and sustenance. It was 10am, spectacularly clear, and I enjoyed a superb all-round panorama, with the topography of my An Cruachan trek particularly well displayed. Still feeling somewhat tired, I descended towards the head of Loch Mullardoch, weighing options and even considering walking out along the north shore of the loch. However, on the lower slopes I began to feel the beneficial effects of my summit nosh and decided to go for a 'short' version of the round, omitting the Ceathreamhnan group.

At the river just west of the head of the loch I exchanged greetings with a party who had transatlantic accents. They were taking a noon break on a camping trek but I was unable to ascertain their itinerary; they said something about planning to walk along the loch and "maybe doing some of those Munros", They looked a little surprised when I splashed across the river without first removing my fell-running shoes.

A refreshing easterly breeze was blowing up the loch, but this did not reach round the corner into Gleann a' Choilich, and the midday heat was enervating. I filled my water bottle and made a slow ascent, with stints of step counting and short rests, to the Bealach Beag between Beinn Fhionnlaidh and Carn Eighe. A threesome who looked like parents and a sprightly teenager were making good time across the bealach and onto Fhionnlaidh. Given my slow pace I deemed it judicious to omit Fhionnlaidh and to proceed directly to Carn Eighe, which I toiled up in bottom gear.

During the ascent I had noticed wisps of mist spiralling into the air between Carn Eighe and Mam Sodhail. This had seemed odd on such a clear day. I now saw the explanation. Although the mist had dispersed by mid-morning from the northern glens it had persisted to the south, and even now filled Gleann nam Fiadh almost to the brim. Mindful of my previous experience on Toll Creagach I was apprehensive of the intentions of this sea of mist, and in the now cooler air I made my way with the limited haste I could muster along the length of the ridge. I arrived at Toll Creagach at about 7.30pm. The summit is for the most part dome-shaped. My previous error in the mist was explained but not condoned; instead of descending to the south I had veered west and then north-west, so dropping down towards Loch Mullardoch in the opposite direction to the dam and precipitating my long struggle along the south shore.

Subsequently, Alec had told me that when descending intentionally to the Mullardoch dam most of the heather can be avoided by continuing from Toll Creagach eastwards to the next, smaller peak before turning downhill. Now, however, the intervening bealach was swathed in mist from the south. Not wishing to chance my luck again with the obscuring vapours, I instead went down the north-east spur of Toll Creagach with my final destination clearly in view. I reached a little col before the slight rise to Creag a' Bhaca. To the right, steepish ground fell to the Allt Fraoch-choire (stream of the corrie of the heather) and I could not get a clear view down. So I contoured easily round to the left. And then I hit deep heather with an almost audible wham! It was still full daylight and I did not have as far to go as last time. The loch shore still seemed the best way, but the water level was higher than before. When I had less than a 100 horizontal metres to go I encountered a cliff that fell steeply for about 10m. into the water. This minuscule obstacle cost me 20 minutes of retracing steps, shinning over deer fences, ploughing through more heather and casting around until at last finding the way down to the road. I had been lucky with the low water the previous time. I part walked, part jogged to the car, drove down to Cannich, and relaxed in the manner to which I had become accustomed, in a B&B.

Footnote:
This description of my fieldwork for *The North-west Highlands District Guidebook* is a personal one, but the book has been very much a team effort. I thank my co-authors Dave and Alec, editor Rob, and production manager Tom Prentice as the major players.

NAE MAIR BLACK BUN

By M. G. Anderson

"You dinnae like Hogmanay? Ca' yersel a Scot?" My interlocuter paused to summon up all his reserves of amazement and contempt. Telling him that more days are lost to British Industry through alcohol etc, would have been a waste of breath. Besides I was used to being impugned for this heresy. If I am guilty of rejecting Scotland's civilisation at her zenith, so be it, but after one December 31, when I walked along Rose Street, saw the drunks stretched head to toe in the gutter and witnessed the bad-tempered fights between friends fuelled by the 'fiery cratur'. I decided enough was enough, although, one of the accessories to this festivity almost makes it all worthwhile. I am talking of Black Bun, that fruity concoction of sultanas and fly cemetery, which makes its fleeting appearance annually at this unhallowed hour.

I was planning to sip a quiet dram, bite down a bit of black bun and retire to bed, before friends in the Edinburgh JMCS, proud new owners of the Auld Smiddy in Dundonnell, invited me to join them. The offer of a retreat from the hullabaloo of Hogmanay, to the unsullied wilderness of Torridon was too good to refuse, so off we went. When we arrived, people were already settling in, laying out their sleeping bags, bagging the best places. Everyone laughing, even some singing, Glen Campbell's, *Galveston,* for no apparent reason, the usual high spirits at the beginning of a promising weekend. A homely glow was provided by the old furnace, crackling and creaking in a most satisfactory manner, but after years of disuse, prodding the blocked chimney with ice axes simply increased the general stour in the air, so that a smoky layer of cumulo-nimbus clouds nestled above the top bunks with the result that, at the end of the weekend we went home with sooty faces, hair clogged with carbon, the auld grey heids a lot happier and all of us coughing intermittently.

But even here, amid the wild and craggy splendours of the Western Highlands, the obligations of New Year couldn't be evaded. The locals, purely out of old fashioned Highland hospitality, had invited us to bring it in *a la Gaeltacht,* so that even I, the Hogmanay hermit, could hardly refuse without appearing selfish and discourteous.

Stepping outside the howff was a pleasant relief from the choke-damp within, the frost on the roof of the Smiddy a glittering white carapace under a crisp, starry sky. When we entered the hotel, still coughing and spluttering, no one greeted us. Lined up in front of the bar in an assortment of deerstalkers and flat caps, each hat sporting a medley of fishing flies, stood an almost motionless rank of drinkers, for all the world like a congregation at prayer. There was no hum of conversation, only a few indistinct orders breaking through the slurping and clinking. Any Englishman happening on this still-life would assume this was Scotland at its dourest, the toper's version of Sunday in the Kirk. But this was purely preparatory. Every man-jack of them was busily injecting the required tonnage of booze into his system in order to get up the requisite head of steam for the arduous night ahead. The muffled orders gradually distilled themselves. There was: "Pint O'heavy an' a hauf, Jimmy," or simply: "Hauf'n heavy, Jimmy."

Jimmy was moving like a whippet from end to end of the bar, dispensing refreshment without pause or interval. All the taps were on, and when one glass was filled its place was taken by a clean glass with ne'er a drop of spillage. And it *was* a clean glass. There was no malingering of the sort that you sometimes get: "In the same glass, then?" There was no doubt Jimmy was the hero of the year's end, the Stakhanov of the Bar.

Towards 10pm, the tempo increased to a frenzy. People were ordering double, treble and even quadruple rounds as the hour of doom approached, when the shutters clanged down on that awful final note. Would we all be flung out at closing time, forgotten by our hosts, and have to celebrate by the frozen lochside? This question was answered when our genial host – not Jimmy; he was merely a superior factotum – appeared and announced: "Ben the Hoose."

Once ensconced in the best room my social sloth took over, so I slunk into a remote armchair, but even hiding in a corner couldn't stop the torrent of whisky coming at me from all directions. A few nips was enough to tell me I'd had more than enough. Refusal was pointless, when my glass was half full, for them it was half empty. Putting my hand over the rim didn't staunch the deluge either. They simply poured over it. Luckily, there was a pot plant nearby. Nobody took any notice of my watering it with pure spirit, but later in life, when I became an environmentalist, I felt a bit guilty about that sozzled flower.

The return to the Smiddy was unmemorable, that is to say I have no memory of it. Getting into my pit was awkward, but eventually, both legs were in and, bodily logistics taken care of, I immediately fell asleep.

I was awoken by the first light of day peeking timidly through the slats of the shuttered door, as it slowly creaked open. Figures were creeping about in the shaft of dusty light coming from the doorway. A louder creak sent a spasm shuddering through my head, my hangover's First Footing.

"A Guid New Year tae yin 'n aw!"

Silence.

"Are ye a' deid?"

More of the above.

Three locals, who had missed out on the party were doing some catching up. Everyone was asleep or dozing half awake, struggling to return to it. Nobody answered their genial salutations. One of them, giving up this thankless task, sat down by the post in the middle of the room and within a moment collapsed into a drunken slumber. The other two split their forces. One Gaelic Goliath dished out cheer to the top deck, while the other catered to the lower bunk. They offered refreshment from their New Year bottles, shook hands or in the case of the girls sealed the moment with a Gaelic snog. As far as I could make out most people blearily complied, even though the liquor must have tasted quite revolting on their heavily encrusted tongues. The Highlanders were fairly forceful with their greetings. Refusing "To tak' a New Year," was asking for trouble. Several slumbering climbers were shaken into the New Year anew and much whisky gurgled its merry way down reluctant throats. The sleeping damsels clearly were not enjoying the mauling they were getting but if their boyfriends were too spineless to intervene, they had better just lie back and think of Scotland.

Two along from me a girl was weeping miserably as the drunken giant plied her with festive cheer. It would be my turn soon. I dived down leaving only my nose poking through as a snorkel. A pointless exercise, for pretty soon my draw-cord was tugged open to reveal a visage that was to provide material for my nightmares for years to come. Worse than the worst hairiest Heelander in *Braveheart.* For no reason at all I found myself talking in an uptight voice as if I had spent my formative years at Fettes.

"No, thank you so much, I have had quite enough to drink and now, my good man, if you wouldn't mind letting me go to sleep. We have a long day on the hill, tomorrow, or rather today, and unless I get to sleep right away there won't be time for brekkers and I can't imagine there will be any place of refreshment open this Ne'erday to supplement our rations."

"Hey Fergus, jusht listen at this English Pfluff. No law de daw plaice o'ar refreshment open todaih. Listen, Twala," he roared, "jusht stuff this boattle, sorry *supplementary ration* doon your place o' refreshment or I'll mak ye remember Prestonpans." He grabbed my sleeping bag jack-knifing me upright, just as I was wondering why anyone from south of Loch Lomond is immediately suspected of Englishry.

"Get a dram of the Fiery Cratur in yer belly and ye won't need tae stoap for refreshment. Ye Mealy Pudden!"

"Well, if perchance you have some of that delicious black bun, I could entertain a nibble."

"A nibble, Ooh entertain a nibble! I'll gie ye a nibble! We've nay mair black bun, an' if we had I'd ram it up your Sassenach erse! Noo tak yer dram!"

"Maybe he disnae want ane." This voice of reason came from the lower deck.

"Whit?"

His chum, Fergus, was upholding a less rigorous standard of enforcement of sharing the cup that cheers. Perhaps being less of a lion-hearted patriot than his pal, or possessed of that other powerful national characteristic, being canny with his bawbees. I couldn't help noticing the bottle about to

Neist – Ed Grindley and Noel Williams: Supercharger attempt number 10, 1981. Photo: Noel Williams.

be rammed between my teeth, was a 12-year-old Macallan, entirely wasted on the furred up tongues of the libatees.

"Haud on, Donhail. I tellt ye. Leave the laddie alane.

"Whit? He'll tak his New Year like a man."

"Go on gie him a break. He doesnae want yer whisky. C'mon doon."

"Whit?"

"He doesnae want it."

"We'll. He's goin' tae get it!"

"Leave him alane!"

"Awa 'n bile yer heid!"

"Whit?" – A favourite word of theirs now swopped over to Fergus.

"He'll tak his New Year."

"No he winnae! Let's awa hame tae oor beds."

"Fergus, awa and bile yer heid!"

"Whit?" A dangerous pause. "Nae-yin tells me to bile ma heid!"

"Well am tellin' ye the noo. Awa an' bile it wi a sheep's heid an'a!"

"Whit!" This was Fergus in case you're losing track.

At that moment all extraneous noise was drowned out as the bottle was upended against my tonsils, and in order to prevent death by drowning I had to swallow the whisky to the last drop.

"Yer a real Scotsman, noo!" was the last bulletin from mine unwanted host, as his legs were dragged down off the bunk by his inflamed friend. Desperately, Donhail scratched for some purchase. Captured in the glimmering fire light was a *Kilroy Was Here* cartoon figure peeking over the bunk, except this one had a raggedy beard, with an expression trapped midway between surprise and anguish.

"And let me wish you a Happy New Year!" I shouted festively.

"Whit?"

This "Whit" was Donhail's Farewell to Dundonnell as Fergus was about to demonstrate precisely his objections to boiling his head. Now preferring action to words, Fergus took off his jacket and threw it at the third member.

"Hector, haud that."

The jacket plopping over Hector's heedless head, to make him a sleeping coat-rack. Down below, there were three loud cracks followed by: "Ye'll no tell me to bile ma heid!"

The brawl was brief. Fergus was a bonny fechter, and briskly sorted out the attempted enforcer. Besides, Donhail was not allowed to take his jacket off, it was stuck midway, half-on, half-off, impeding efficient combat. Unfair perhaps, but these Highlanders never learned to play cricket.

The commotion at last managed to wake Hector – the third reveller. He was completely taken aback, blindfolded in addition to being befuddled by drink.

"Whair am? Turn on the light! Mah e'en, mah e'en!" He shrieked panic stricken.

Mountain Painting Weekend 2003: John Fowler, Neil Quinn and Iain Smart view their subject – The Three Sisters, Glen Coe. Photo: John Mitchell.

John Mitchell's interpretation of Gearr Aonach and Aonach Dubh.

"Help! I've been blinded. I've lost mah sight! Oh Jings! I should have never hae drunk yon porridge whisky at the bothan!"

He rushed about the Smiddy and I watched in fascination as he smacked straight into the anvil with a horribly painful crack then neatly pole-vaulted over it. He looked about him like a lost dog. The jacket-cum-blindfold had fallen onto the floor. Silence. He touched his eyes.

"It's a miracle! It's a New Year miracle! I was blind and now I can see! – see?" He pointed to his eyes in case anyone was interested, and limped out at a run.

"I'm going to the kirk right noo. Whaur is it?"

Far away I just caught him practising his New Year Resolution: "I'll never, Meenester. I'll never touch a drop again. So help ma, Boab. No hooch onyway."

* * *

As sometimes happens Ne'erday turned out to be extremely fine, bringing with it the promise of a bright fresh new start. Kissing goodbye to the lame half-life of mediocrity and failure of the previous 12 months, a delusion lasting as long as snow in the Lake District. There was a fiery lurid dawn of orange and yellow cloud, while we tramped the frozen bog to the foot of the ridge. So far it was like any of a 100 grey days in the hills. Another day, another set of wet clothes. Mounting up to the shoulder of the ridge the team was sucked into a thick clammy mist. The wind blew, the wet drizzle spat in our faces. Hunching down into our anoraks, we resigned ourselves to another dreary outing. Sheets of mist billowed down in long columns, each one damper than the last, first grey, then brighter and sparkling with little sequins. An Teallach, clad in veils of swirling mist, coyly wrapped up, then slowly revealing all. A stone Salome, its gorgeous towers uncannily bringing to mind the first sighting of Dracula's castle in an old Hammer Horror Movie.

Then, all petty thoughts disappeared as the mist boiled away evaporating as a glorious winter sun took over. All the regrets, the melancholy of the past year were burned out in that spectacular array. Set in front were row upon row of pinnacles, crags and battlements glistening white, giants' milk-teeth under a cloudless sky. The snow, a flawless satin, so bright that even with sun glasses, we had to turn from the mountains and look to the plain for relief. In contrast with the monochromed heights, the heather, gorse and broom of the lowland provided a patchwork of amethyst browns and greens, fragmented by a myriad of startling blue lochans stretching towards the horizon where it melted into the snow whitened hills. To the west the Atlantic shimmered in a calm sea broken only by the Summer Isles, rubies in a saphire setting.

Nothing could disturb our harmony with the mountain that day. Surmounting the brow we all whooped in exultation, voices carrying easily in the still air. Even the creak of crampons and the snap of crisply crackling snow could be heard clearly. No other human sounds disturbed the calm. Brushing snow off the handholds, we discovered the rock warm and dry within minutes, the midwinter sun hotter than on many a summer day.

The climbing itself was beyond perfection, névé, safe, solid and plastic, affording technically interesting moves in a scenario of apparent drama, but well-secured with ropes and runners. Balancing and tiptoeing over spikes, spillikins and gendarmes we saw, peering up, a never ending series of delights. Snow covered bushman's huts and pot kilns all in a line, the towers, bulbous haystacks out of a painting by Courbet. Sitting on the leaning tower known as Lord Berkeley's Seat, with all around us the lavish splendour of a winter's day in the Northern Highlands, mountain upon mountain varnished with silver, strewn about in prodigal abundance, the thought occurred that if there was a magic carpet, there was nowhere else to be, not even the Karakorum. The little breeze that had sprung up when the trip started, died away. A century ago Mummery, atop the Matterhorn, noted the air was so still that cigarette smoke ascended directly heavenwards. None of us smoked to put it to the test, but today, would have been such a day.

Too soon we left behind the last ice-crusted pinnacle and descended to a grand sloping plateau, wind polished into an icy mirror, its surface changing into a burnished gold by the lowering sun which, dropping behind the ocean, set the Atlantic afire with molten red. On that last slope down to the Smiddy the dusk air turned chilly and lifeless as if the sun's going had switched the magic off.

Minutes later we were in the hut chattering away over a warming brew and hot soup, the cold forgotten, a row of blue-flamed primuses purring away like happy kittens, dixies on the boil dancing, and everyone burbling away in the *joie de vivre* of this wonderful day. Each team coming in had given their verdict. We had been dancing with the gods and angels in the empyreum. No one exactly said that, the English language failing miserably to meet the demands put upon it, so we had to fall back on hackneyed expressions of exuberance for this once in a lifetime day on the hill, as in: "Whit a great day!"

Absolutely trounced by: "It was better than a fish supper!"

Bringing it down to a common experience we had all enjoyed. One bright spark who fancied himself as being in touch with the great world outside, came out with: "It was better than a fish supper when W. H. Murray dined alone." But this was met by deservedly blank stares all around.'

Or so they all told me. I was part of that ecstatic crew only by proxy. My great day had been spent, head over a bucket clenched between my knees inspecting my very own Jackson Pollock therein, my headache thumping away to a perpetual, *Galveston,* while afar off, as if in a distant glen, my stomach was erupting on a diminishing ration of nutrients.

And you wonder why I avoid Hogmanay.

THE SCOOP

By Jamie Andrew

"Oooooffffff!!!"

Another rusting piece of iron crumbled and snapped as I tried to stand up on it, sending me thumping back down into my harness.

Hanging free from the rock, 200ft. up, my harness digging painfully into my side, I sat for a moment, exhausted and frustrated, my head pounding, arms aching and knuckles oozing blood. Once again I found myself questioning my motives for coming here of all places, Sron Ulladale, for a holiday. We could have all gone to the south of France in the same time for much the same cost, but here we were in Harris, messing about in a tangle of ropes, etriers and pitons, dizzy-headed, high above the windswept moor.

When I first began rockclimbing, in the mid-Eighties, aid climbing was well and truly extinct as a branch of the sport. In Britain at least, the cliffs no longer rang to the sound of hammer on piton and brightly clad, super-fit free climbers had moved in to clean up the remains.

However, one great British aid climb in particular was not to be forgotten, preserved forever in Ken Wilson's coffee table classic, *Hard Rock*. Situated on the impressively overhanging north-west face of Sron Ulladale in the Outer Hebrides, *The Scoop* remained as a testament to a style of hard climbing which had all but faded away.

The Scoop was pioneered by Doug Scott back in 1969. 450ft. high and overhanging by 150ft., it was climbed over six days with several bivouacs and more than 30 hours' climbing and was given the grade A4. At the time it was hailed as a pointer to things to come, but actually, it turned out to represent the high point of British aid climbing.

In 1987 the inevitable happened when the talented duo of rock stars, Johnny Dawes and Paul Pritchard paid a visit to Harris. Their free climb of the face took a line based on *The Scoop* and weighed in at a mighty E7 although they avoided the A4 roof pitch which remained unviolated by the free climber.

Ever since first reading about *The Scoop* I had longed to do it and was fascinated with the thought of swinging free in etriers, high above the desolate moor with nothing but space below me. The thought of it also terrified me. Year after year passed by and always I found other ways to pass the summer, subconsciously putting it off until finally, in 1994, the excuses had all worn thin and *The Scoop* could be delayed no longer. The approach of midsummer spurred me into rallying some support.

Dave Kirk, an uncompromising Aberdonian and stalwart climbing partner was readily roped into the idea. My old friend Al Matthewson was also keen to come along but was careful to stress his purely supporting role, muttering something about taking photographs. Ric Davies, another level-headed friend wanted to come too, but "only for a holiday".

So it was that in May of that year, the four of us found ourselves rattling northwards from Edinburgh in an overloaded mini on a mission of discovery (and, it must be confessed, in pursuit of that elusive 'puerile tick').

Twenty-two hours, 230 miles, two ferries and a two-mile walk with ridiculously heavy sacks later, we arrived at base camp beside lonely Loch Ulladale. It was 3pm and as it doesn't get dark in the Outer Isles in midsummer until…well at all really, we planned to make a start immediately.

Dave and I sorted through the gear we'd brought: Six ropes, countless karabiners, a fortune of Friends, great arrays of pegs and nuts and all sorts of other interesting bits and bobs. After some discussion we elected to take all of it.

"Better safe than sorry," warned Dave. Hopelessly overburdened, we stumbled up the jumbled boulders and steep, slippery slabs that led to a dripping stance at the foot of the route. Feeling totally awe-struck by the humbling monstrosity of black rock over our heads, we fell silent as we fumbled on harnesses and wrestled nervously with tangled ropes. Eventually, we were ready.

Dave put me on belay, growling the helpful advice: "Don't take too long," and with no little trepidation, I set off. A couple of free moves across a slab brought me out over the void to the first of the difficulties. Difficulties which gave no indication of letting up till the top of the crag. *Oh God!* To say I felt daunted gives no impression of the utterly oppressive nature of the place: 450ft. of frowning overhang loomed above me while I pathetically tried to fiddle in a small nut. I was now having serious doubts about the sanity of this whole scheme. What was I doing here? I might have turned back there and then had it not been for the thought of the expense and effort of merely getting to the foot of this route. I couldn't simply come back next week when I felt a bit braver.

Al and Ric joined Dave on the belay and spurred me on with various encouraging jeers and insults.

Blocking the wider view from my mind, I concentrated on the few feet of rock in front of my nose. Clipping an etrier into my nut, I clumsily stood up in the first rung. Another nut went in, a friend and then I could reach a peg. Soon, I was totally absorbed. My mind became completely focused on puzzling out the next manoeuvre and I became unaware of everything else around me; Dave, Ric, Al, the wind, the loch, the moor. Only the next section of rock mattered. And the next section of rock suddenly looked very blank indeed.

A bolt head protruded from the rock just above me, hangerless and slightly downward pointing. I looped the end of a wire over and jammed up the nut to hold it in place. Then I clipped on my etrier and cautiously eased my weight up. Teetering precariously on the top rung I could just reach a tattered length of cord hanging down from goodness knows what above. There was no loop to clip into so I had to simply wrap the cord round my wrist and haul up. To my horror the cord was attached to a rusted rurp wedged into a blind, schisty crack. There was no going back now so, holding my breath, I tied a loop in the cord, clipped in an etrier and stood up. With relief I grasped a more secure piton higher up.

After that little scare, progress continued steadily, if painfully slowly until I eventually reached a hanging stance. "Safe!" I shouted down, but I didn't sound very convincing.

Now it was Dave's turn to begin the learning process. Unpractised in the art of jumaring and unfamiliar with aid stripping techniques, his progress was slow and his curses were frequent as he swung out into space, out of reach of runners and rock. Finally, he arrived sweating at the belay and announced in his inimitably resolute manner that I would be doing the rest of the leading.

Unable to argue I set off up the second pitch, consoling myself with the knowledge that this was a more straightforward section, being only A2. Straightforward it certainly wasn't and several loose blocks conspired to give me a worrying moment or two, as did some *in-situ* pitons which disintegrated under body weight. Meanwhile, back on the hanging stance, Dave was wrestling with the three ropes which were being carried high up into the sky by strong updraughts, and twisted round and round each other, like a huge nest of snakes. But at length the pitch was completed and I landed panting on the beautiful sanctuary known as the First Lie-Down Ledge. Perfectly flat, clean, a golden rectangle in proportion with an overhead crack bristling with pitons, it was a horizontal haven in a world of horrible overhangs. Not long later Dave joined me on the ledge and as it was now 8pm we decided to call it a day there. We stashed the gear on the ledge and set off down our abseil rope, spinning in space, to the welcome relief of horizontal ground, our tents, and a large meal.

Rain swept across the moor that night, lashing our little tents and swelling the nearby stream (and carrying away Al and Ric's treasured supplies of yoghurt and crème-fraiche which had been left there to cool). I slept fitfully, tossing and turning most of the restless night, unable to relax while the route was only part done.

The morning dawned fine, bringing with it, for me, mixed emotions of relief and dread – dread at having to return to do battle with that great black monolith which seemed to almost overhang the loch.

We set off early and a brutal 150ft. jumar shook our chilled bodies awake and returned us to the First Lie-Down Ledge. Dave made himself comfortable and I made a start on the big, third pitch. It took a while to get going again but soon I was back into the swing of things (literally).

The third pitch consists of a huge, soaring corner, interrupted by three block overhangs which are all turned by the left wall. Climbing the corner proved straightforward enough but the overhangs caused considerable problems with gear placement and rope drag. Moving round the first overhang provided one particularly memorable moment. I managed to reach the lip on Friends but couldn't find any placements in the band of earthy schist around the lip. Standing high in my etriers I could reach another strand of cord, very similar to the one I had encountered on the first pitch.

"Here we go again," I muttered and, throwing caution to the wind, I grabbed the cord, swung out, and hand-over-handed up it. This cord, I discovered, was attached to a very manky looking peg. However, it wasn't the state of the peg which worried me, rather the state of the karabiner which connected the cord to the peg. About a third of the krab, including the gate, was missing. The remaining section was about a third of its original thickness and was white and crumbly with corrosion. In short, it was no longer a UIAA certified krab. I gulped and carried on heaving until in a position where I could slot in a nut and breathe a large sigh of relief.

When finally, the third roof was reached, a tension down and left brought the Second Lie-Down Ledge, a near perfect replica of its brother 150ft. lower down. Dave followed, leaving the original abseil rope in place and another rope down the third pitch to protect our retreat – a distinct possibility as the next pitch was the A4 crux tackling the final 40ft. roof. This great black overhang dominated the rest of the route, looming monstrously overhead as a final threat to those brave enough or stupid enough to venture this far.

But, by now, I was numb to the effects of such intimidation and launched wearily upwards. The leaning wall leading to the roof proved difficult. A thin crack leading round a bulging section was too shallow to take knife blades and so I resorted to using microwires. Carefully, I eased up onto an RP and, craning my neck, surveyed the crack above me.

Whoooosh!!! Suddenly, the world was spinning round my head. Loch Ulladale swung into view above me, the nasty black overhang and the blue sky were beneath my feet and several kilograms of gear was jangling round my neck. There was a brief silence, then Dave began to giggle. The release of suspense overcame me and soon I was swinging around upside down laughing, until Dave pointed out that the outward pull on the ropes had jerked out every one of my wires leaving only three very rusty pitons between me and the belay.

Back to business. This time the RP held long enough for me to ram a Friend in higher up and I was soon clipped into Doug Scott's bolt at the start of the roof. A very long tension and stretch rightwards gained the thin wet crack which split the roof. Until this point it hadn't been necessary to do any pegging as nuts, Friends and *in-situ* pegs had always been available, but now it was time to unholster my hammer.

Al, who had by now ascended to the First Lie-Down Ledge and was curled up with a good book, looked up with interest.

"What d'you bet he drops the peg, Dave?" he challenged.

"Bound to!" shouted down Dave.

Ignoring their pathetic attempts to unnerve me, I held a small leeper at full stretch and began feebly to tap at it, an action which only resulted in me spinning slowly round out of reach of the crack. After several attempts the peg began to bite and I was able to attack it with a double-handed stroke.

Ping! The peg arced out into space and floated gracefully down through the abyss to land inaudibly among the jumble of boulders 150ft. out from the base of the crag. Dave and Al sniggered. Cursing my clumsiness I began again, this time managing after some effort to get in a body weight holding peg. Getting the hang of it now, my progress accelerated to a snail's pace, and eventually, feeling decidedly space sick, I pulled round the lip and collapsed with relief onto a slabby belay, three hours after leaving the Second Lie-Down Ledge.

Dave followed, totally out of sight from above, his various aerial antics going unseen. Meanwhile, Al began a series of spectacular free-hanging jumars, a long way out from the rock, removing the fixed ropes as he climbed to join us.

The final 'easy' pitch is graded A1/HVS and is merely vertical. However, it still felt bloody hard to me and by then, quite frankly, I'd had enough. Dave and Al were still refusing to take up the lead, explaining that it would be much quicker if I just led it. It was with huge relief that I finally pulled out onto the top, in the early evening sunlight, totally exhausted, both mentally and physically.

It was June 4, 1994, 25 years to the day after Doug Scott and his team completed the first ascent. Theirs' was certainly a far greater achievement than ours – that stands to reason. Nevertheless, it was not without some feeling of dazed pride that I staggered back down the hill, my body struggling to readjust to the strangely normal feelings of gravity and perspective. A mouth-watering meal of fresh trout which Ric had hooked out of the loch and then sleep, oblivious to the driving rain which once again battered the tents.

I had never done anything like *The Scoop* before and I'll probably never do anything like it again. But to have been there, just the once, and tried it, at least I know something of what it was all about. Doug Scott hit the nail on the head with his immortal description of *The Scoop* as "a unique experience in fear and fascination". It certainly provided a unique, fearful, and above all fascinating experience for me.

LAST SHIFT ON THE GROSSHORN

By Jamie Thin

I LURCHED down. Fear grabbed me by the throat, and kicked me awake, but I wasn't spiralling down the face as I had half-dreamed – the ice-screw was still there. I was just swinging over space in the dark. I must have been rocked by the wind or a heavy slough of powder snow from the summit ridge. The belay was crap - it would never take a leader fall - but was just enough to hold our weight on a hanging bivvy.

We were halfway across the crux ice traverse on a veneer of black ice over slabs. I had got a few turns on the ice-screw before it hit the rock below It was sticking out lamely and flexing every time I shifted my weight. Rog was clipped into another ice peg, little better. We'd ground to a halt after Rog broke his crampon, darkness had fallen and the temperature had plummeted. Now the wind was picking up, sending streams of freezing powder snow down the face. Rog seemed impervious to it. Maybe it was Yorkshire grit or bravado. He half-smiled, or perhaps it was a rueful grin. For me, the fear was seeping into me with the cold. We each had a bivvy bag, but no warm gear or sleeping bags - we couldn't get into the bags anyway - I just stuck mine over my head and sheltered under it.

The plan had been to get up and down in one push and now we were at about 3500m on the North Face, in the thick of a winter storm and the temperature was -25°C and dropping. We were too far up to consider descending. The ice conditions had made any belays difficult - so we had soloed the first 300m up the initial couloir. We had tried to pitch the crux traverse, but the belays were at best psychological.

We ate some chocolate in the first grey light of dawn, and then I had to think about moving. By now I couldn't feel my fingers and was fumbling with the gear. Rog was in no fit state to lead. With only one crampon left, he had been forced to hop the last few pitches before dark, with most of his weight on his arms. Step cutting was impossible. It had been a dry, lean winter and what in some years would have been nice névé, was black ice as hard as marble. Even the axes could only bite in a few millimetres on the second or third attempt.

I didn't want to start climbing again, my muscles were stiff and cold, but neither did I want to stay. Movement is sometimes better than waiting for the sunrise.

After a few shaky moves, I got into balance and worked my way across and up. I was desperate to reach the headwall for a decent belay, knowing our gear below would never hold a leader fall. Eventually, I reached the shelter of the headwall and hammered a peg into the first crack in the rock. Rog hopped up to join me.

The finish to the route was a long traverse left below the headwall and then an escape up the ice cliffs above.

I led off again crossing more black ice, sweeping off any remaining powder and trying to keep high so I could place pegs in the rock. Placing one awkward peg on a bulge, I was out of balance and couldn't get my crampons to bite. I got the peg in and hung off it with relief. I continued the traverse, placing a drive-in ice peg halfway along and the confidence began to return, even if my fingers were still numb. I reached a prow of rock and hammered in another couple of pegs for a belay. They went in easily, but I was just happy to be on solid ground and off the black ice. The rope was frozen and I couldn't squeeze it into my belay plate, so I just took a waist belay, and shouted to Rog to follow across.

Rog hopped and jumped over on his one crampon boot, he reached the awkward peg on the bulge, and had to stretch up to try and knock it out with his ice-hammer. It was just out of reach, he edged a little higher up and leaned over…shhhumm…his foot shot out and he was off, swinging down on the 15ft. of slack to the next runner.

The first I knew of it, I was arcing out into space to meet him.

The impact had pulled both the pegs in my belay and I found myself still clutching the rope hanging from the ice peg I had placed as a runner. We stared hollow-eyed at each other, and then at the ice-peg above, from which we were both swinging. I got an axe back in the ice and steadied myself from the swinging on the rope. Rog hammered in a wart-hog and made a makeshift belay. We were back safe, but had been inches from total belay failure and 1000m of free-fall. All we could do was blot the thoughts from our minds and focus on the next move, the next belay.

When I climbed back up to the ice-peg, I found it had been bent into a right-angle and the ice all around was fractured. We took another bivvy in a crevasse on the summit ice-ridge and then were left with the tortuous descent route, first over the main summit, so we could reach the long traverse on a narrow corniced ridge, and then two abseils down to the Schmadri-joch.

By now Rog was doing all the leading - we were both dehydrated after 48 hours without liquid – and I was barely rational, wracked by hot aches up both arms. I couldn't hold my ice axe or rope and just tumbled down the soft snow slopes onto the glacier. Rog disappeared down one crevasse, but managed to pull himself back out. We could see the hut now. But it was still a long way through the powder snow before we could finally dump all our gear and collapse.

The hut was as we had left it, empty and silent, but still with the big bowl of water on the table. We drank and felt the wonderfully cold liquid rush down our throats, moistening our dry cracked lips and painful swollen tongues. We just sat for a long time, happy to be alive and to have the leisure to relax. Then we began the slow painful process of shedding boots, gear and gloves. I left my inner-gloves till last, not wanting to see the blue-black creep of frostbite on my hands.

***

Thirteen years later I'm reading the spidery script of my hospital diary:
Interlaken Regional Hospital
"By an almost inevitable progression we have arrived in the hospital wards. I'm clutching my pen with swollen, clumsy fingers dyed bright red by mercurochrome paint. While my left hand is still all bandaged to keep the fingers immobile and free from infection.

I'm beginning to adapt to the daily routine - getting woken by the night nurse for the first of my six-hourly injections to thin my blood and dilate my capillaries.

The slow rising awareness of where I am. The confusing twinges of sensation which come from my hands. I play games with myself trying to analyse the myriad of seemingly unconnected sense impulses and working out how my hands and fingers are lying…but always I'm surprised to find my hands in some other position to the one I imagined."

On that same winter climbing journey, cycling across northern Europe, climbing in the Tatra mountains and the Alps, I read Tolstoy's *Resurrection* - lamented by the critics for its sentimentality. Re-reading it now many years later, it is still sentimental, but the last words strike a chord with my half-remembered feelings…

"And a perfectly new life dawned that night for [him], not because he had entered into new conditions of life, but because everything he did after that night had a new and quite different significance than before. How this new period of his life will end time alone will prove."

Footnote:
My friend and regular climbing partner, Roger Lawson, was killed on the Dru the following summer on August 13, 1992, when an abseil point failed.

HEAVY DAYS IN THE LABYRINTH

By Nigel Kenworthy

As A local boy from Ayr, Arran was one of Heavy's favourite adolescent haunts. He wanted to relive past glories, whereas I was selfishly ticking Classic Rock (The Scottish ones first, the rest could wait.) It would be a pleasure to sack-haul the old man again. In fact, Heavy had a pedigree – he had been dragged up some of the best routes in Scotland.

I said *Labyrinth,* he said *Sou'Wester Slab,* I said: "Both." He said: "Okay." For Heavy it was his fifth time on Sou'Wester, my third. However, an ascent of *Labyrinth* would be a first for me. Heavy had done it before, 25 years ago with Wee Jock, but it was much harder then. Wee Jock had carefully positioned glowing fag ends on vital holds. Simmering hatred between the pair led to violence and culminated in a massive stramash on Brodick golf course. It was evens, blow for blow until Heavy decided to use his watch as a knuckle-duster on the sixth. By the ninth it was all over. After making up, it was into the club bar for a few beers before an alcohol fuelled final nine holes later on that evening.

Cir Mhor, that most impressive of Arran peaks, rises magnificently at the north end of Glen Rosa. It was just a pity that it was such a long way from the end of the road. However, a bit of begging and subterfuge by Heavy and the old pre-rehearsed 'bad knees' acting routine, gained us a key to the gate, which cut a few kilometres off the walk in.

"It looks a bit wet," says Heavy. "Better have a go at Sou'Wester first." This was the usual Heavy ruse, go for the climb you have done many times before to get the confidence up a bit. I still found the first pitch awkward . Heavy had [kindly!] lent me a pair of red suede Scarpa vibrams with no tread. Apparently, these were in vogue Seventies footwear, whose previous owner had succumbed to the big C a decade earlier. His taunts of: "Dead man's boots you're gonna fall off" did not help. Nevertheless, pleasant meandering across the great west-facing slab on the next pitch led to the superb three-tier chimney, followed by a relaxing veteran's lunch of sardines among the midges.

Now for *Labyrinth*; a wholly different affair. The route has not always been known by this name, as it was originally christened East Wall Climb by the first ascensionists (G. C. Curtis and H. K. Moneypenny in 1943) and described as "severe (strenuous) giving about six hundred feet of continuously interesting climbing, with magnificent situations" – SMCJ Vol. 23.

However, it has now been downgraded to V. Diff and straight-forward. The greasy alleyway at the foot of the first pitch was identified eventually, from the pages of the old crusty guidebook. The first 70ft. were easier than they appeared. A haul on loose, grey, weathered granite and a belay on a spatially inadequate, vegetated platform, led to a right trending crack. This was a good old-fashioned thrutch, just too wide for a thigh jam, but not wide enough for back and fronting. Of course, Heavy had great fun with it. On the whole of Sou'Wester he had let out with irreverent pleasure only two: "Oh my Gods" and one: "Oh God," but he now surpassed himself and with blasphemous gratification let out three: "Oh my Gods" and four "Oh Gods," in only 10ft. of climbing. It was okay though, his father was a minister and Heavy must have heard that sort of language at home all the time.

We were now on a diagonal grassy shelf and a pleasant (he said 'exposed') horizontal traverse led leftwards. I was all set to go, but the lack of protection made me dither on the stance. Fortunately, Heavy was able to point out that even though he had brought me for my technical expertise, he was the 'Maister' and had brought along the experience. "Try the crack lower down son, and do as you're told." He was right; it was a better proposition for the second, as it offered some protection. This ended abruptly on a little grass ledge, the largest midge nest in Scotland.

The crack above was the crux. While I attempted this, Heavy, to keep his spirits up, had decided to raid a convenient blaeberry bush next to the belay. The first 5ft. were trickier than expected and I came back down for a rest, only to have squashed Blaeberries rubbed into my face. "Ah ha! it makes you look like Braveheart," says he with a titter, "straight on up, English." So with Blaeberry juice coagulating up my nose, I swung up the crack spurred on by a need to escape. This was a short pitch of 50ft., so he was soon beside me, purple not only from the exertion, but from the blaeberry crosses that he had rubbed on his own cheeks, giving him the appearance of a bespectacled Pict. However, he soon turned ashen after a closer inspection of the next pitch. This was a chimney of two tiers and vertical. Up over the first chock stone, behind a second and then strenuously up 70ft. of protectionless crack. I began to smile inwardly with malevolent glee during the grimaced exertion of the last 10ft., eagerly anticipating the antics to follow.

"Climb when ready."

"Climbing...PULL!" came the reply. I soon forgot about the midges and listened instead to the groaning, scrabbling, grunting, sighing, effing and blinding, punctuated with the occasional: "Oh my God." All too soon and with the last move being an air-cycling, toe-scraping, two–handed pull-up, he landed on the eyrie beside me. "I need to lose two stone he says." My pumped forearms bore testament to that.

The direct line, which was first climbed in 1950, now went up the Hard Severe crack above. However, it was agreed unanimously that the original line off to the right was more traditional, in keeping with the character of the route and, more importantly, looked much easier. Unfortunately, after a rope length of vegetation, I reached a jumble of boulders with very muddy boots. The last, little chimney had a sting in the tail, no protection. This was not a bad thing, as by this time Heavy was either using it to stand on or leaving it in.

We were quite tired at the top and I was aching all over from all the heave-ho exploits, with my new jacket torn to shreds (bad climbing technique, as Heavy pointed out).

However, we were pleased with ourselves and soon forgot our tiredness to jog silently down Glen Rosa, satisfied and at peace in our private meditations.

LIFE'S DAY

The sunrise brings green chuckling on the fabric
so the tent is set sailing on its hopes;
we crawl out to bathe in blue sky,
dancing in bare feet, shouting down
the gabbling grouse that tell us to go back.
The mountain waits, patiently as peace
before the gods of war we chase.
We will go up and be no less blessed
than all the saints and prophets
who thought they had a monopoly of heights.
(They could have done with better belays
and a friend or two.) We eat greedily,
pecking food, and view, in turn,
like nodding hens.

The gear is rucksacked, in a robber's rush,
and feet itch for godlike wings to soar
to the hard place where we would drink
the cup that will not pass from us.
Much later, much later, hard won,
when only the perfect sky is higher
and the tent a green dot in shadows
laid like plaid across the world's moor
then, only then, we praise, or fall
like the lost leaders gone before,
who leave us tempting chalk marks
on a shadowed wall.

                                        Hamish Brown.

THAT BIG CORNER

By Colin Moody

I CROSSED to The Misty Isle with George Szuca in 1988. We camped in Coire Lagan. On the third day we couldn't find The Cioch and stumbled into Coir' a Ghrunnda. We then moved to Kilt Rock but it also misted over.

The following year, George told me about the Upper Tier at Neist on Skye. "Man there's room fur two hunner routes". He had not let me in on a secret, he told everyone, even wrote about it in the new routes book.

Six years passed before I drove over from Torridon with Yan Taylor. After a disappointing time on *Supercharger*, Yan wandered up towards the Upper Tier and after a while he returned proclaiming "Just like Auchinstarry quarry, we're back to going to Torridon". After a slight protest, I did what I was told.

In June two years later I had got hold of Noel Williams' manuscript for the Skye Sea Cliffs and Michael Tweedley and I repeated most of the routes in the 'Financial Sector.' We were impressed, both with the quality of the climbs and also the amount of cleaning that had gone into them. Some of the lines had been put up that year and the rest the previous one, so the debris was still fresh.

The obvious feature was the big unclimbed corner just to the north. It was slightly overhanging for about 180ft, below that was steep grass for a 100ft or so, then below that another 100ft of vertical rock face plunging to the sea. To add to the atmosphere the corner was north facing and the top 50ft or so was wet. It was a classic feature, but probably about E5 and so, beyond us. I didn't want to waste any time on it but Michael was keen to abseil down for a look. I got out the old static rope and tied it to the two bombproof belay stakes beside 'The Tower', then backed it up with three or four unnecessary rock belays. Michael went down the rope, spinning uselessly in space. After his abseil he admitted he had been scared. I was only two stone heavier, so I had little excuse not to launch into space as well.

Michael didn't know about the rope! I had bought it twelve years earlier when it looked fine but it wasn't new and had possibly fallen off the back of a lorry at some time! I had left it to bivvy out at a big cliff one autumn and when I took it out of the survival bag in the spring it was soaked. Caving Supplies said it 'should' be ok. Fortunately it had no sheath so any damage was easily seen, but conversely it was easily damaged and spun you round too much, preventing you from getting a good look at routes.

I set off down the abseil trying to keep my mind blank (more difficult than it should have been)- if I didn't think about the rope it wouldn't snap! It reminded me of the end of the film *Village of the Damned*, but I was keeping my thoughts from a rope rather than aliens! I fed the rope through the plate trying to keep it as smooth as possible. Relief on reaching the ground at a controlled speed didn't last, as Michael wanted to move the rope slightly and go again to get a better look.

We both went again. There was an obvious belay ledge occupied by a loose flake which I left in situ, my thinking being that if it was missing on my return I would know someone had been there and would leave the route to them. Below that, unbelievably, there was a weakness at the overhang which made the line seem almost feasible.

Michael wanted to spend our remaining two days of holiday on the route but the idea appalled me. I wanted to climb, not waste time getting greyer on abseil, cleaning a route for someone else to do. I talked him out of it then drove him to Torridon. Afterwards I went back to work on Mull and Michael returned to college in Leicester.

I was back climbing at Neist with Bruce Taylor the following month and I showed him the corner; we thought it was a fine route for Neil Smith. For climbers of our modest ability Neil was a sort of Rope Gun. If you showed him a route he would take your rope up it so you only had to follow and remove the runners.

In September Neil, Bruce, Roger Lupton and I set off to climb the route. When we got to Neist it was raining hard, blowing in from the southwest, so we did a few routes at Staffin instead. Whenever I spoke to Michael on the phone I got the inevitable "Have you done that big corner yet?" He also informed me that it was 'wicked', a fact that I was not aware of. I also had a lot of mixed feelings about the route. It was a compelling line which I really wanted to do, but didn't want to fail on.

The following year I was back on Skye with Louise Gordon Canning and a new(ish) length of static rope. I started the abseil to look at the line again. I went down twenty feet then without warning my belay failed and I was plunging to my death. My life didn't flash before me. I woke up at Sligachan, my heart pounding. This was getting ridiculous. After a few minutes I calmed down and went back to sleep.

Back at Neist (in day time) I talked to a Glaswegian on *Bridging Interest* who said, "Have you seen that big corner?" Someone else had noticed one of the most obvious lines on Skye (aren't they all?) It was time to spring into action.

Next day Louise went off to do her Yoga while I set up all the belays and abseiled down the corner. After sticking the rope end out of rockfall range, I went up the gully to the belay. The next abseil was to dislodge the flake. I felt that I was now committed to the route.

A further ten abseils and the first pitch was ready to climb. Because of the angle there was not much loose rock and it was a bit tiresome unclipping

On an un-named peak in the Roscoe Bjerge, Greenland. Photo: Peter MacDonald.

and reclipping runners to keep me from swinging into space. The bottom twenty feet had a thick base of clay which was difficult to dislodge with a pick. Each time my legs started to go numb I would finish the descent and trudge back up *Tower Gully*. It would have been sensible to have a plod around then reclimb the bottom twenty feet of rope, but this did not occur to my scared brain. The cleaning was interrupted when we reclimbed a few routes in the area - a day without climbing was not an option for either of us.

Next day we did the pitch to the missing flake ledge. Louise was not impressed at being lowered from the belay as she had been expecting to do the whole route. I had had enough of the place and had invested too much nervous energy; the best part of the route had been climbed.

Back home it was obvious that a return was needed. Next month I met Neil and Roger at Kyle, Neil wanted to go to Rubha Hunish but I persuaded him we should do the corner and, with a highland start, we were away by the crack of noon, or soon after. I have witnessed Neil arrive at the Cioch for a day's climbing after six p.m., but he would be climbing in the sun while others were in the pub. When we got to Neist I thought ten minutes and we'll be there, but no. Certain protocols have to be followed, out came the coffee and Rizlas. Eventually I left them to it and set off across the moor. After the climb, which Neil led in his usual casual manner, the coffee and Rizlas reappeared. Done at last, time to get back to some proper climbing.

Bad Dream E3 5b,5c, Neist, July 1997.

Dansketinde, Staunings Alps, from Col Major. The S Ridge starts from the "Douglas Boulder" (L foreground) and takes a line directly to the summit. The SW Ridge forms the L skyline. The Original Route gains the col on the right and then takes a hidden couloir just right of the R skyline. Photo: Stephen Reid.

Stephen Reid starting the first pitch of the main part of the S Ridge, Dansketinde on the second (successful) attempt. Photo: Stephen Reid collection.

FLASHBACKS

By Iain Smart

TOTAL recall is a disconcerting experience, at least in the way I experience it. I will be engaged in some task or other when, without warning, for a second or two, I will be back in an event in the distant past. For a few fleeting moments I experience all the sensations of the five senses that were arriving at some particular moment that happened long ago. Most interestingly, I experience the moment with the unsophisticated psyche I had at the time, not with the psyche I have now which is battered and disillusioned by the attrition of subsequent living. These flashbacks seem to arrive spontaneously without being triggered by Proustian madeleine cakes or any other contextual reference. Ordinary memory by comparison is a woollier picture, an old dog-eared snapshot pulled out consciously from the filing cabinet of the mind and seen by the 'me' I am now, not by the previous unsophisticated 'me' that was there at the time the event happened. The total recall I am referring to is a sort of epilepsy of the memory centres in the temporal lobe, an involuntary replay of some event in the past. Some of these recalls are pretty dreadful others are happy. Here are three happy ones.

***

I was on top of the Cat Nick on Salisbury Crags. It was a peaceful morning. The whin was yellow and the grass a fresh green. Beside me was Bob Grieve. I could smell the smoke of coal fires and a whiff of Bob's asthma tobacco. There was no sound of traffic. I could hear church bells striking all over the old and new towns. I could see the pall of smoke from the household fires over the tenements of the Dumbie Dykes and the Pleasance. My hands were glowing from clutching holds all morning. I heard Bob speaking. I could make out only one word of the sentence he was uttering. It was: "...morning...". I had at that instant no memory of anything that had already happened in my later life, just a feeling of being aware of the present and feeling happy before the whole scene vanished.

The greenery and yellow whin indicates that this scene must have taken place in early summer. It must have been just before 11 on a Sunday morning to judge from the quietness and the church bells. The date must have been some year of the late Forties.

There is a lot of social history in this transient flashback. Sunday mornings were quiet because there was no traffic. Car ownership was low and I seem to remember you were not allowed to park cars in the street after dark unless you left the lights on. In those days cars were kept in the local garage and taken out at weekends, a bit like yachts in marinas today.

The breakfast fires were lit late because a Sunday morning 'lie in' was for most people less of a luxury than a physical necessity after a six-day week under what today would be considered brutal and illegal working conditions. Our future President, Professor Sir Robert Grieve, was at that time a minor functionary in the Civil Service with his coming greatness unsuspected. He was smoking asthma tobacco in his pipe because it was cheap. By smoking this dreadful stuff he was gradually saving enough to buy records of the Beethoven symphonies. The records would have been 78rpm, played on a wind-up gramophone with a fibre needle. In those days technology was basic and affluence was not widespread. Many Edinburgh professional families were satisfied to take their annual holiday in remote resorts like North Berwick or the adjacent slightly more upmarket Gullane (pronounced 'Gillin', if you were the sort of person that went there).

I was standing outside the bothy at Upper Steall. It was dark. It had just been raining. A warm wind was blowing clouds across the stars. I could hear the roar of the great waterfall across the glen. Two people were standing next to me. One was saying: "We are sib to the wind....". I could hear his accent and voice as if it was happening in real time, whatever that is. I felt an overwhelming sense of freedom and discovery as if I had escaped from a cage into a magic world where few others had entered.

This embarrassingly naive event I now remember took place one April in the mid-Forties of last century. I was 15 years old and going through an animist phase. Every rock and tree had its spirit, every glen and mountain a presence of some kind. In lonely places the sense of the ambient world was at times quite frightening. In those days Upper Steall had a roof and walls that kept out the rain, if not the wind, a battered caravanserai in the wilderness of remote upper Glen Nevis. Now all that is left of its once-sheltering halls is a crumbling gable end and a pile of rubble. It is passed by scores of walkers each weekend, if not each day.

On the occasion of the flashback I can recall from ordinary memory that I had arrived at this battered caravanserai late, late in the gloaming about the hour that Kilmeny came home. I had been camping alone for some days in the Mamores and White Corries. I tried to enter the darkness of the surviving habitable room. Compared to a tent the place seemed a haunted cavern wherein a presence lurked. I was on the point of pitching my cotton tent outside instead of braving the unknown forces within the gloom of the ruined house when another rain squall arrived and provided the courage to enter. I gritted my teeth and stepped into the wood-smoked darkness and lit my candle. Things weren't so bad once I got a fire going, better still after a primitive meal. My memory of these days was of constant hunger kept inadequately at bay with dried egg, baked beans, bad margarine and Beattie's bread. Only the beans survive to the present day, the rest are now happily extinct. But there were still shadows moving around and the wind soughed in the roof tree and there were of course 'unidentifiable sounds'. We animists find it bad enough in the daylight but in firelight and shadow the world is full of unchancy things. Then I heard footfalls. Panic and a flood of adrenalin.

Fortunately, the footsteps came from mortals, two boys from Falkirk. The elder was a soldier on leave and the other was about my age and being taken on his first trip to the glens. The fear and emptiness vanished. We talked far into the night of bothies in the snowy north and places ill tae ken. We felt that our presence here showed we had broken out of the conventional world and discovered the real world for ourselves. Having done this we were 'special' in some way and belonged to an elite group; we were 'sib' - to use a forgotten term that describes that feeling of brotherhood between free and equal spirits who had independently broken through into the real world without any psychological support. Youth leaders had yet to be conceived, let alone invented; indeed, their very parents had yet to be conceived. I think at the time we would have regarded youth leaders and adventure training, even if we could have imagined such things, as akin to loose gorgon heads wandering around turning adventure into stone. Anyway, in this war period such things were psychologically out of context: 'adventure activity' at this time was compulsory and for real.

My independent reading was limited and embarrassingly unsophisticated, probably only Ratcliffe Barnett, Alasdair Alpin MacGregor and Wendy Wood, all now forgotten romantics who put emotion before logic. Scott, RLS, John Buchan, D. K. Broster and Seton Gordon who also influenced us are still remembered and indeed still have priesthoods to tend their flame. I also remember reading Omar Khayam with empathy from whence the repeated intrusive references to the 'battered caravanserai' in this story must be derived. We had read Frank Smythe and Tilman, but their adventures seemed to take place in some unattainable never-never land; we discussed them with awe in our voices.

We had also, I regret to say been influenced by the disastrous example of Captain Scott. I had, of course studied SMC Guides and Journals in the gloomy cathedral-like halls of the Public Reference Library in Edinburgh's George IV Bridge, reached by a walk across the blacked-out Meadows lit by the grudging brown gaslight from every second veiled lamppost. These sacred leather-bound volumes with round-cornered pages and evocative sepia illustrations were hidden deep in the stacks and were handled reverently. They smelled of old books and old lore, a bit like the Bible except that you had some hope of actually approaching the holy ground where the events described had taken place. The stars of Bill Murray and Tom Weir had yet to shine upon us. At the same time as we were sitting round our fire in Upper Steall Bill may well have been writing the first draft of *Mountaineering in Scotland* with a blunt pencil on toilet paper by the light of a similar candle in a bleak prison camp in Germany and Tom, the gun-layer, working out the mathematics of counter battery fire in a howitzer emplacement on the Channel Coast. The psychological map we were using was worn, dog-eared and out of date. School leavers at the end of the war fell between two dispensations. We were schoolboys among war veterans and understandably deferential. A few years later youthful energy could get away with being arrogant and disrespectful. Alas, this luxury was not available to us.

I find the scene I have been describing unbelievably Arcadian. Was the world ever really like that? Could three reasonable intelligent teenagers be so unsophisticated as to raise their arms in the night air, to the throbbing waterfall and say sincerely and without embarrassment: "We are sib.... sib to the wind!"? In spite of the commercialism of the present outdoor industry there will surely always be unprofitable people, the despair of admen, who wont buy what they are told, who walk through the prevailing fashions without noticing them in the way ghosts pass through walls as if they weren't there. You occasionally pass a youth, obviously in the possession of a vision of his own, walking Alastor-like uphill into the gloaming while the rest of us are proceeding downhill to the pub as fast as our fading nervous systems will allow. Sometimes I feel as if the figure might be me walking out from the past through a chink in spacetime which just shows that even a hard-bitten realist can write sentimental nonsense.

I was lying on the stern of a boat. I could smell the aroma of old rope and hear the beat of a big engine. Around me there was space and light and colour and the mellowness of a summer evening. I felt luxuriously fulfilled and happy and being acutely aware of the ambient world.

Rummaging around in the untidy filing cabinet of ordinary memory I recall that this must have been another clip from the late Forties. We were returning from an illicit visit to the forbidden Isle of Rum where we had spent a week climbing on Ruinsival, Trallval, Hallval and Askival, but for some reason not Barkeval. I was with young versions of the Great Slesser and the Great Dutton. (Even at that distant time they were under heavy suspicion of future greatness.) We had stayed in Canna after our return from Rum while the rest of the party had returned to Embro. Lorne Campbell had given us permission to sleep in the loft of an outhouse down by a little bay below the old castle where the princess was held prisoner. We had intended to achieve fame by making daily first ascents on the cliffs above the harbour or on the precipitous north coast. The weather was against such crass activity. We were in the middle of a long heat wave. (There used to be such things.) The sea was glassy calm and had been for a long time. The atmosphere was too heavy and soporific to do much except eat of the Tennysonian lotus flower. We passed the time serenely watching yonder amber light that would not leave the myrrh bush on the height and so on. Even the Great Slesser was moving in slow motion. Canna and Sanday at that time had a substantial native population and was not often visited. As rare strangers we were treated with distant politeness. When we first asked at the farm for butter and milk we were provided with it diffidently. The next day we were judged by our polite behaviour to be harmless and were invited in for a strupach and a ceilidh. Milk, butter, eggs and home-baking survived unrationed in these quiet places.

The next boat to come was a dilapidated freighter inward bound from green Barra of the waves. In the glory of a summer's evening she wove her way into the harbour and amid a flurry of ringing bells she hit the pier with a crunch that cracked the pier's woodwork. The captain peered over the bridge, looked at the altered geometry of the wood and muttered: "That bloody pier is always getting in the way."

Macbrayne's had freighters in those days - old tramp-like vessels with a proper straight cylindrical funnel that emitted abundant smoke. These picturesque vessels took occasional passengers and we were given deck accommodation to Mallaig. Sobriety among captain and crew was not considered essential in these less prissy times. For most of the voyage the crew including the stoker assembled on the bridge absorbed in some discussion. Meanwhile, this latter day Birlinn Clann Ranald steered for Mallaig, imparting from time to time an interesting pattern to its wake - an occasional shallow curving zig followed eventually by a more positive zag. In those days the Western Isles still had a whiff of the old frontier between two civilisations.

Anyway, back on the coiled rope hawser on the stern of this romantically ramshackle vessel I was surrounded by an extravagant sunset reflected in a smooth oily sea, full of the reflections of the surrounding mountains. For a brief second or two I had been who I used to be with no memory of the future. But that's normal - not being able to remember the future, I mean, unless, of course you have the second sight.

NEW CLIMBS SECTION

OUTER ISLES

LEWIS, GREAT BERNERA, Creag Liam (SMCJ 2002):
Note: Grade opinions from from I. Taylor – Interactive E2 5b *, The Prow E2 5b ***, Ticallion Stallion E3 5c ***, Garden of Eadan E2 5c **, Bostadh Strangler E2 5c **.

VALTOS/REIFF , Traigh na Berigh:
Rainy Days and Golden Evenings 40m E2 5b. K. Magog, S. Crowe. 7th July 2003.
A high level girdle of the wall at Traigh na Berigh, starting on the right and traversing the break below the top to finish on the left.

Geodha Maladale:
The following routes lie on the big west-facing cliff in Geodha Maladale just north of Valtos. An old boundary wall runs towards the cliff edge at NB 0893 3785; an abseil can be made from here using a threaded embedded boulder in the wall some way back from the edge.
A large tidal shelf runs beneath the cliff and the abseil gains this close to where it terminates at a sea cave. The shelf can be easily traversed southwards for 100m or so. There are very few breaks in the steep lower band of black rock at the left end of the shelf.

Shallow is the New Deep 40m E1/2 5a *. R. Anderson, C. Anderson. 19th April 2003.
This takes the wide shallow groove that runs the height of the cliff above the initial band of black rock towards the left end of the shelf. Start just to the right of the groove where there is an obvious break in the steep lower wall. Climb steeply to the break and then move up left and across into the base of the groove. Climb the groove to the top. Both the gear and the rock are poor at the top.

Some 20m or so farther along the shelf to the south (right) an obvious square-cut tower feature can be identified at the top of the cliff. The next route climbs a crack leading into the blocky corner forming the left side of this tower.

Easy Does It 40m VS 4c. R. Anderson, C. Anderson. 19th April 2003.
Start at the edge of a tidal pool just off to the right of the line, then traverse up left past a groove and climb up the slabby wall to the base of an obvious crack. Climb the crack to a recess at the base of the blocky corner running up the left side of the tower and climb this, gingerly in places, to the top.

UIG SEA CLIFFS, AIRD UIG AREA, Gallen Beag 1:
This is the continuation of Gallen Beag 2. A narrow inlet/geo cuts into the large platformed area leading out towards the island of Gallen Beag. The wall overlooking this narrow inlet is composed of excellent waterworn rock, its northern end overlooks Gallen Beag 2. In the centre of the wall a right-angled corner can be located, the line of North Atlantic Drift. Routes are described from here, first right then left.

North Atlantic Drift   25m   E2 5c **. R. Anderson, C. Anderson. 13th July 2003.
The right-angled corner, gained by abseil.

The arête to the right is broad and has a good ledge on it. Scramble out to this from
the base of the corner.

Seven   25m   E2 5b **. R. Anderson, C. Anderson. 13th July 2003.
Climb a crack-line just left of the edge to a steepening, then pull over left on to the
wall (Camalot#0 useful). Climb to a break, move up right, then pull steeply up left
and finish more easily.

Tidal Rift   25m   VS 4c **. R. Anderson, C. Anderson. 13th July 2003.
Climb cracks in the front of the broad arête.

An abseil down the slim corner to the north gains a ledge. The first route climbs
the left edge of the right-angled corner taken by North Atlantic Drift.

Washed Out   25m   HVS 5a **. R. Anderson, C. Anderson. 13th July 2003.
Move out right onto the arête, climb this on the right and then on the left to finish.

Competitive Stress Disorder   25m   E3 5c **. R. Anderson, C. Anderson. 13th
July 2003.
Climb thin cracks in the black wall right of the slim corner with an awkward
finish just left of the final moves of Washed Out.

Panic Attack   25m   HVS 5a **. R. Anderson, C. Anderson. 13th July 2003.
The slim corner.

Rising Tide   25m   HVS 4c *. R. Anderson, C. Anderson. 13th July 2003.
The bigger corner to the left, finishing up the crack just left of the corner.

Eightsome Reel   Very Difficult. R. Anderson. 18th July 2003.
The corner and steps at the northern end of the wall.

The Boardwalk:
Face Off   30m   E2/3 5c **. R. Anderson. 18th April 2003.
The obvious groove-line just right of Shadows in the Sun. Climb directly into,
then up a left-facing groove-line and continue via a right-facing groove-line to
easier ground leading to the top.

Jagged Little Thrill   20m   HVS/E1 5a **. R. Anderson. 17th April 2003.
Climb up to the right-bounding arête and climb steeply up its left side via a shallow
groove, stepping left at the top to pull over the final jutting shelf.

Edgy   20m   E1 5b *. R. Anderson. 17th April 2003.
Just left of Quartzvein Crack. Climb a crack-line in the arête to a finish on its left
side.

The Point Wall:
Spaced Out 25m VS 4c *. R. Anderson, C. Anderson. 19th July 2003.
Immediately right of Black Sabbath, climb thin cracks just left of a chimney to step across this and gain a ledge. Climb up on to a ramp and follow this across the top of the wall.

Geodh a' Bheannaich Area:
The following routes lie in a shallow square-cut recess between Geodh a' Bheannaich and Chapel/May Day Geo. The recess can easily be located on the cliff top, as can the big exit corner to Seal Dive (SMCJ 1988). An abseil can easily be rigged down the back of the recess, down a deep groove just right of Seal Dive. Ledges at the bottom appear safe from all but the biggest seas and they can be traversed left to a deep rift where the Abyss (SMCJ 1988) starts, or rightwards towards the tidal pond area just north of Geodh a' Bheannaich itself.

From the slabby shelf at the base of the big groove forming the back of the recess, traverse left to a deep and narrow tidal rift, The Abyss. The next two routes start from ledges just up to the right.

Pushed Over 30m E2 5b. R. Anderson. 18th April 2003.
Climb a short corner and crack leading to a ledge at the base of a wide crack. Contrive moves up the wall just left of the crack directly into a shallow groove and follow this to the top.

Edged Out 30m E3 5b. R. Anderson. 18th April 2003.
Climb to the ledge as for the previous route, then continue up the wide crack on to the edge, just left of the upper corner of Seal Dive (SMCJ 1988), then make some bold moves to a large hold and some gear. Finish up the short groove above.

Heatwave 35m Difficult. R. Anderson, C. Anderson. 18th April 2003.
From the shelf at the base of the left-hand corner forming the square cut recess, climb up right towards a higher recess then follow corners and ledges back up left to the top of the left-hand corner.

Geodha Caol:
The following route lies on the west-facing wall on the seaward side of the Geodha Caol promontory.

Vein Glory 30m E1 5b **. R. Anderson, C. Anderson. 20th April 2003.
Start in the corner at the top left of the large sloping shelf at the base of the recessed section of the cliff, at the start of Backslip Way (SMCJ 2001). A two-foot wide pink vein of quartz starts on the floor of the ledge and snakes its way out left and up to the top of the crag. Follow this vein of quartz out left above the void and then up corners and an edge to a small shelf, gear on right can be arranged and extended. Climb the protruding vein for a steep and spectacular finish.

The Red Wall:
Just beyond the first cliff north of Seil na Berie is a south-facing reddish wall with an obvious hole in the wall. Walk over the top of the crag just beyond Seil na

Berie to locate a wide fault running down the side of the reddish wall. An abseil down this wall gains a spacious ledge below the hole, which is a body sized solution pocket. Continue the abseil to ledges just above the sea at the base of a large right to left-slanting fault.

The Hole Solution   30m   E2 5b *. R. Anderson, C. Anderson. 9th July 2003.
1. 10m 5b. Climb into a V-groove, then go right to the arête and climb to the spacious ledge.
2. 20m 5b. Move up left into the hole, then climb thin cracks above to the top.

Seil na Berie:
Beneath the northern top of the Berie headland is a sheltered rocky bay, an impressive spot when there is a big sea running. The most prominent feature is a slabby rib of blocky corners overlooking a right-angled quartzy corner, then a series of crack-lines through an upper section of quartzy rock. The routes finish beneath the two Gloop Holes.

Cornerstones   30m   Severe. R. Anderson, C. Anderson. 11th July 2003.
The central corner system in the slabby rib.

Edgeway   30m   Very Difficult. R. Anderson, C. Anderson. 11th July 2003.
The slabby right arête just right of Cornerstones.

Whitecap   30m   VS 4c *. R. Anderson, C. Anderson. 11th July 2003.
The thin crack just right of the quartzy right-angled corner.

Torcaso Geo (SMCJ 2000):
Note from I. Taylor: Running Scared E1 5b ** and 42nd Street are 25m not 40m, Life in the Old Dog Yet is 25m E3 5c **, Happy Returns is 15m E2 5c **.

UIG SEA CLIFFS, MUNGERSTADH AREA, Eileen Geo:
Takeaway   HVS 4c. R. Anderson, C. Anderson. 8th July 2003.
The right side of the large quartz streak just left of Breakout gained by starting as for that route to the accommodating ledge, or tide permitting directly.

Red Veil   E2 5b *. R. Anderson, C. Anderson. 8th July 2003.
The obvious corner between Sea Pink and Deep Blue.

Painted Geo, The Friendly Wall:
Becalmed   20m   HVS 5a **. R. Anderson, C. Anderson. 6th July 2003.
Start at the same point as Isle Be Back in the centre of the seaward wall on sloping ledges just above the sea. Climb the shallow corner and where Isle Be Back steps left to a small ledge on the wall, continue straight up a crack-line and finish up a slim quartzy groove

Beguiled   20m   HVS 4c **. R. Anderson, C. Anderson. 6th July 2003.
A direct line up the juggy wall and crack-line 1m-2m right of Becalmed.

Bewildered   20m   E1/2 5b *. R. Anderson, C. Anderson. 5th July 2003.
The thin crack-line in between Beguiled and Bewitched.

Bewitched 20m E1 5a/b **. R. Anderson, C. Anderson. 5th July 2003.
The thin crack-line immediately left of the arête taken by Swell Time. Pull over the initial steepening and climb the crack-line to the top.

Painted Geo, The Black Wall:
The following routes are reached by abseiling down the large west-facing slab which forms the outer edge of Painted Geo. A short wall lies at the base of the slab.

Veinity Fare 50m VS 4c/5a *. R. Anderson, C. Anderson. 7th July 2003.
Climb a wide quartz vein in the centre of the short wall and climb the slab easily to the top.

Edged Out 50m HVS 4c **. R. Anderson, C. Anderson. 7th July 2003.
Climb the slabby left arête of the short wall to a junction with Foaming at the Mouth, then climb the right side of the arête to finish easily up the slab.

The following routes lie just around the edge where there is a small tidal ledge that can be gained by traversing in from the base of the slab, or by a more direct abseil. This is the far end of the Black Wall. Four routes start from this ledge with the first taking the right edge, just left of Edged Out. A belay can be taken at a horizontal crack on the slab.

Foaming at the Mouth 50m E1 5b **. R. Anderson, C. Anderson. 16th July 2003.
Move up right and bridge across a short chimney to gain the right edge, then climb the thinner, right-hand of two cracks to gain the slab via a short v-slot. Finish easily.

First Cut 50m E3 5b **. R. Anderson, C. Anderson. 16th July 2003.
The thin crack-line in the blunt edge a short way left of the right edge. Boldly climb the thin crack-line to a ledge, then continue up the edge to the right of a groove.

Divided Loyalty 50m E2 5c *. R. Anderson, C. Anderson. 16th July 2003.
The wider crack immediately left of First Cut leads to ledges where moves up right gain a V-groove leading to the slab and an easy finish.

Gear Shifting 50m E3 5b/c **. R. Anderson, C. Anderson. 16th July 2003.
The crack-line immediately left of Divided Loyalty. Move up left into the crack-line and climb this to a blocky protrusion, then climb steeply up thin cracks to easier ground leading to the slab. Finish up the slab.

Magic Geo:
Gas 30m E3 5b *. T. Fryer, I. Taylor. 1st June 2003.
Start at the base of Campa Crack and follow a right-slanting pink dyke to join Limka after 20m.

Magic Geo, Mitre Wall (SMCJ 2001):
Too Wild for Feral Fyffe   40m   E4 6a. E. Tresidder, T. Bridgeland. 9th June 2003.
The prominent crack right of Black Crack. Good climbing with lots of poor small
gear (RP's and aliens). One crucial Friend#2.5 at half-height. Climbed on sight.

Screaming Geo:
Shonkey   50m   E2/3 5c. T. Fryer, I. Taylor. 6th June 2003.
Lies on the same wall as Conundrum and climbs the left-hand dog-leg crack.
Some suspect rock in the upper half. Abseil to a small stance 5m above high tide
level. Trend left following the crack to below roofs. Move left 1m to pull through
at the point of least resistance and continue more easily on quartzy rock to a slab.
Follow discontinuous cracks to the top.

Great Gig in the Sky   25m   E4 6a. S. Crowe, K. Magog. 5th July 2003.
Climbs the wall right of Hughies Cocktail.

Notes from I. Taylor: A direct start to Bonxie (SMCJ 2001) was climbed at the
same grade, E3 5c *. The Alchemist is between The Sorcerer and Am Burrach.

MINGULAY, Rubha Liath, Seal Song Geo:
Five routes on the south wall, all starting from the mid-height band of ledges, in
the vicinity of The Power Of The Ocean. Abseil approaches to comfortable stances.
All routes on immaculate rock and about 15m.

The Boat   HVS 5b *. R. Durran, A. Taylor. 9th July 1999.
The striking left to right slanting groove in the wall left of the top corner of The
Power Of The Ocean. Much pleasanter than first acquaintance would suggest if
dry. Good jamming and bridging to a steep finish. This may be the line climbed in
1998 by Sarah Gardiner.

The Girl In The Boat   E4 6a ***. R. Durran, A. Taylor. 4th July 1999.
The thin flake/crack in the right wall of the top corner of The Power of The Ocean.
Climb the wall to a good side-pull at the base of the flake. Make hard moves with
improving protection to a good flake below the top. Finish more easily.

Boat Song   E2 5b **. R. Durran, A. Taylor. 9th July 1999.
The arête to the right of The Girl In The Boat. Start down and right of the arête
and climb past a large flake to a bold and airy finish.

The Mooring   E1 5c **. R. Durran, A. Taylor. 9th July 1999.
The unappealing corner to the right of Boat Song has a crack in its right wall.
Steep, but with excellent protection.

The Wake   E4 6a *. R. Durran, A. Taylor. 9th July 1999.
An eliminate up the wall right of The Mooring with some excellent moves. Climb
a steep broken crack and then make harder moves between thin breaks to the top.

A further route starting from the extreme left end of the ledge beneath the obvious
hanging groove capped by a small roof.

The Extraordinary Relief Map of Iceland 25m E2 5b **. R. Durran, H. Lawrenson. 13th August 2003.
Start below the groove. Climb very steeply up, move left, then up and back right to the base of the groove. Climb the groove and turn the capping roof on the right.

The following route climbs the full height of the wall and is well right of the above routes.

The Sun Has Got His Hat On 40m E3 5c **. C. Henderson, R. Durran. 23rd July 2000.
Abseil from the lower apex of the slabby area about 50m right of The Power Of The Ocean to a good ledge just above high tide level at the foot of a prominent corner system split by a clean roof at half height. Climb leftwards and then turn the roof on the right to gain a good ledge. Continue up the corner using the fine finger crack in the left wall. Exit rightwards below a second roof in an exposed position to reach easy ground.

The following route lies on the opposite side of the Geo.

The Girl With Extraordinary Eyes 25m E3 6a ***. R. Durran, C. Henderson. 23rd July 2000.
Down and to the right of the wall taken by Fergus Sings The Blues is a clean wall undercut on its right side by a low cave. Abseil to the slightly tidal platform below the wall. Surmount the left edge of the cave and move right to the prominent line of right-trending flakes. Climb these to a rest below the capping roof and surmount this with difficulty in a fine position to finish.

Rubha Liath, Geirum Walls:
The following three routes are easily identified by the prominent right-facing corner. It is possible that others may have claimed the first and possibly second ascents of them.

Seal Of Approval E1 5b **. R. Durran and partner. July 1999.
A crack in the left wall of the corner. Climb the corner for 3m and then move left along a break to the base of the crack. Surmount a bulge (crux) and continue to the top.

Seal Clubbing E2 6a *. R. Durran and partner. July 1999.
The arête left of the corner. Make a boulder problem start from the left and then climb direct to the top.

Sealed With A Kiss E3/4 6a/b **. R. Durran and partner. July 1999.
The shallow arch to the left of the arête. The difficulty is reach dependent. Climb the wall to a good break and make a long reach for the obvious hold on the lip. Pull on to the wall with further difficulty and continue direct to the top.

Guarsay Mor:
The Mushroom Of My Fear 50m E3 5c **. R. Durran, C. Henderson. 21st July 2000.

Five metres right of the start of Hill You Hoe is a left-facing corner capped at 10m by a small roof. The usual high quality climbing on this wall.
1. 15m. Climb the corner and surmount the roof and short wall above with difficulty to gain the right end of the ledge of Ossian Boulevard.
2. 35m. Climb up and slightly leftwards for a few metres, then slightly rightwards before continuing directly through some entertaining bulges to reach easier ground. A superb and sustained pitch.

Sruth na Fir Gorm   50m   E5 6b. R. Campbell, P. Craig. 13th May 2003.
This route is on the southerly section of the main Guarsay Mor cliff. The ledge at the base of the wall terminates at the flake-crack of Taxing Macphee. From the top of the flake an intermittent ledge runs rightwards under the smooth bulging wall to disappear into a quartz recess that is the first weakness in the wall and is part of pitch 1 of Save Our Souls. Lost Souls climbs the wall just to the left of this recess breaking through the bulge via a niche (the rightmost of several similar features). This route is a counter-diagonal trending leftwards through the first weakness in the bulge 10m left of Lost Souls. Move up and right along ledge into the quartz recess on Save our Souls. Belay. Move left round rib and climb up wall to flake hold on Lost Souls. Move up left to a position under centre of overlap, move left again before making a hard move up into groove. Continue steeply to easier ground and finish as for Lost Souls.
Note: Save Our Souls was repeated by R. Campbell, P. Craig at E5 6b on 11th May 2003.

Note from A. D. Robertson: *Crystal Daze* should be E3 6a (not 6b).
Lost Souls (E4 6a, 5b). The route description for the first pitch was found to be misleading. A more accurate version would be:
1. 30m 6a. Climb rightwards off the ledge, then move up to a higher ledge. From near its right end make thin moves out right and up to a small flake. Step right and go up past small quartz holds up a narrow wall between two small roofs. Step left to the edge of the second roof and climb through the break to better holds. Move up to a small roof, step right under it then climb to a horizontal crack. Follow this leftwards to belay in a niche.

PABBAY, The Pink Wall:
Cormorant your Way to the Top   E5 6b,5c. R. Campbell, G. Latter. 14th May 2003.
Climb monster flakes up wall left of 'I Suppose…' past a hard move to an impasse 3m below roof. Step right into 'I Suppose…' and follow this to top.

What! No Puffin   85m   E6 6b. S. Crowe, K. Magog. 15th May 2003.
Climbs the grooved arête on the right edge of the Pink Wall, starting right of Ancient Mariner but eventually finishing in the same place. Hard moves gain the ledge; move up to the Y-shaped crack. Move up, then left to climb a steep bulge, before moving left again to join and finish as for Ancient Mariner.

Fondue Macpac   70m   E6. P. Robins, J. McHaffie (alt.). 2nd July 2003.
A line in between In Profundum Lacu and Raiders of the Lost Auk.
1. 20m 6b. From the small pinnacle at the top of the gully, gain the right-hand side

of a small overlap above. Move left and up to a good flake and steepening. Strenuous moves gain a crack and then a belay on the left-hand side of a small ledge.
2. 50m 6a. Go up a corner and move right to join IPL. Pull over the bulge as for that route, then move up and right to gain protruding flakes and an undercut break. Continue more easily to the top, first right then left.

Night Terrors (or The Haunting?)   E4. L. McGinley, T. Leppart. July 2003.
A route between Tomorrow People and Tickled Pink.
1. Goes up right of Tomorrow People to the same belay.
2. Traverses into Tickled Pink.
3. (Crux – 5c?) Follows a slanting groove left then up to top.

Notes: A. D. Robertson and P. Craig made the second complete ascent of In Profundum Lacu. Thought to be E5 6a 6a 5b *** and superb. The second pitch was very strenuous then bold, certainly not 5c. The final pitch (common with Raiders of the Lost Auk) is worth 5b, not 5a.
P. Robins and J. McHaffie thought the following grades: A Cormorant's E5 5b,6a/b,5b; The Bonxie E5/6 6a,6a; Ancient Mariners E4 5c; The Guga E5 5c,6a,4c.

The Grey Wall:
A. D. Robertson and P. Craig made the second ascent of Spits in Paradise/Elysium and agreed with E4 5c 6a 6a. It should be noted in the description that the second pitch has a very loose initial chimney. The rest of the pitch is solid and excellent.

The Great Arch:
Prophecy of Drowning was thought to be E2 5b 5a 5c 5b **** by P. Allen and M. Atkins. A truly outstanding climb and worth four stars. The original E3 grade understandable given the position, as escape would be very interesting.

The crux sections of Child of the Sea and Sturm und Drang were thought to be the same by A. Arnott and R. I. Jones despite being graded 6b and 6a (i.e. the routes overlap).

P. Robins and J. McHaffie climbed a very good combination, climbing the first four pitches of the Arch project, then up the corner to the left-hand end of the arch and round the arête into Prophesy of Drowning. E6 5a, 5c, 6b, 6a, 5b, 5b, 5b.

Banded Geo:
Spring Squill: M. Gear suggests an improved way of approaching the route, by the abseil to the bottom of Spooky Pillar. This gives a 15m pitch, following Oh No, Norman's in Reverse! across the top of the black slab (4c) and then climbing down and traversing left (facing in) at about Difficult to the distinctive eyehole flake belay. The route was then climbed in three pitches, 25m 5a, 25m 5b, 15m 4b, since the belays seemed better. Pitch 2 as in the guide is 5a at the start.

Oh No, Norman's in Reverse! To reduce rope drag and with better belays, climbed as three pitches, 1. 25m 5a, 2. 25m 5a, 3. 15m 4c. Description provided.
At The Drop Of A Hat (Endolphin Rush Direct Finish)   5c. C. Henderson, R. Durran. 11th August, 2003.

Pull directly over the roof above the stance into a small hanging corner. Step left to the arête, pose for photos and finish up and left. No change in overall grade.

Vomtanion and the Three Punterneers 50m E5 6a. J. McHaffie, T. Badcock, P. Robins. 4th July 2003.
A line up wall right of Ship of Fools. Start from the left-hand end of the main ledge at the bottom of the geo. Climb easily up a shallow groove for about 10m to a steepening. Step left beneath the upper of two overlaps; continue awkwardly left for 3m to some larger undercuts and a rest. Move up on small holds (crux) to gain a break. A short traverse right gains a flake. Climb more or less directly past some small ledges and a vague crack to a final bulge and the top.

Fat Les 60m E3. P. Robins, T. Badcock, J. McHaffie. 4th July 2003.
The obvious overhanging crack left of Endolphin Rush.
1. 40m 5c. Climb the crack on good holds to a step right and rest. Climb up to a short hanging corner and up to join Endolphin Rush on pitch 2. Follow this left and over a bulge to belay on a large block.
2. 20m 4b. Straight to the top.

Ug-Spudchucker E3. M. Perrier, J. Spanken. 3rd July 2003.
A line left of Fat Les, gaining the right-facing corner.
1. 5c. Climb steeply up a crack to gain the corner and follow it to a roof. Traverse left beneath this to belay.
2. 4c. Climb easily to the top.

Copper Got a Pollock E3. R. Pullen, J. Spanken. 2nd July 2003.
The obvious diagonal line running from bottom left to top right of the geo, starting by Chockarockaholic and finishing as for Spring Squiril.
1. 4c. Follow the fault to belay before Ship of Fools' wall.
2. 5c. Traverse steeply across the break of SOF's wall to easier ground.
3 and 4. 4c. Continue in the same line to reach and finish up Spring Squiril.

Banded Geo, South Face:
Ice Box Prose 35m HVS 5a *. R. I. Jones, M. Gear. 6th June 2003.
This is the next route right of Cereal Killer (SMCJ 2002), but is probably best described in relation to a right-facing corner. Four metres left of the corner crack of Corn Choked Chimney (SMCJ 2002) is the right-facing corner. Climb this and the cracks up the wall system above. Shares the last 5m with Wine Box Chimney.

Wine Box Chimney 35m E1 5b *. A. Erskine, J. Wardman. 6th June 2003.
A chimney sits 2m left of the corner. Climb this and the short right-facing corner above (crux). Finish up the steep wall.

The next two routes use a belay at the bottom of the corner of Corn Choked Chimney.

Refrigerator Poetry 35m HVS 5a **. R. I. Jones, M. Gear. 6th June 2003.
Takes the wall between the corner and Muses from Afar. From the bottom of the corner step right to the wall and climb the centre to the top.

Jonathan Preston emerging onto snow from the niche above 'Impossible Wall' on the S. Ridge, Dansketinde. Photo: Stephen Reid.

Muses from Afar   35m   VS 4c *. R. I. Jones, M. Gear. 6th June 2003.
From the corner traverse right to the crack in the centre of the wall. Climb this to
the top.

Rubha Charnain, Small Buoys Geo:
Time for a Cormorant   15m   Very Difficult. H. Salisbury, V. Hennelly. 3rd June
2003.
Climb the corner left of the crack of Reprieve until an awkward step right into a
shallow sentry box. Climb up and left of this to easier ground,

Rubha Charnain, Evening Wall:
Nom   8m   4c. R. I. Jones (solo). 7th June 2003.
Climbs the centre of the wall 2m left of Sandgorgan to the right end of a ledge and
direct to the top above.

The Sandgorgan   8m   5b. R. I. Jones (solo). 7th June 2003.
Two metres left of Stalking the Corncrake are two small cracks at 1.5m height.
Climb these and the wall direct above.

Stalking the Corncrake   10m   VS 4c. D. Carr, V. Hennelly. 7th June 2003.
Left of Beach Bums. Climb the crack to a prominent thread on the left and climb
this direct. Continuing up the crack right of the thread lowers the grade to 4b.

Pleasant Rib   10m   Very Difficult. D. Carr (solo). 7th June 2003.
Climbs the rib immediately left of Beach Bums.

Allanish Peninsula, Hoofers Geo:
Skuaed   35m   Hard Severe. H. Salisbury, V. Hennelly. 4th June 2003.
Climb the crack right and parallel to The Ramp. Move slightly right on to the wall
at 5m and up to a ledge. Continue up the crack 2m on the right and chimney
above.

Cast and Shadow   40m   HVS 5a. D. Carr, A. Arnott. 4th June 2003.
The prominent sharp arête to the right of The Ramp. Climb up to the arête. Climb
this first on the right and then up the arête to a large ledge and easier ground
above.

Boosh   25m   E5 6a. P. Robins, J. McHaffie (both led), N. Dyer. 3rd July 2003.
Climbs the striking left-slanting crack on the right side of the deep chimney just
left of the first described route, right of the descent (looking in). Gain the crack
and go up to a small overlap. Tricky moves over this lead to better holds as the
crack approaches a corner. Climb straight up the wall above to the top.

Big Bloc Sloc:
The following routes climb the wall left of the deep sea cave. To access scramble
down to a small terrace above the wall and abseil.
Ying   15m   Very Difficult. R. I. Jones (solo). 5th June 2003.
The wide crack on the left.

The unclimbed West Face of Vinson Massif from Camp 1. Photo: Rob Milne.

Rob Milne and Heather Morning at Vinson High Camp with Mount Shinn behind. Photo: Rob Milne.

Yang   15m   Severe. R. I. Jones, A. Erskine. 5th June 2003.
The central crack to a short steep wall and the crack above.

Yo   15m   Difficult A. Erskine, R. I. Jones. 5th June 2003.
On the right via a shallow groove.

Shags Geo:
A Semblance of Reason   50m   VS 4c. R. I. Jones, M. Snook. 31st May 1999.
Three metres right of Quartz Waltz and left of the next prominent corner. Climb
the wall and cracks to the large ledge. Climb through the roof on the left above as
for Quartz Waltz.

The following routes are concentrated around the conspicuous groove/corner of
Wok On The Wild Side which is midway between the corner right of A Semblance
of Reason and the next corner of Hunting the Gripper. It has a distinctive quartz
patch at its base and a large triangle shaped rock at quarter height in the corner.
Access is gained by abseil down the corner from a block on the terrace that can be
thread.

Sweetness   35m   E1 5b **. R. I. Jones, J. Wardman. 4th June 2003.
Climbs the rib between Mussel Crack and Hunting The Gripper. Belay at the
bottom right of the rib. Step onto the wall and make delicate moves up the wall
(double zero cam essential). Trend slightly rightwards as you gain height moving
to easier ground. Finish direct through the overhanging finishing slot.

Note: Hunting The Gripper thought to be VS 4c *.

Groovy Attitude   35m   VS 4b *. J. Wardman, R. I. Jones. 4th June 2003.
Six metres right of the corner is a groove with a spike at the bottom. Climb the
small right-facing corner to an overhang. Take this on the right to a ledge. Step
right and climb the corner above to a steep juggy finish.

The Galley: The buttress at the foot of the twin corners of *The Abridged Version*
and *The Complete Works* has fallen away. However, a solid belay ledge remains,
so it is still possible to abseil in to do these routes, plus Wiggly Wall, which now
goes at HVS 5a and remains superb.

Rubha Greotach, The Galley:
N. Morrison thought Winos in a Barren Land to be E3 5c, not E3 6a.

The Poop Deck:
Pabbarotti   25m   E1 5b *. N. Morrison, W. Moir. August 2002.
The meat of this route is the flakey wall right of the crack-line on Geovannie.
Start right of Geovannie and climb the left side of the slab running into the corner-
ramp of The Immigrant. Join that route just below the ledge. From the ledge step
out right on to the wall and follow flakes and juggy breaks in a fine position to the
top.

Pause For Jaws 25m E2 5c **. C. Henderson, R. Durran. 27th Jult 2000.
The slim left-facing groove 5m right of Incommunicado gives surprisingly technical and interesting climbing. Finish direct above the mid-height ledge.

Allanish Peninsula, Allanish Wall:
Zen Left-hand 15m E2 5c *. N. Morrison, W. Moir. August 2003.
Where Zen and the Art of Corncrake Management's dog-leg moves right, climb direct in the line of a crack to a ledge. The crack-line continues up a steep juggy headwall.
Note: Zen seems best started from the ledge below the crack, as such it is 15m not 25m.

Rosinish Wall:
Taxi For Tam 10m E3 6a. W. Moir, N. Morrison, M. Atkins. August 2003.
The left-slanting groove 8m left of The Ethics Police.

Bay Area:
Baywatch 10m E3 6a. W. Moir, M. Atkins. August 2003.
The roof and rib left of Stoney Middleton.

Irish Rover 14m E3 6a. W. Moir, P. Allen, M. Atkins. August 2003.
Cracks on the left side of the wall left of Rum, Sodomy and The Lash. Start up black rock, then make a hard pinch move to better holds.

Small Box Geo, Squall Wall:
Squall Wall is the bounding wall immediately left of the Small Box inlet, providing short climbs on immaculate rock. Routes are described left to right.
Descent: Abseil down the line of Squall Wall to reach a ledge system.

Tempest 15m VS 4c *. P. Allen, M. Atkins. 8th August 2003.
The obvious crack line to the right of Squall Wall.

Eliminator 15m HVS 5a. M. Atkins, P. Allen. 8th August 2003.
Takes the sheet of rock right of Tempest, starting at a small box corner. Climb straight up to join the stepped ledge system. Good climbing on in-cuts, but unfortunately escapable leftward.

Zephyr 15m HVS 5a. P. Allen, M. Atkins. 8th August 2003.
The fault line to the right of Eliminator provides pleasant technical moves to finish.

The following route is on the island opposite the camping place.
Bouncing Bim 20m E3 5c. P. Robins, R. Pullen. June 2002.
Climbs the wall left of the deep chimney which becomes more closed at the top (right again is sharp overhanging arête). Move up on slots and then left to gain the arête near the top. Climbed in the rain so the grade may be wrong.

COLL:
Routes by J. Spencer, J. Sadler, L. Spencer and party in July 2001 and August 2003 (the An Caisteal Slab routes may have been climbed before).

Hogh Bay, An Caisteal:
Park by the Project Trust Hebridean Centre at Ballyhaugh (NM 175 581) and follow the track NW for 200m, then join a faint path running along a fence. Follow the dogleg in the fence, turn left through gate and head for highest point on skyline (named as An Caisteal at NM 172 583). Pass through a notch on the left (south) of the high point. Immediately to the left is an easy angled slab 'Beginner's Slab', and to the right, a dyke 'The Gully'. Straight ahead for 75m, bearing right along a platform reach an undercut, west-facing slab 'The Slab' and surrounding walls. The rock is gneiss, ranging in colour from black to orange through pink, and mostly of excellent quality. Nearby Traigh Hogh (10 minutes) is widely regarded as one of the most beautiful beaches in the Hebrides.

Beginner's Slab:
Izzy Whizzy 8m Very Difficult. Up the middle of the slab by a black streak.
Emma's Dilemma 8m Severe. Direct line to the left of Izzy Whizzy.
One Move Wonder 8m Hard Severe. The overhang over the water at the right-hand end of the slab.
Many variations are possible.

The Gully:
The bottom of the dyke is boggy. From right to left.
Yo Hogh 7m Severe 4a . Up twin cracks formed by a hanging block.
Hogh 10m VS 4b. Start at boulders at lowest point of rocks, beneath twin overlap. Climb up over the overlaps, bearing left into a hanging corner (bearing right at the top gives a 4c finish).

Hogh, Hogh 8m VS 4c. Start below the highest point of the wall. Straight up to the break and over the overlap via a 'thank god' hold.
Hogh, Hogh, Hogh 7m Hard Severe 4a. The blocky crack at the left end of the wall. Break out right at the level of the overhang.
Hogh Hum 5m VS 4b. Up the brown streak.

The Slab: From right to left.
Grooved Slab 8m Very Difficult. The grooved slab on the right side.
Scorpion 10m Severe. Follows left-slanting crack reached by a strenuous move over the overhang to its right. Continue direct up thin crack.
Skid Marks 10m Hard Severe. Climb the brown streak, moving in from the left on small holds.

Callum's Callisthenics 10m Severe. Step on to the undercut slab, move right and follow crack and groove, moving right at the top.

Basking Shark 10m Very Difficult. Step on to undercut slab then straight up blocky crack to the overhang, turning on either left (easier) or right.

Abseil Slab 10m Very Difficult. Turn the big overhang at the left end on its right, then straight up the slab (harder and thinner towards the right side).
High Hogh 10m VS 4b. To the right of The Slab is a steep section with a left-leaning groove system. Climb the slightly overhanging groove on big holds.

Black Wall: This short wall of black, sea-worn rock lies several tiers below The Slab.
X 7m VS 5a. The crack on the right.
XX 7m VS 5a. Climb the centre of the wall.
XXX 5m VS 4b. The crack on the left.

About 200m north of The Slab cross a barbed wire fence to find a solitary pinky grey buttress with *The Missing Hat* 8m HVS 5b. Climb the buttress via a faint crack-line.

Picnic Rocks (NM 171580):
From the gate in the fence, instead of heading for the An Caisteal notch, turn left and walk (SW) towards Traigh Hogh. Pass by a rocky knoll on the right, and cross grassy meadows, heading for a rocky shelf which leads down to the Picnic Rocks, a short section of pink, grey and black slabs riven by cracks and corners, with a green pool at its base. From right to left:
Route 1 5m Very Difficult. Climb the right-trending flakes up the grey wall at the right hand end.
Pets' Corner 8m Hard Severe. Starting to the right of the green pool, climb the corner.
Pet Scorner 8m Very Difficult. From the green pool climb the blocky corner. A variation finish takes the short hanging corner to the left.
Renroc Step 8m VS 4c. Surmount the overhang and climb direct to the top.
Route 2 8m Very Difficult. Up the black wall left of above.
Anerr Corner 8m Very Difficult. Climb on to the overlap at its lowest point, and move right into the corner. Veering left at the top is harder.
Flake Crack 8m Severe. Up the flaky crack.
Crax 8m Severe. Climb the next set of cracks on the wall between the two main corners.
Yet Anerr Corner 8m Very Difficult. Good bridging up the corner.
Crax Crax 8m Severe. Climb the crack-line just left of the arête.
Trident Right Hand 8m Severe. The right-hand (widest) crack.
Trident Central 8m Very Difficult. The central crack.
Trident Left Hand 8m Severe. The left-hand crack.

Creag nam Clamhan: The SMC District Guide mentions "of particular note" Creag nam Clamhan (crag of the buzzard) at NM 237 622. To reach, it park by the cattle grid (NM 234 628) where a stream flows under the road. Follow the stream (keeping ears and eyes peeled for corncrakes in season) veering rightwards (SE) onto boggy ground, flanking the right hand (S) side of a boulder strewn grassy hillock. The crag is about 40m long, 8m-10m high and of grey and pink gneiss of variable quality. Some large boulders beneath the mid-point of the crag provide a useful reference point. Right to left.
I'd Rather Be At The Beach 8m VS 5a. Follow the obvious left-slanting flake-crack at the right-hand end, bearing right at the top. Left finish via a block is harder.

Incy Wincy 8m VS 4c. The square-cut groove to the left of the boulders.
In the Groove 8m Severe 4a. The vegetated crack-line 5m left of Incy Wincy.

MULL, Scoor, Horse Wall:
Note: Paul Tattersall thinks Eat My Shorts is E5.

Ardtun, Yellow Block:
Gone Again   12m   E2 5b **. C. Moody, C. Grindley. 12th October 2003.
The obvious off-width crack right of Everything He Hates About Climbing.

Back From China   10m   HVS 5a *. C. Moody, D. Brooks. 11th June 2003.
Left of White Heather Club, move round the overhang to start.

Ardtun, Stirk Crag:
This is between Green Hill and Blow Hole, about 60m east of the fence; north and
east facing.
Gribun Phone Box Vandals   10m   VS 4b. C. Moody. 29th February 2004.
Twin cracks on the east face.

Erraid, Asteroid Chasm:
Mars Watchers   22m   VS 4b. C. Moody. 27th August 2003.
Gain the shallow chimney right of Asteroid Groove. Follow the ramp up left, go
over a bulge and finish up the wide corner crack. The easy start was not climbed,
but had been climbed before with a low tide.

ISLAY, Lossit Bay Area:
Blackback Stack   20m   Difficult *. G. E. Little. 22nd April 2000.
This is the highest stack at the south end of Lossit Bay. The south face of the stack
is split by a distinctive wide crack. Gain the base of the crack from the right (at
low tide for a dry crossing) and climb it on big holds.

Geodha Cam (MR 176 562):
This narrow geo lies on the north side of Lossit Bay. Its east flank comprises a
slab of immaculate rock. Two short routes have been done, the centre of the slab
and the obvious slabby rib (both about Very Difficult).

The west flank of Geodha Cam is a vertical, part vegetated wall.
Small Boy Waiting   15m   VS 4c. G. E. Little, C. Woodrow. 2nd April 2002.
This route climbs the highest and cleanest section of the wall. Start below the
point where a leftwards-slanting turfy fault reaches the top of the wall. Climb
easy rock to pull on to the steeper face. Climb straight up on strange pocketed
rock to finish at good jugs.

Black Face (NR 172 565):
This fine north-facing slabby black wall lies on the east side of Lossit Point and is
relatively sheltered from the waves that pound this stretch of coastline. The rock,
contrary to its appearance, gives good friction and the climbing is on (mostly
sound) incut flake holds. All the routes start just above normal high tide and are
accessed by abseil.

Blackjack   30m   Severe *. G. E. Little. 4th April 2002.
Start at the foot of a long crack that springs from a small ledge at the bottom left-

hand corner of the face. Follow the crack to a short black corner. Climb this and then pull on to the slab above. Climb the long scoop (staying right of the clumps of vegetation) on excellent, often hidden holds.

Ace of Spades 30m HVS 5a *. G. E. Little. 4th April 2002.
Start at a small ledge slightly up and to the right of the foot of the initial crack of Blackjack. Move right and climb incipient cracks to an obvious undercut flake overlap. Pull over this and continue via the obvious crack (first crux). Surmount a short wall and then climb straight up aiming for the slight rib forming the left edge of a clean triangular slab. Pull directly on to the rib (second crux) and climb it to the top.

Darkness into Light 30m VS 4c **. G. E. Little. 4th April 2002.
Start at plaque-like flakes near the bottom right-hand corner of the face. Climb an immaculate black slab to the left-trending black overlap. Continue up the slab parallel to this until forced to move left. Cross a short wall and then go up to climb a short stepped groove. Finish up the centre of the clean triangular slab above.

Sanaigmore Area, Leac Dubh (NR 229 719):
This very fine slabby wall, displaying dramatic dipping strata, lies in a grand position on the east face of a rocky promontory on the east side of Port na Diollaidh. The promontory is accessed by a short scramble. The black wall of Leac Dubh is footed by a wide easy angled grey slab. All the routes start from this footing slab (which is sea-washed in its lower part). Access to the footing slab is by abseil from a big block at a little grassy trench situated just before the top of the promontory. The first few metres of the abseil are down a vegetated scoop and all routes converge to finish up this scoop.

Rampant Razorbill 25m VS 5a **. G. E. Little. 13th July 2002.
Start a few metres above the high tide mark below some distinctive splodges of quartz. Climb to the quartz then straight up on excellent holds to below steeper rock. Traverse up and right to a little right-facing block overhang (of doubtful stability). Pass the block without using it (crux) and then gain and climb the vegetated scoop to finish (in common with Gallus Guillemot).

Gallus Guillemot 20m VS 5a **. G. E. Little. 13th July 2002.
Start near mid-way down the footing slab below a little stack of flakes wedged in a horizontal crack. Climb straight up on immaculate rock aiming for the little right-facing block overhang (in common with Rampant Razorbill; finish up this).

Crafty Cormorant 25m VS 4c **. G. E. Little. 13th July 2002.
Start a couple of metres down from the top end of the footing slab. Move up to gain a wide horizontal crack. Foot traverse this left for a couple of metres, then trend up and slightly left on small holds until a left traverse gives access to the vegetated scoop and thence the top.

Portnahaven Area, The Fan (NR 173 513):
This splendid wall, in the shape of an open fan, forms the west flank of a little hidden geo (Geodha na Toine Moire) half a kilometre east of Port Wemyss. Access

to the base of the wall is effected by scrambling over the top of The Fan then traversing back along its base on a perfect dipping dyke gangway. The routes, all of good quality (one or two stars), are described from left to right as approached along the dyke gangway.

Rust 6m VS 5a. G. E. Little. 12th July 2002.
Start a short distance down the dyke gangway where a rounded flake fault runs up rightwards. Climb straight up the steep wall on small holds.

Pretty in Pink 15m Severe 4b. G. E. Little. 5th April 2002.
A short distance down, at a level section of the dyke gangway, a right trending rounded flake runs up and across the wall. Gain it, follow it to a slight ledge then finish straight up.

Burnt Umber 10m HVS 5a. G. E. Little. 5th April 2002.
Start at a blank wall between the start of Pretty in Pink and a right-facing flake lower down. Climb the wall on excellent small holds to join Pretty in Pink at the slight ledge.

Raw Umber 15m VS 4c. G. E. Little. 5th April 2002.
Gain and climb the obvious dark right-facing, right-trending flake to its end. A weakness runs up and left. Follow it for 2m, then climb directly up to finish on generous holds.

Aquamarine 15m VS 4b. G. E. Little. 5th April 2002.
A second right-facing flake system lies to the right of Raw Umber. As the name suggests, the start of the route is below high tide (as is the start of all the routes further right). Gain the flake, climb it and continue straight up on rock displaying an embarrassment of good holds.

Amber 18m HVS 5a. G. E. Little. 12th July 2002.
Start at the lowest point of the dyke gangway (well below high tide) a couple of metres right of Aquamarine. Climb boldly up the centre of the 'blank' wall on small flakes, then continue by a profusion of generous holds.

Yellow Ochre 20m Severe. G. E. Little, C. Woodrow. 12th July 2002.
Start at a black pod-like crack below the left end of the prominent roof high up. Climb the pod and continuation crack to reach the left end of the roof. Surmount bulging pink rock above to finish.

Chrome Yellow 20m Difficult. G. E. Little. 12th July 2002.
Start below the right-hand end of the prominent roof high up. Climb straight up passing the right-hand end of the roof on steep rock festooned with good holds.

Graphite Edge 20m Very Difficult. G. E. Little. 12th July 2002.
Climb the right edge of The Fan, in a splendid position, at a surprisingly friendly grade.

Dead Truck Geo (NR 158 535):
This narrow cliff-flanked geo lies 150m north of the Wave Energy Plant. Despite

the fact that the head of the geo has been used as a dumping site for old vehicles, it offers some worthwhile climbing. Access by abseil.

Sacrum Crack 25m Very Difficult **. G. E. Little, C. Woodrow. 17th April 2003.
This diagonal crack is the most striking feature on the south wall of the geo. Start at a big wedged block (just sea washed at high tide) and follow the flake-crack, in a magnificent position, to finish up a short corner at the highest point of the wall.

Sunshine Slab 10m Difficult. G. E. Little, R. W. Little. 17th April 2003.
This line takes the pink slabby face on the north flank of the geo. Start above a wedged block (above normal tidal influence), then gain and climb the pink slab covered in a profusion of small holds.

SKYE

SGURR NAN GILLEAN, Lota Corrie, South-West Face (SMCJ 2003):
Cuddy 50m VS 4c *. S. Kennedy, R. Hamilton. 18th April 2003.
To the right of Arbroath is a deep chimney. The buttress right of the chimney contains a huge flake in the upper section. Start directly below the flake at the left end of a ledge. Climb flakes to a another ledge which is followed rightwards, past a perched block, to a small corner. Climb the corner, then move left into another short corner. Continue up slabs on the left to the base of the flake (25m). Pull on to the flake, step right, then finish straight up (25m).

GLEN SLIGACHAN CRAGS, Low Crag, Panoramix Wall:
Journey Into Space 60m E5. S. Broadbent, K. Wigmore, A.Baugh. 30th May 2003.
A devastating climb up the blank right-hand side of the wall. Easy for the grade, but bold with some heart-stopping run-outs. Probably the big line of the crag with some of the finest sustained climbing the wall has to offer.
1. 35m 5c. The epic first pitch has three good runners with long sections of interesting climbing between them. Start up the sloping ramp as for the previous route, but after 4m head straight up to break through a weakness in the overhang above (Peg in wall just above overhang). Traverse rightwards on the basalt until a line of holds leads back leftwards to another basalt dyke and good nut runner. Hand traverse along this dyke to belay on a cluster of cams close to the right side of the crag.
2. 25m 6a. The blank wall on the upper-right part of the crag provides the crux of the route, and amazing exposure. Move back left to pull through the overhang on small holds. A very poor peg runner provides the last protection on the route. Trend up and left on improving holds across the superb blank wall until the ledge of Grand National is reached. Step right and climb the shallow groove as for that route, before continuing straight up on excellent holds to the top of the crag.

Panoramix Left-Hand:
Pulse 25m E2 5b. A. Baugh, K. Wigmore. 30th May 2003.

Interesting climbing which skirts the vegetation on the right side of the wall. Start at a series of mantelshelves below the right-hand end of the half-height overlap. Climb 10m to the overlap and good protection. The overlap is then turned using the crack on the right (cleaner than it looks!). Move left up a ramp (tiny cams) to gain handholds in the basalt. From here, climb direct to the top using imagination to move between the well spaced holds. Airy.

COIRE A' GHREADAIDH:
Note: C. Moody notes that Eag Dubh from this side has been climbed at I/II ***.

Stag Do   100m   III. S. Muir, R. Hewison. January 2004.
A gully to the left of White Wedding with about 8m of steep ice. The upper gully was easy apart from a short ice step that could bank out.

SGURR DEARG, South Buttress:
Hobo   65m   E3 *. J. Lines. 22nd April 2003.
This route climbs the obvious slabby arête right of Styx.
1. 25m 5c. Start at a small basalt dyke 3m right of an undercut rib and follow it over a ledge to a resting point at 8m. Make thin moves left to the arête and follow it to its apex.
2. 35m 5a. Step off the pinnacle and make a thin traverse rightwards to gain a niched crack, then direct up slabs to a large ledge.

SRON NA CICHE, Cioch Buttress:
Integrity, Variation   15m   Severe (original grade). P. Fletcher, B. Ripley. June 1962.
Where the crack-line of pitch 1 enters a corner and is then blocked by an overhang (optional belay), instead of climbing over the overhang, pull out left on to a triangular ledge on the left arête of the corner and climb the superb arête to the normal stance. Similar standard to the normal route.

ORONSAY (Loch Bracadale) – NG 311 357:
The island is accessible only at low tide. At the SW tip of the island, a descent can be made at low tide to the sea via a grassy promomtory, passing an intriguing cave. Now traverse westwards to gain *The Twins*. These are two small stacks. The left-hand finger gives a 10m Very Difficult up the southerly face. The right-hand stack is climbed via its SW Edge, 12m Very Difficult. Despite some trundling, the stacks still remain rotten basalt (C. Dale, 20th May 2003).

NEIST, The Upper Crag, Financial Sector:
Red Currantcy   22m   E1 5a. C. Moody, C. Grindley. 20th September 2003.
The wide crack just right of Loom of The Land. Abseil to the start of the crack, or start up the heather for a 30m route. Finish slightly left, a bit intimidating at the top.

Poverty Point:
The landward side of the point forms a large non-tidal bay bounded by a large loose looking groove on the right and a prominent jutting pillar on the left.

Golden Shower 30m E4 5c ***. M. Reed, G. Robertson. 23rd August 2003.
A groovy route, with technical climbing all the way, taking the obvious line up the front of the jutting pillar (immediately right of a deep chimney come cave). Pull directly up on to the pillar, then step left and follow the slim groove to a precarious move right onto a sloping ledge. Gain the steeper upper groove (bold) by means of a spooky undercut, then exit this immediately left to finish up good cracks.

The Man from Ankle 25m E3 5c ***. G. Robertson, M. Reed. 23rd August 2003.
Moving left from the previous route, passed a series of steep black walls and grooves, one arrives at a big crumbly corner/recess (this approximates the high tide line). This first class route, technical and well-protected, takes prominent thin cracks and grooves just right of the recess. Follow the dwindling lower cracks until thin moves lead to a small ledge at the base of the right-hand groove. Climb this direct (crux) to the top.

The following four routes are just north of the main cliffs.
Shelter 18m E1 5b *. C. Moody, C. Grindley. 20th July 2003.
The second corner left of Any Spare Change?

Any Spare Change? 20m Severe **. C. Moody. 20th April 2003.
Between Keeler and Chugger's Elbow are two short corners. Climb the crack between the corners.

Thrift Is A Virtue 14m Severe *. C. Moody, C. Grindley. 31st May 2003.
The corner right of Any Spare Change?

Fool's Gold 16m Hard Severe 4b *. C. Moody, C. Grindley. 31st May 2003.
At the right end of the cliff is a pinnacle. Start at the right side of it and climb up left behind it, then go up to bulging rock. Move right through the bulge and continue to the top.

Conductor Cove:
Note: M. Hudson notes that a massive block of rock went missing a few years ago, presumably removed by a winter storm. The block is most of Conductor's Arête. Desmond the Slapper (SMCJ 2002) more or less re-climbs the resulting sandy scar.

Baywatch Area:
Juniper Rib 15m Severe *. C. Moody. 19th July 2003.
Going to Baywatch from the concrete ramp, this route is 12m before the drystane dyke.

Call International Sheep Rescue 20m Severe. C. Moody, C. Grindley. 19th July 2003.
About 20m left of Baywatch is a pale flake. This is left of a black corner which is left of a rib with overhangs at 5m. Climb the pale flake and continue up to overhangs above. Go through the gap up left, then step right and finish above.

Note: An HVS has been climbed just left of Sonamara. Start up a corner-crack, then climb the rock left of the continuation grassy corner.

The Lower Crag, Yellow Walls:
Comeuppance   20m   Severe. M. Hudson, A. Holden. 17th April 2003.
A short diagonal line starting about 20m right of Sugaree (SMCJ 2000) and higher up the blocky ledges. Take cracks diagonally leftwards towards a groove exit.

JCB   25m   Severe. A. Holden, M. Hudson. 17th April 2003.
The open grooves immediately left of A Type of Cooker (SMCJ 2001).

The next two lines are reached by turning right after the descent, towards Supercharger. Immediately right of the recess taken by Smeg is a square tower holding the following routes:
Senora   20m   E1 5b. M. Hudson, N. Bassnett. 28th October 2003.
The strenuous front face of the tower via a pod. Gain the pod from the right and exit precariously. Follow the open chimney above.

Angora   20m   VS 5a *. M. Hudson, N. Bassnett, R. Brown. 28th October 2003.
The grooved right-hand arête of the tower. Start directly below the arête, and exit the small niche with a strange move to reach jugs above. Follow the blocky groove above more easily.

TROTTERNISH, Dun Dubh (394m, NG 442 666):
NE Face/North Ridge   Difficult. C. Dale. 15th May 2003.
A fine pyramidal peak with a triangular NE slope consisting of steep grass cut by rotten basalt bands. Rigid boots used for step kicking. Start from a grassy shelf on the left edge of the face. Traverse diagonally rightwards across the first turf field. A short rock hose gains the second turf field. Another rock hose gains the slender third turf field. Follow this rightwards to gain the exposed crest of the north ridge. Ascend the ridge steeply over a couple of reed cornices and a rock step to gain the knife-edge summit ridge, taken a' cheval to gain twin boulders which are the airy summit. Reverse the ascent route.

North Ridge Direct.   C. Dale. 3rd June 2003.
As titled. The ridge can also be gained at half height by "the traverse of the sods", a very exposed track passing three bad steps and which traverses the vertical west face.

Druim an Ruma (385m):
West Face   50m   Difficult. C. Dale. 15th May 2003.
Start 15m right of the grassy apex abutting the west face. Climb through a basalt band to gain a ledge. Follow this rightwards for 10m, then climb through a short dolerite band. Follow a vegetable weakness leftwards, then naturally up (a botanical paradise). Below the final vertical band, follow a vegetable cornice on hands and knees to one last pull through the cornice to gain the "Lost World", a flat summit with dwarf trees and a tiny pool. Reverse the ascent route.

STAFFIN SLIP NORTH, Toy Buttress:
The routes are described from right to left.
Toy   20m   VS 4c *. M. Hudson, A. Holden, P. Arden. 7th May 1999.

In the centre of the buttress a clean boot-width jamming crack leads past an awkward bulge at half-height.

Bow Crack 25m VS 4b. M. Hudson, A. Holden. 7th May 1999.
Two metres left of Toy lies a slimmer crack system with a bow-shaped deviation halfway. Start up a subsidiary slab and finish carefully up ivy.

Above & Beyond 25m HVS 5a *. M. Hudson, A. Holden, P. Arden. 7th May 1999.
Ten metres left again a clean tower is split by a striking crack which narrows to nothing at two-thirds height. Follow the crack pleasantly then mount a suspicious flake with care. Finish on rounded bulges.

FLODIGARRY, South Tunnel Buttress:
Routes described from left to right:
1. *Spantastic* – as in guide
Sea Slaters Crack (variation to Spantastic) HVS 5b. S. Sadler, J. Richardson. 5th June, 2003.
From the belay ledge, climb to the opening of the cave (as for Spantastic). Make a rockover move right, 5b, on to a ramp which rises diagonally leftwards. Follow this to a small shelf on the right. Move up and right to reach a large flake/block. Continue up the crack which rises diagonally leftwards to the belay of Spantastic (pitch 2 as for that route).

2. Lucy in the Sky – as in guide.
3. Captain Mainwaring (1997). This route was not climbed by W. Jeffrey as earlier reported.

4. *Raindance* 35m HVS 4c. S. Broadbent, K. Wigmore, A.Baugh. 26th May 2003.
Fascinating and varied climbing up the centre of the face, crossing the grassy ledges at half-height. From the hanging belay at the bottom of Raining Men climb the crack for 3m until an awkward step left can be made into a shallow left-slanting groove. This is followed with interest to the grassy ledges (possible belay). From here, follow a series of cracks straight up the steep headwall above to finish close to the right arête.

5. Raining Men (2000) is definitely the route climbed by W. Jeffrey in 1990 and not thought worthy of reporting! On pitch two, W. Jeffrey finished up the arête, whereas the Raining Men traversed left to finish up Spantastic.

6. *Singing in the Rain* 45m HVS. S. Broadbent, K. Wigmore, A. Baugh. 26th May 2003.
A delicate climb up the groove in the arête right of Raining Men.
1. 25m 4c. From the hanging belay at the bottom of Raining Men make an exposed traverse rightwards on good flake holds. A series of hard moves to enter the groove above provide the crux of the route, and are poorly protected by small wires. Follow the groove more easily to belay at the top of Raining Men pitch 1.
2. 20m 4b. Follow pitch 2 of Raining Men.

South Stack:
North Face 20m VS 5b. S. Broadbent, K. Wigmore, A. Baugh. 28th May 2003.
A rather artificial route up the centre of the stack's north face. The difficulties are all easily avoided but are very well protected and enjoyable. Start from the rock ledge at the foot of the East Face and traverse rightwards on big ledges to the centre of the North Face. The first real difficulty is a steep thin crack which leads to the right end of the Captain Quibble traverse. From the top of this move back left to finish up the strenuous flake crack that bisects the headwall at the left side of the face. Finish gracefully if you can…

KILMALUAG, Balmacqueen (NG 445 749):
At the right-hand end of the bay at Balmacqueen there are some short cliffs. At the right-hand end of the obvious easy angled slabs lies a small zawn relatively unaffected by the tide and with the following three routes.

Romeo 12m Very Difficult. R. Taylor, B. Mitchell. 31st August 2003.
The left-hand of the obvious twin crack-lines to the left of Tango.

November 12m Very Difficult. R. Taylor, B. Mitchell. 31st August 2003.
The right-hand of the crack-lines.

Tango 12m Hard Severe. R. Taylor, B. Mitchell. 31st August 2003.
The obvious crack-line on an arête running through a series of small bulges.

RUBHA HUNISH, Meall Tuath:
Willey's Last Stramash 75m E4/5 ***. B. Birkett, G. Sharp (alt.). 21st September 2003.
Climbs the great corner system just left of centre (left of Drifting Too Far From Shore). A route of two halves with the first offering a classic pitch on denatured rock – not unlike Mousetrap on Gogarth. While technical difficulties are reasonable and the climbing good, there are limitations of the rock. On the second pitch both rock and protection are excellent. The initial 40ft corner overhangs continually and the hand traverse left along the lip of the overhang to the final crack up the headwall is sensational. Start beneath the shallow cave-like recess.
1. 40m 5b. Steep grass and easier rocks lead to the corner. Climb to the black cave. Move up and right out of the cave to pull into the right-hand corner groove above. Climb this until possible to move into the left-hand corner-crack which is followed with interest to a ledge.
2. 35m 6a. Climb the impending corner with sustained interest to the roof. Gain the hand traverse which is followed leftwards across the lip until moves up gain the crack. Climb the crack to the top.

The following line is on Tulm Island, the steep island in the bay facing Duntulm Castle.
West Face 40m Severe. M. Hudson, D. Hudson. 1st November 2003.
Launch from the slip below the Duntulm Castle Hotel and put ashore on the east coast at a rock shelf. Scramble round the south end of the island to reach slabs on the west face. Start below the summit of the island at a huge square block. Follow the slabs above the square block, taking care with steeper turfy grooves to finish. Belay on blocks well back down the grassy slope.

NORTHERN HIGHLANDS NORTH

BEINN DEARG, Diollaid a' Mhill Bhric (Gleann Sguaib):
Note: Sidewinder (SMCJ 1999) and Inverlael Buttress (SMCJ 1999, on The West Buttress) were accidentally missed out of the new guide.

Cona' Mheall, Coire Ghranda Face:
Tower of Enchantment II. D. McGimpsey, A. Nisbet. 21st March 2004.
Below the final tower of the route is formed a vague ridge which descends well down. Climb the ridge to the final tower. This was climbed up its crest, which is much easier than the right side.

SEANA BHRAIGH, Luchd Coire, An Sgurr:
Summit Rib 250m II. D. McGimpsey, A. Nisbet. 15th December 2003.
The second from the right of the six ribs, leading directly to the summit of An Sgurr.

Nether Rib 250m II. I. Small, D.McGimpsey, A. Nisbet. 15th January 2004.
The third from the right of the six ribs, with a steeper start.

SEANA BHRAIGH, Luchd Coire, Central Massif:
Note: The following route is in SMCJ 1999 but was accidentally missed out of the new guide.
Saxifrage 210m IV,4. M. Bass, J. Clamp, S. Yearsley. 18th April, 1998.
This route takes the rightmost of the three icy corners on the face left of Flowerpot Buttress, etc.

BEINN AN EOIN, Sgorr Deas, West Face:
Sgorr Deas Chimney 120m IV,4 *. D. Moy, D. Allan. 31st January 2004.
The obvious chimney at the north end of the face. The chimney is climbed direct with the half-way chokestone turned on the left side. Approach the climb from the east end of Loch Lurgainn via the lochan on the col between Sgorr Deas and Sgorr Tuath.

STAC POLLAIDH, East Buttress, South Face:
Underground Resistance 170m V,6. E. Brunskill, D. Morris. 27th February 2004.
This climbs the left edge of the large south face and takes the easiest line through the impressive headwall. Start at the left side of the very steep bottom tier about 20m right from the left edge at an obvious left-slanting ramp/corner. Climb the ramp and continue up and right via ice smears and turfy walls (35m). Continue up and right over steep turfy walls aiming for a short but prominent left-facing corner in the next tier (directly below an impressive corner cutting through the headwall) – (45m). Climb the wall just to the left and continue up heathery ground left to some roofs on the left edge of the buttress (30m). Climb through the roofs and continue up steep blocky walls near the left edge until a short flake-crack is reached below a large snowy niche. Climb this and belay in the niche (40m). Above is a short chockstone-filled chimney; climb this and easy ground to the top (20m).

CUL MOR, Coire Gorm:
Steeplejacks Climb 200m IV,5. D. Allan, D. Moy. 2nd January 2004.
Start about 10m up and left from the start of Three Chimneys.

1. 40m. Traverse rightwards up an easy ramp, then cross the ice pitch of Three Chimneys to continue up a turf rib. Traverse up left about 15m, bypassing a short continuation chimney and a further break in the wall above. Where the ground steepens, step up on to the wall beneath a small semi-detached block and swing right (good thread). Continue up awkward turf steps (crux).
2. 50m. Follow easier ground to beneath the upper chimney of Three Chimneys.
3. 45m. Traverse right beneath this and the right-hand chimney and climb an open turfy groove.
4 and 5. 65m Follow the easy gully above.

Far West Buttress 150m II. V. Chelton, D. McGimpsey, A. Nisbet. 14th January 2004.
A series of ribs to the right of the main wall. Much less steep and with a higher base, they may hold snow when the main cliff is bare. This is the best defined rib, second from the right (west). Climbed solo by varying lines.

REIFF, Pinnacle Area:
Old Fart At Play 9m VS 4b. B. Trevelyan, M. Phillips, S. Bostock. 25th March 2004.
Pleasant climbing up the black wall between Kiddies Corner and Toddler's Crack, following a thin crack trending left, then back right. Start from the very bottom of the cleft.

Seal Song Area:
Note: *Modern Thinking Direct Start* (E4 6b) was climbed by I. Taylor, T. Fryer in August 2003.

Pooh Cliff:
Fish Fingers E2 6b. W. Moir, R. Hewitt. July 2002.
The scoop right of Body Swerve, aiming for crimps on the left.

GLAS BHEINN:
Eas a' Chual Allan 75m IV,5 *. D. Allan, D. Moy. 2nd March 2004.
Unlike its illustrious neighbour, this is one of the shorter waterfalls in Britain. Visible from the road, it lies at NC 248 281 above the south end of Loch na Gainmhich. The first 15m is near vertical.

QUINAG, Spidean Coinich, Bucket Buttress:
Paily Wally 55m III,5. E. Christison, D. McGimpsey. 31st January, 2004.
Climbs the north-west facing wall round to the right of the existing routes. Best approached by a short descent of the north-west ridge from the top of Spidean Coinich and traversing in.
1. 25m. Go up into a small bay and gain a turfy groove on the left which leads to a terrace.
2. 30m. Climb grooves up the wall, trending slightly left.

FAR NORTH WEST CRAGS, Serendipity Crag (Guide p253):
Outside Right 18m E1 5a. R. Anderson. 17th February 2004.
The thin blind crack immediately right of Central Wall.

Jamie Andrew on the summit of Kilimanjaro. Photo: Jamie Andrew.

· *Serenity* 18m E2 5b **. R. Anderson. 17th February 2004.
The obvious blunt arête where the crag changes aspect. Start just left of the edge taken by Right Arête and climb the slab to a horizontal crack where a step up left gains the base of the blunt arête. Climb the arête on its left side to gain a short groove and move up right on to a ledge where an interesting finish awaits directly up the edge.

Creag Gharbh Mhor, Red Wall (Guide p255):
Note: Many of the routes here were climbed by D. Wheeler and partners in 1994 and 1995, also Jewel in the Crown (Glaciated Slab), Prester John (Polin Geo), some of the easier routes on School Buttress and much bouldering, most notably at Sandwood Bay on the hilltop between the second and third beach.

Wrycrack 15m E2 5c *. R. Anderson, C.Anderson. 20th February 2004.
The thin crack-line 1m left of Rhicorner, after the initial section the crack is climbed on its left side. A touch eliminate but as with the other routes here, good

Note: R. Anderson started up the ramp of Rhikkie Tikkie Tavie, stepping right but then going straight to the top and presumably cutting through that route as it comes back left before finishing as for the 4c finish up horizontal breaks to the highest point of the crag – E2 5b. Description for Goosemon-mon seemed a bit vague and grade odd.

Oldshoremore Beach Crag:
Go down the steps, past a neat little slab (*Turn Around and Take it in*, Very Difficult, J. Price, May 1989), and keep going till at very low tide, an orange flake-crack is E1 5b. Next right is a barnacled steep wall to a good hold, then finish slightly right up flaky folds (*Down by the Seaside*, HVS 5b). The best line is right again: *Surfin OSM*, E1 5b/c. Right again is a blunt arête and crack (*Led Zep Rip Off*, HVS 5a). Routes by D. Wheeler, B. Leng, G. Howard, 1st August 1995. Routes are 10m, low tide required.

CREAGAN MEALL HORN:
Moonlight Shadow 300m II. B. Davison. 28th February 2004.
A big left-slanting gully left of Cesfall has several short icy steps and two interesting chockstones, the first passed by a squeeze on the left side and the second by ice on the left wall. Much of the rest of the gully is easier.

MEALL HORN, Creag an Lochan Ulbha:
This is the cliff above Lochan Ulbha.

Guantanamo 150m V,4. D. McGimpsey, A. Nisbet. 28th February 2004.
At the right end of the cliff, west of the west end of the loch, is an easy gully leading into a steep corner-chimney with icy turf (and little protection) and finishing by an iced ramp, well seen on the approach.
Sedna 150m V,4. A. Nisbet, D. McGimpsey, B. Davison, D.Allan. 28th February 2004.
Towards the left end of the cliff is an obvious big hanging slab. About 100m right of this is an icefall flowing from a gully on to a big slabby wall. This gave a fine

Keith Anderson traversing past a tower on the Flèche Rousse ridge, Aiguille d'Argentière. Photo: Adam Kassyk.

exposed pitch on sometimes thin ice, hence the grade. A fine route on continuous ice.

Sunlight Shadow   150m   III. B. Davison, D. Allan. 28th February 2004.
Above and left of the hanging slab, an icefall can be seen. Start up an iced groove system leading to a large ledge and move across to the base of the icefall. On the first ascent the lower section of this was poorly formed and so it was mixed climbed on the left. The continuation of the route is a pleasant icefall cutting through the buttress at the back of a broad terrace.

BEN LOYAL:
Marathon Corner Direct   280m   VIII,8 ***. G. Robertson, P. Benson. 31st January 2004.
A magnificent natural winter line, one of the North West's finest, climbing mainly frozen turf, with short sections of snowed-up rock and ice. The winter ascent follows the lower and upper corners direct throughout, with the crux being the barrier wall connecting the two. The hard sections are very precarious and protection is poor throughout.
1. 50m. Start below the lower corner and climb steepening turf to a rib of rock with a small niche on the right.
2. 45m. Climb the corner direct, harder than it looks, to an impasse, then step across left to belay.
3. 35m. Move left to gain a snow ramp leading up round the crest to a huge perched block.
4. 30m. The crux pitch. Climb the crack behind the block and continue up grooves to where a hard mantelshelf gains a small sloping niche. Make committing moves into a blind crack above, then lurch right to a haven of turf. Continue up steep turfy walls to a bay below a chimney.
5. 40m. Climb the chimney, then easier ground up left towards the big upper corner. Gain the base of the corner by a tricky step on to a slab, then climb the corner for 10m to step left to large detached blocks.
6. 45m. Climb the corner direct to the capping overhang, then make difficult moves up and right to a ledge.
7. 35m. Climb the continuation corner direct to the top.

BETTYHILL CRAGS, Farr Point:
The Dark Mennis   60m   Severe. P. Gorry, M. Dennis. 20th July 2002.
On Farr Point sea arch. Scramble down the grass slope on the left-hand side of the promontory and across a large rocky ledge to arrive at the left hand side (when looking out to sea) of the tunnel. This route takes the slabby landward wall of the tunnel, opposite the overhanging wall of The Farr Side. An enjoyable little route, the first pitch of which requires low tide or a snorkel. Start on the large wave-cut platform at the entrance to the arch.
1. 50m 4a. Traverse into the tunnel and along the black slab. Wriggle through the porthole at the far end (semi-submerged at high tide) and belay at the corner beyond.
2. 10m 4b. Continue traversing to a sea level ledge.
Either climb Bombs Away or reverse the route.

Bombs Away!   60m   E1. P. Gorry, M. Dennis. 20th July 2002.
Start from the ledge at the end of The Dark Mennis (a sea-level ledge on the

landward side, on the right-hand side of the promontory, looking out to sea, at the mouth of the arch.). Impressively loose.

1. 30m 4b. Traverse diagonally right up to a black boulder situated at the apex of the arch. Traverse diagonally left a little further to a broken ledge.

2. 30m 4a. Continue diagonally left up a grassy ramp, past Fulmar nests, to a shallow groove. Climb up the grassy headwall to the top. Belay on a turf bollard.

CAITHNESS EAST COAST, Noss Head:

The Ugly Sister 35m VSL (Very Severely Loose). S. M. Richardson, M. Robson. 6th July 2003.

The prominent stack at ND 385 550, east of Castle Sinclair Stack. Abseil from the fence post at the end of the Lighthouse boundary wall to non-tidal ledges opposite the stack. Swim 10m to a platform on the north side of the stack and climb a short wall to gain the west ridge that leads to the summit. Abseil descent down east wall.

Fantasy Golf Stack 35m HVS. M. Robson, S. M. Richardson. 7th July 2003.

The rectangular grass-topped stack at ND 378 549 directly beneath the west side of Sinclair Castle. Discovered after a lengthy search for a stack once featured on a fantasy golf calendar. Can be approached by stepping across a narrow channel either side of high tide.

1. 20m 4c. Starting on the north side, climb a pillar just right of a prominent arch, step left across the arch and traverse left on to the west wall. Belay on a large ledge next to a steep crack splitting the wall.

2. 15m 4c. Climb the crack to the top. Simultaneous abseil descent.

The Tee 10m HVS 5a. M. Robson, S. M. Richardson. 7th July 2003.

The small non-tidal needle-like stack 100m west of Fantasy Golf Stack at ND 378 548. Climb cracks on the west face. Abseil descent.

South Caithness:

Ramscraig Stack, Alternative Start. R. Benton, R. I. Jones. 31st August 2003.

This provides better climbing and allows the stack to be climbed in two pitches. It joins the original route by pulling up through the bad step on pitch 2.

1. 30m 4b. Start from the ledge at the corner right of the south-eastern arête on the east face of the stack. Climb this and pull through onto a ledge, step right and climb the steep wall above to a grassy ledge. Follow this leftwards to the arête.

ORKNEY, Yesnaby:

The Numbtease Dance 20m Very Difficult. I. and M. Miller, C. and H. Clarke. 3rd March 2004.

Approx. 8m to the left of Old Man's Folly, climb a right-trending, left-facing fault on big holds/small ledges. Finish either direct or continue on the fault to a wee niche and the top.

The Tower Area:

The Forgotten 18m E1 5b *. I. Miller, H. Clarke. 4th March 2004.

Climb the thin full-height groove come crack immediately to the left of Bobbin's Groove (right of Deceptively Groovy). Easy at first to a ledge, followed by crimping through a black slab, then strenuous jug pulling up the last steep 6m. Excellent rock and adequate protection.

NORTHERN HIGHLANDS CENTRAL

AN TEALLACH, Toll an Lochain:

Lady's Gully, Swiss Approach   90m   III. J. Preston, M. Hirsbrunner, C. Koenig. 26th January 2004.

A more direct approach through the rock barrier. Start about 100m right of the left end of the barrier wall where there is an obvious line of weakness. Traverse a few metres right, then step up steeply through a rock band. Continue up and diagonally right on turf to below and left of an obvious corner (45m). Traverse right again for a few metres, then up through two rock bands to the base of the snowfield, directly below the gully.

AN TEALLACH, Glas Mheall Mhor, North Face:

Easily seen from the An Teallach path from Dundonnell, this cliff comes into condition during a prolonged freeze. The routes are all spring fed, giving good water ice when higher cliffs may not be in condition. The cliff is more than 500m long with an easy descent at the west end. A diagonal ramp at the east end also gives a steeper descent (a short icefall joins the ramp part way up, one of the routes previously reported). To the right of the ramp are a series of icy left-facing corners, then the steepest section with a hidden chimney. The centre of the crag holds the largest ice sheet of GOB. Continuing rightwards the crag gradually tapers away but contains several lower angled icefalls.

Descriptions are from left to right starting to the right of the short icefall on the descent ramp.

Crystal Clear   100m   IV,4. I. Small, I. Collier. 2nd January 1997.

This climbs the thin hanging ramp that forms the leftmost of three corners. Climb the ramp on ice and follow rightwards to a steep final wall.

Plasticity   100m   V,5. I. Small, A. Hume. 28th February 2004.

About 70m right of the previous route are two parallel groove come chimney lines. Climb easy ice to gain the left-hand line, then take the chimney to a ledge below a steep ice pillar. Ascend this and easier ground above.

The Slit   100m   IV,5. I. Small, A. Hume. 28th February 2004.

The right-hand line. Climb easy ice to gain a prominent V-groove and follow this to beneath a hidden icy chimney, climbed to a ledge. Finish up a steep ice column directly above and easier ground.

Resolutions   100m   IV,4. I. Small. 1st January 1997.

Immediately to the right is an obvious icefall which forms a big open groove at the top.

GOB's Day Out   110m   IV,5. D. McQuaker, A. McQuaker, D. Martin, I. Collier, I. Small. 2nd January 1997.

Fifty metres to the right is the largest icefall, forming a wide sheet. This starts on the left side at the foot of a diagonal fault and climbs the icefall on its left side with two steeper sections near the top.

To the right, three other ice lines were climbed by I. Small on 1st January 1997 at 90m IV,4; 80m, III,4 and 80m III,4.

Badrallach Crags, Goose Crag (NH 107 896 Alt. 240m West facing):
The closest climbing to the Badrallach road is this scruffy crag with the best looking rock on the left side. Once the road leaves the forestry, there is a sheep fank on the left by the junction of fences. Park in the next passing place or verge on the left. The crag is directly above, reached in about 10 minutes.

Cow Dumped In JR's Soft-Top 40m VS 4c. A. Cunningham, K. Geddes. 13th September 2002.
At the left side is an undercut pillar of rock with short corners bounding either side, the left-hand corner crack has a small rowan tree at the top. Start at the lowest rocks and climb a crack to a ledge under the pillar. Move leftwards and up the corner-crack and finish easily up the slab.

SGURR NA LAPAICH, Sgurrr Na Clachan Geala (NH 162 343):
Practice Lap 120m III,4. A. Hume, I. Small. 17th February, 2004.
This route lies on a short steep buttress on the north side of the terminal end of Sgurr na Clachan Geala's South-east ridge (NH 168 338). Climb the obvious ramp past a steep rocky section to a crest and turf ledges (50m). Move up on grassy ledges to easier ground and directly to top (70m).

STRATHFARRAR, Sgurr na Muice, North-East Face:
Ribsticker 140m III. J. R. Mackenzie, A. Nisbet. 24th March 2004.
A reasonable route starting from the terrace and climbing the shallow rib between Tusker and Three Little Pigs.
1. 50m. Start below and right of Tusker at a thread and climb directly up the steepening rib over short walls.
2. 50m. Continue in the same line up the rib over more short walls.
3. 40m. Follow the vague crest to the top.

Three Little Piggies 300m II *. D. Broadhead, J. R. Mackenzie. 22nd February 2003.
To the right of Pigsty Gully another shallow break runs up the three-tiered face, with the top tier split by a shallow gully. The climb starts opposite the northern end of the loch. The lower tier gave continuous ice at a moderate angle followed by snow to the middle tier which gave a fine 25m ice pitch to snow. Another short ice pitch above then leads to a long snow slope and the final tier split by a fine gully that gives a good mixed pitch to finish up snow.

The Trough 200m II *. J. R. Mackenzie, D. Broadhead. 11th January 2004.
A long turfy ramp borders the right edge of the bay containing Slaughterhouse Blues and gives a pleasant excursion up a natural line. Approach for that route but start lower down and to the right of the slab which bottoms it. Easy climbing keeping to the left for two pitches arrives at a short steep wall. This is climbed centrally or on the left for most interest. The ramp now steepens and the route keeps near the rock on the left to arrive at a slabby pinnacle. Move up left to a wide groove to gradually easing ground and the top.

Sgurr na Fearstaig, South Top, East Face:

Torque of the Devil 165m IV,5 **. D. Broadhead, J. R. Mackenzie. 9th February 2003.

A good natural line up the buttress right of Red Campion. The climb takes the leftmost buttress which has a conspicuous triangle of snow 50m up and is bounded on the left by the snow ramp of Red Campion. To the right of a small icefall at the toe of the buttress is a left-slanting turfy ramp.

1. 45m. Follow the ramp past a bulge to traverse left along the top of the snow triangle to reach a small recess with a large block.

2. 40m. Continue the traverse to the left-hand edge of the face where a prominent notch will be seen 20m up the edge. Climb up to this notch steeply to below an overhang. Twin cracks then enable difficult moves leftwards to the base of a turfy ledge, a well protected crux, and continue for 10m past a step.

3. 40m. Continue left for about 10m, then climb up or near a thin ice smear and some steep mixed ground to an easing to where the summit snowfield begins.

4. 40m. Continue up steepening snow to the top, sometimes corniced but usually outflanked to the left.

Tendril 50m II. D. Allan, J. R. Mackenzie. 6th March 2004.

About 30m up the right-slanting section of Sea Pink Gully it is possible to gain entry to the slab above. Above, move up left then back right to finish up a scoop; sometimes heavily corniced.

Dancing With Calluna 90m III *. J. R. Mackenzie, D. Broadhead. 22nd February 2003.

The buttress that separates Sea Pink Gully from Enchanters Nightshade has a good initial pitch.

1. 50m. Start at the foot of the buttress and follow a line of weakness up left then back right to below the final step.

2. 40m. The short step, then snow and a possible cornice at the top.

To the right of the main crag lies a smaller one split by a gully and overlooking the Bealach Dearg.

A Wee Cracker 75m III *. J. R. Mackenzie. 21st February 2004.

A good steep climb with attitude. It takes the prominent narrow gully just right of a thinner cracked groove. Snow leads to a minor pitch followed by steepening snow to the obvious crux, a near vertical rocky corner (potentially good gear on left wall). Struggle up this to finish in a good position; possible cornice. Often in condition.

Fuar-tholl Mor (NH 237 437):

This open corrie has mixed ground below the summit of Sgurr Fhuar-thuill. Besides the route below, other much longer Grade I and possibly Grade II climbs could be made here if not swamped in snow. Often in condition with a base of around 900m.

The Glass Scribe 120m III,4. J. R. Mackenzie. 21st February 2004.

Just left of the summit is a broken buttress with snow ramps and steps and below that another slabby buttress. Contour in or descend Grade I slopes to the foot of this. A fine icefall runs down the middle of this lower buttress issuing from a spring. Climb steeply up a groove to a large iced slab and up the middle of this to a short fat vertical pillar. Ascend this and easier ice above to snow and mixed ground to the top. A good contrasting climb with reliable ice.

Creag Ghorm a' Bhealaich (NH 245 435):

A slender ridge falls directly from the summit into upper Coire na Sguile. Either side are narrow gullies. Often in condition with a base of around 930m.

SE Passage 80m I/II *. J. R. Mackenzie. 21st February 2004.

The left-hand gully is scenic, quite steep and well defined, having a small but interesting pitch at some narrows.

NE Passage 80m II. J. R. Mackenzie. 21st February 2004.

The right-hand gully is blocked by a rock buttress at half-height. Above are two ramps; traverse left across to the top one and make airy moves across and up to finish up the last few metres of the ridge.

CREAG GHLAS, East Buttress:

Oh Dearie Me 250m III,4 *. A. Dennis, J. R. Mackenzie. 9th February 2004.

A good technical exercise with mainly good protection. It takes the thin discontinuous turf streaks to the right of the slab edge of Oh Dear and Oh Dearie Me and finishes up the last two summer pitches of the latter route. The route is graded for the slab section as the headwall can be avoided by easier ramps and grooves on the left. As climbed it is a technical 5. The route is probably only in condition after north-westerly blizzards.

Turn the short bottom slab on the left and move right to the turf streak. Climb this past a thin section to belays left of a small tree. Move right to the tree then up increasingly tenuous slabs to a large cracked block on the left. Move right and climb a groove and then easier ground. The climb as described takes the steep short wall via a vertical ice slot followed by easier ground to a large flake below a steep wall. This and the next pitch can be turned on the left by more broken ground. Climb the corner to the right of the flake and then the awkward crack and chockstone above, as for the summer description of Oh Dearie Me. Now finish up the optional V-slot as for the summer route.

West Buttress:

Cut Glass 90m E3 5c **. R. Brown, J. R. Mackenzie. 25th June 2003.

A good but serious route up the narrow slabby buttress to the left of Sweet Charity.

1. 45m 5b. Climb the centre of the lower slab as for Sweet Charity to below the niche where that route escapes (crucial nut runners in the niche). Step left and climb thin moves up the fine slab, past a flake to left-trending edges and go up these to follow a short heather rake to a good crack on the left.

2. 45m 5c. A short wall leads to the slab. Step up on this and climb it delicately to a narrow ledge and welcome gear. Continue to the left of a steeper crack on knobbles to vital Rocks#7 and 5 runners at the end of the crack. Climb up and left delicately to a rounded horizontal edge, step up right then straight up to a

tricky final move. Finish by 5m of scrambling. Escape up left to reach the descent gully.

The Unknown Soldier 25m E7 6b *. J. Lines, R. A. Biggar. 18th July 2002.
An eliminate offering extremely bold slab climbing on impeccable rock. Start 2m left of Victory Crack and just to the right of Tales of the Old Days. Climb directly up the bald slab to some quartz blocks at 12m (RP 5). Stand on the quartz and make a long reach for a fingerhold, make a rockover on to this and stand up (crux). Reach a good hold on the left and clip the peg on Tales of the Old Days. Stand on a good hold and move diagonally left, then up to a horizontal break. Step left to a vertical crack and finish up this (as for Tales of the Old Days).

BEN WYVIS, Coire Mor, No. 2 Spur:

Fox Gully Arête 200m II. J. R. Mackenzie, D. Allan. 18th February 2004.
This is the left bounding edge of Fox Gully clearly seen as a strip of snow or turf near the left edge of the steep buttress left of the gully. Scenic and a pleasant way up the cliff.
1. 50m. Climb the broken walls and ledges left of the edge, steeper than they look.
2. 50m. Continue up the narrow snow or turf strip and arrive at an arête.
3. 100m. Continue up the level arête then over two towers, best climbed on the right, then up a steepening snow slope to finish.

The Last Resort 200m IV,4 **. J. R. Mackenzie, D. Allan. 13th March 2003.
A steep and natural line up the main buttress right of Fox Gully. It is sustained at the grade and twists and turns amidst good crag scenery. To the right of the left edge, bounded by Fox Gully, is a shallow bay perhaps 30m or so right of the edge, bordered to its right by a right slanting gully ramp. In the centre of the bay is a steep wall leading up left to a narrow ramp and chimneys below a prominent pinnacle. The climb starts up the wall and ends up on the top skyline just right of the first of three horns. The direct start is described; an easier break to the left would reduce the grade to IV,4.
1. 40m. Climb a steep turfy wall that leads to the base of the left-slanting break. Follow the break up and left to chockstones in the chimney that leads to the pinnacle.
2. 45m. Step down and move right along a vanishing ledge for 10m to a tricky step right. Move up and then back left along a ramp for 15m to below steep walls right of a left-slanting break. Climb the difficult stepped walls then move right.
3. 45m. Above is a steep wall. Step down and move right below this to a bay and climb a splendid narrow chimney to its top. Move left past a rocking stone to gain a hidden chimney. Climb this steeply over delightful bulges and chockstones to a chockstone below the final bulge.
4. 40m. Climb the tricky bulge above and then more easily an isolated outcrop.
5. 30m. Steepening snow leads to the top.

Temptress 180m V,5 ***. J. R. Mackenzie, A. Dennis. 8th March 2004.
Probably the best line on the crag giving excellent varied climbing that is exposed,

scenic and adequately protected and with a sensational finish. It starts up the big right-facing corner in the central bay and ends up the hanging corner by the second horn.

1. 35m. Climb the corner direct to the overhanging wall. A foot traverse left to the edge is followed back right via turf. Continue up the left branch and poor belays back left on the shelf above; possibly better to belay slightly lower.

2. 50m. Cross the shelf to below a left-slanting ramp. Climb the difficult wall on its right to turf and climb straight up past a serendipitous spike to and over a yellow chockstone and up into a shallow bay and ledge above.

3. 25m. Move up left along a narrow shelf to a below a steep groove below the final wall. Climb the groove to a tiny shelf.

4. 20m. The overhanging wall has an off-width crack and chockstone; climb the wall to its left first by turf then by torques, step right and climb the blocks and shelves in an amazing position.

5. 50m. Easy snow to the top.

Interrupted Gully 200m II *. D. Allan, J. R. Mackenzie. 18th February, 2004. A good interesting climb with only the start visible from below. It takes the right-slanting ramp at the right of the bay.

1. 50m. Climb ice or turf up the ramp to a snow patch. Instead of continuing to its end (and a possible escape) belay below a prominent slanting flake-crack midway along the patch.

2. 50m. Step left and climb a very awkward short wall to a ledge, crux, and then up the narrow turfy gully above which then slants right.

3. 50m. The gully now jinks back left and up. Climb steeper ice or turf up the gully to a cracked block on the left.

4. 50m. A steepening snow fan and probable cornice to exit.

Creag Bealach Culaidh (NH 447 726):

This remote, south facing, quartzite crag lies above its namesake loch about 4km west of Wyvis Lodge. The most distinctive features are a vertical pink holdless wall and a two-stepped corner to its left.

Badger up a Plum Tree 35m E1 5b **. G. E. Little, J. Lowther (alt.). 7th June 2003.

This excellent climb takes the obvious two-stepped corner.

1. 25m 5b. Climb the fine corner until it is possible to pull out left on to a slab (the lower corner-line turns into a wide messy crack above). Climb the upper corner to a grass ledge and tree.

2. 10m 4b. Climb the block-filled chimney and thence to the top.

Sett Up 25m E1 5b. J. Lowther, G. E. Little. 7th June 2003.

This route lies well to the right of the vertical pink wall on an obvious rib lying between an open vegetated groove (holding a rowan) on the left and a wide tree-filled grassy gully on the right. Start at the very toe of the rib. Climb over a huge flake, then up past a sapling to better rock. Move up to below an overhang. Traverse hard right until moves back left give access to the slabby face above. Climb the unprotected slab and vegetated ground to finish (no belay).

THE FANNAICHS, Garbh Coire Mor:
Tormentil 200m IV,5 *. A. Nisbet. 18th November 2002.
A narrow ramp across the steep wall parallel to and overlooking Primrose gully.
Start right of the depression and Ramp Tramp and climb steeply on turf sods to
reach the ramp. Follow it to a short corner which gives a couple of strenuous but
well protected moves to gain a continuation of the ramp, less well defined but
which leads in the same line to the top.

Triffid 220m VI,7 **. D. McGimpsey, A. Nisbet. 4th January 2003.
Climbs the right side of the buttress, passing right of a band of overhangs which
cap the central area of the buttress. Start about 10m left of Burdock.
1. 40m. Climb a groove with thin turf to the right end of an overhang. Traverse
left and pull through the left end of the overhang to another longer groove which
is followed curving right to a slight crest below steeper ground.
2. 20m. Move right and climb a turfy corner. Traverse back left along a ledge for
about 10m and pull through a bulge. Traverse left again and pull leftwards through
another bulge to reach a flake below a steep corner. There may well be icicles,
or even an icefall, just right of the corner.
3. 20m. Climb the steep corner (or the icefall) to turf. Continue slightly rightwards,
then up to a good ledge.
4. 50m. Go rightwards, then up steep turfy ground to finish up a short bulging
chimney.
5. 50m. Trend left into a broad fault and up it.
6. 40m. Continue up the fault to the top.

Coire nan Eun:
The cliffs are divided into three distinct buttresses, East, Central and West
separated by two gullies, Descent Gully and Inner Sanctum (1994).

Lava Luvva 100m III. D. Morris, H. Stagg. 1st February 2003.
This route climbs an icy recess and the gully above in the centre of the east
buttress. Climb the ice recess via the right wall to gain a right-trending ramp and
easier ground (40m). Continue above to a fork, take the left branch up a defined
gully and finish up the right wall to the top.

Kitekat Rib 90m II. D. Morris, H. Stagg. 1st February 2003.
This route climbs the rib overlooking Descent Gully. Start on the right side of
the buttress at the foot of Descent Gully, attain the rib and climb direct to the
top.

Feral Buttress 75m III,4. E. Brunskill, D. Morris. 10th January 2003.
Start at the base of Inner Sanctum and traverse leftwards on to the front face of
the Central Buttress via the obvious ledge to a large block. Climb left-trending
turfy grooves to a bay below twin parallel grooves (30m). Climb the left-hand
groove and continue in the same line to the top (45m).

Slam 90m VI,6 *. E. Brunskill, D. Morris. 10th January 2003.
This route climbs the turfy groove system on the left edge of the West Buttress.

Protection is generally spaced and of dubious quality. Start at the bottom left toe of the buttress and climb the deceptively steep left-trending turfy groove system to a recess below the very steep upper section (50m, similar first pitch to Fatal Attraction). Continue up the continuation ramp leftwards until it levels out below a steep flaky wall. Climb thinly up this to another ledge and traverse left to a protruding block. From the top of this climb boldly up and right through the blocky overhangs to easy ground and the top (40m).

Bunny Boiler 100m III. D. Morris, H. Stagg. 15th February 2003.
On the western side of West Buttress several icefalls form readily. This route tackles the second of two parallel falls. Climb the icefall direct and continue above trending right up a ramp to the top.

Saddle Up 120m II/IV,4. D. Morris, H. Stagg. 15th February 2003.
This climbs a vague right-trending icy recess starting to the right of the main icefalls at the right side of West Buttress. Climb the icy recess for 50m to a snowfield. Cross the snowfield to below two ice falls. The wide left-hand icefall is II. The narrow central fall is IV,4.

SGURR NAN CLACH GEALA:
Summiteer 180m II. D. McGimpsey, A. Nisbet. 26th January 2004.
A route up the right face of the summit buttress. Start on a terrace above and right of Fusilier's gully. Climb a prominent groove to a steep wall (25m). Go diagonally left, then back right to reach the top of the groove's continuation (45m). Cross a snow ramp slightly leftwards, then move right under a wall to reach a line of weakness (40m) which leads naturally (45m) to the upper crest, and finish as for Fusilier (25m).

Fionn Bheinn, Creag Toll Mor:
Crystal Visions 65m IV,5 *. D. Allan, J. R. Mackenzie. 14th December 2002.
The hanging chimney provides the line of the crag.
1. 25m. Climb the turf over a step to below the wall guarding entrance into the chimney.
2. 40m. The wall provides the crux. Climb to an overlap, move back right and gain and surmount a turfy overhang to another similar overhang immediately above. Once in the chimney things ease; another short chimney can be taken on the left or avoided on the right.

The Kilted Raven 80m II. J. R. Mackenzie. 10th December 2002.
A well defined ramp runs up right to left beyond Prophetic Voices. It has only one point of difficulty, a short rocky block which needs to be climbed over to reach the continuation and the top.

The Plaid and The Bonnet 75m III. J. R. Mackenzie, D. Allan. 14th December 2002.
About 50m to the right of Crystal Visions are some narrow grooves leading to a black summit crag, prominent from below. Some good climbing particularly on the first pitch.

1. 40m. Climb the leftmost and most interesting groove over a series of short steps to below the summit crag.
2. 35m. Continue along the dwindling ledge to a steep pull up on the left at its termination and continue up turfy ground above.

GRUINARD CRAGS, Jetty Buttress, Back West Wall:
After the Storm 20m HVS 5b. R. I. Jones, S. J. McNaught. 12th April 2003.
Start as for Gruinard Corner (the crack-line directly beneath the arête) for 5m to a shelf. Continue but before reaching the main corner, step right into the bottom of a corner on the arête above an overhang. Climb this and the arête to the top.

Trespass 20m E2 5c **. C. Meek. 5th May 2001.
The crack-line just right of the arête, with a move right after the bulge.

The Rowan 20m E1 5b *. C. Meek, C. Dryer. 20th May 2001.
Another crack-line 2m to the right.

GRUINARD CRAGS, Inverianvie Wall, Optic Wall:
Lock-in 15m E1 5b. C. Cartwright, N. Wilson, S. Campbell. 30th March 2003.
Climb the slab between The Parting Glass and Gill to the widest section of the overlap, pull through and then follow a faint groove trending slightly right.

BEINN AIRIGH CHARR, Martha's Peak:
2003 Route 380m III. M. Shaw, I. Humberstone. 29th December 2003.
This route zigzags up the main face of Martha's Peak, finishing on the summit. It is only the second route up this impressive face and follows a natural winter line up a series of ramps and shelves. Initially the 2003 Route follows a line left of the 1910 Original Route (which was climbed in winter in 1999 by Lyall/ Webb). At the "platform halfway up the upper crags" it crosses the Original Route and finishes up an easier chimney line to the right.
    Start near the bottom left corner of the main face and follow an obvious ramp line up and left. This leads to a platform overlooking Staircase Gully. From the platform a large shelf leads easily up and right to beneath a deep chimney slot (obvious from the base of the crag). From beneath the slot a short rock band needs to be climbed up and left to gain access to another left-trending ramp line. This leads to a shallow gully which is followed back right up to the "platform halfway up the upper crags". The well-defined chimney of the 1910 Route could be climbed from here but, instead, a separate chimney line further to the right was climbed in two pitches, finishing just beneath the summit.

LOCH TOLLAIDH, Hidden Crag:
Back to Business 20m E1 5b. F. Fotheringham, A. Tattersall. 4th May 2003.
The blocky looking line through the bulge to the right of Frog Dance, then directly to the top.

CREAG BHADAN AN AISC, Curtain Wall:
Tired of Creation 10m E5 6a/b. P. Tattersall, T. Doe. 18th February 2003.
A central line on the overhanging right-hand sector of the crag, finishing by a

hanging groove. Climb the wall, stretch right to reach and climb the slim hanging groove.

SLIOCH:

Avalanche Goose 225m VI,7. I. Small, N. Wilson. 1st February 2004.
To the left of The Slioch Slim Plan are a line of narrow chimneys. Start as for The Slioch Slim Plan but climb 15m of easy ground to below the line.
1. 25m. Climb icy/turfy grooves to the base of the lower chimney.
2. 20m. Climb the first chimney to belay on a terrace.
3. 25m. Climb the second chimney, which is more of a flake at the bottom (crux), to belay out to the left on the terrace above.
4 and 5. 80m. Traverse right, then up short walls to gain an obvious gully on the left.
6 and 7. 60m. Climb the gully, with one steepening, to the crest of the main ridge. From here about 150m of easy scrambling leads to the top of the hill.

Pinnacled Gully 450m III,4. C. Cartwright, R. Webb. 1st February 2004.
This line initially follows the right-hand base of the "three pinnacles" overlooking Surprise Gully before entering a continuation gully. This gully gives access to some very impressive rock scenery.
1, 2 and 3. 150m. From the start of Surprise Gully climb out leftwards towards the first pinnacle (Pinnacle Buttress). Follow relatively easy ground skirting the base of the pinnacles to reach a small crest overlooking a col and the intersection of the gully running up behind the pinnacles.
3, 4 and 5. 150m. Follow the crest a short way, then drop down to the col. Continue up the gully, bounded on the right by the main cliff and on the left by further pinnacles, for three pitches until it ends at a final narrow col. This col separates the main cliff from the top of a further pinnacle.
6. 20m. Facing the main cliff, traverse leftwards a short way to enter a left-facing corner come shallow groove. Climb this to a bulge, tackled on the left, to reach easier ground.
   Follow easy ground for three pitches to the reach the top.

THE BONAID DHONN:

Scales of Justice 40m E3/4 5c *. G. Robertson, T. Woods. June 2003.
Start from the very left end of the first belay on Vertigo. Climb straight up a thin overhanging crack with difficulty to better holds and a rest below right-curving overlaps. Climb straight up to the overlaps on dwindling holds and with dwindling protection, then follow the overlaps more easily rightwards into the centre of the headwall. Finish direct up cracks. Probably joins the very top of Balances of Fate (SMCJ 1997).

Consolation Prize 70m E1. T. Fryer, I. Taylor. September 2003.
A line up the wall right of Stoater. Start at the large block as for Vertigo.
1. 15m. Go up and left to belay just right of the flake-crack of Stoater.
2. 20m 5a. Climb up a wall then a short groove; trend left, then up to a ledge.
3. 35m 5b. Go up a scoop and flake, swing right, then go up via a short corner. Finish up slabs and overlaps.

NORTHERN HIGHLANDS SOUTH

SOUTH GLEN SHIEL, Creag Coire an t-Slugain:
Trumpet 140m III,4. D. McGimpsey, A. Nisbet. 3rd January 2004.
Start below the central ridge (climbed by The Ridge Direct) and take a groove
which leads to the right side of the ridge (50m). Continue into the left corner of
the triangular snow patch, then leave it by a line of turf and flakes which leads
slightly left into a well defined groove in the crest of the ridge (40m). Finish up
this (50m).

Tipperary, Direct Start 40m III,4. A. Nisbet. 5th March 2004.
Gain and climb an obvious chimney set in a left slanting slab-corner. Continue
left up slabby corners to join the normal route at the end of its right traverse and
where it starts to rise rightwards.

Hypotenuse 120m III. A. Nisbet. 5th March 2004.
A line of grooves parallel and right of the bigger grooves of The Triangle. Start
just right of The Triangle and climb a parallel groove (may not be distinct with a
good build-up). Exit right through a slot in a right-bounding wall into the main
groove system. Follow this to the top, finishing close to The Triangle.

SGURR A' BHEALAICH DHEIRG, Ghlas Choire:
Resolve 50m IV,5. J. Preston, M. Kinsey. 8th March 2004.
A steep icefall 50m right of the prominent pinnacle flows over two vertical rock
walls interspersed by a sloping ledge with a large block belay. Ice screw protection.
An easy traverse off left and down a ramp reaches the base of Resolution Gully.

FIVE SISTERS, Coire na h-Uaighe:
Canine Buttress 150m IV,4. V. Chelton, D. McGimpsey, A. Nisbet. 27th January
2004.
The most prominent buttress, which lies between a dog-leg gully of grade I and
another shorter gully with a steep finish (Grade I/II) to its right. Start just right of
its base and take the rightmost of three possible turfy lines slanting left to a short
steep wall (30m). Climb the wall to a bay, then make a descending traverse left to
pull through a shorter wall (20m). Climb a groove to the crest and follow it to a
barrier wall (40m). Go up a turfy fault on the right to regain the crest and follow it
more easily to the top (60m).

Flying Ridge 120m IV,4. D. McGimpsey, A. Nisbet. 8th February 2004.
The ridge left of Grovel Gully features twin crests at its base, the right-hand crest
being a prominent rock arête. Start up a well defined V-groove between the crests
and from its top, gain the right crest. Move steeply up left (crux) and up a shallow
groove to an easier section. The crest becomes a well defined arête. Climb this for
a few metres, then move right into a long groove. Climb the groove to finish up
the crest.

Hanging Garden 120m II. D. McGimpsey, A. Nisbet. 8th February 2004.
The rightmost ridge on this section of cliff, just left of a wide open gully which
separates it from Babylon Buttress. Climb shallow grooves in the lower crest,

then easier ground to where the crest steepens (easy escape right here). Move right on to the gully wall, then left up two short steep walls to regain the crest. After a small descent, go up left to finish just left of the crest.

BEINN FHADA, Sgurr a' Choire Ghairbh, North-East Face:

Needle's Eye Buttress Direct 150m IV,4. M. Shaw, I. Humberstone. 30th December 2000.
This climb follows the crest of the buttress up slabby rock, threading the needle halfway up the buttress. It thus follows the line of the summer Difficult mentioned in the Volume I guidebook and is a completely separate line to the 1994 Grade II climb which follows an obvious turfy trough to the left.

BEINN BHAN, Coire na Poite:

Realisation 370m VI,6 ***. S. Yearsley, M. Bass. 31st January 2004.
A sustained climb of great character with superb situations which takes a direct line up the front of the buttress between March Hare's Gully and Mad Hatter's Gully. Good protection except for the precarious slabs on pitch 3. Start at the lowest point of the buttress.
1. 60m. Climb the lower toe of the buttress and continue to the first large snow terrace via a steep corner. Belay at a large rock finger at the foot of the second rock tier.
2. 40m. Climb a groove 2m left of the belay for 10m, then take a groove on the left to gain a large snow ledge. Move to its left-hand end and climb a short steep corner. Continue up and slightly rightwards to the second of two parallel snow terraces.
3. 50m. Move 4m left and climb an open groove. Continue trending right then up via precarious slabs to another snow terrace. Move up to the foot of the next steeper rock tier and traverse right to a flake-crack. Climb this for 3m, then move left at its top and continue up a steep groove until it is possible to step right in a superb position on to the rocky crest. Move up and right round the toe of a small buttress.
4. 55m. Climb easier ground for 20m, then a wide open fault-line cutting through the next tier.
5. 55m. Continue up an open groove to easier ground.
6. 55m. Up easy ground to climb a large corner cutting through the next tier.
7. 55m. Easy ground to finish.

Coire an Fhamhair:

Biblical Knowledge 300m VI,5. J. Edwards, G. Hughes. 17th January 2004.
Takes the arête left of Genesis. Start on a ledge left of Genesis some 10m up from the very toe of the arête.
1. 40m. Climb a corner for 20m until a zig-zag right then left allows a ledge on the left to be gained (this pitch could be shortened by coming out of Genesis from higher up).
2. 40m. Climb up a niche and gain a ledge on the arête via a flake. Move up the right side of a cracked slab and follow a rising left-trending ramp until below a stepped wall.
3. 40m. Move up and right to a right-facing corner, then go right and up via turfy

ledges until a move back left leads up to an apexed ledge right of a steep wall.
4. 60m. Climb the wall on the left to reach easier ground. Go up a snow slope trending right to a large detached block, 30m right of the easier exit gully.
5. 50m. Go up and right above the block to reach a left-trending break in the wall above. Climb this to reach easier ground.
6-7. Climb easy ground to reach the broad crest leading to the summit cornice.

Revelations   300m   VI,6. J. Edwards, S. Barron. 30th December 2003.
Start left of the barrelled arête of the line of Biblical Knowledge below some small roofs.
1. 40m. Climb up through the small roofs on thin ice to trend left to an open corner.
2. 25m. Climb the corner on the left wall moving right at its top. This was tricky on the first ascent but would be easier with more ice in the corner.
3. 40m. Go right along the ledge system for 7m to a short steep corner which is climbed to easier ground trending up and right to the base of a weakness above.
4. 30m. Go up the right wall of the weakness to a spectacular belay on a block overlooking Genisis (or continue to make the next pitch shorter).
5. 60m. Go up a short steep wall to much easier ground.
6 to 8. 105m. The ground is now much easier. A hidden easy gully leads left up to the arête which is followed with a short tricky mixed section at its start to the summit.

APPLECROSS CRAGS:
Cas Chrom   12m   VS 4c. S. Kennedy, R. Hamilton. 28th September 2003.
Situated a short distance west of Fearnbeg on the west facing crags on the east side of a large bay (NG 731603). The crags contain a natural arch. Left of the arch is a tree. Start just left of the tree and traverse out leftwards to gain a left-facing slabby corner. Climb the corner.

BEN DAMPH FOREST, Creag na Speireag:
Note: The unnamed E3 6a in SMCJ 2003 was led with a rest point.

BEN DAMPH:
Aquila   235m   VI,7 **. (2004) A. Nisbet, J. Preston. 26th February, 2004.
Staying as near the crest as possible, but bypassing a steep second tier. Start on the right side of the ridge, below the base of Aquila Gully.
1. 30m. Go up to and climb an awkward wide crack on the right side of a tier to a terrace below a steep wall. It has a clean cracked corner on its right side but instead, go to its left end.
2. 30m. Climb a grassy groove until possible to move right above the steep wall. Climb up steps to belay on the crest below flake-cracks.
3. 10m. Climb these to an overhang, then crawl left to a small corner.
4. 30m. Climb the corner and the cracked overhang above to an easy section of crest. Walk along this and climb a corner-chimney.
5. 25m. Climb cracks to a rest on the right, then move up left to a steep but short wide crack. Above this, reach the easier upper crest.
6. 50m. Follow the crest.

Matthew Priestman on the SE Ridge of the Obergabelhorn in mixed conditions. Photo: Adam Kassyk.

7. 60m. Continue in the same line (Aquila Gully takes the gully at right angles heading right) to a crest on the skyline.
Easy turfy ground leads to the top.

TORRIDON CRAGS, Seana Mheallan, Western Sector, Bedrock Buttress:
Mind The Trench   20m   Severe. C. Moody. 19th April 2003.
The left side of the slab is separated from the right by a left-slanting corner. Start about 4m left of the corner at some white patches. Climb up past the right side of the bulge, step left and continue up the slab to the grass ledge. Climb the short steep wall between the overhangs.

Trench At Top   20m   Very Difficult *. C. Moody. 19th April 2003.
Climb past the left end of the first overlap on Lapland, go past the second overlap by a shallow left-facing corner to a grass ledge. A short easy wall leads to the top.

BEINN EIGHE, Far East Wall:
Divine Ambition   50m   E1 6a. S. Ritchie, J. A. Edwards. 19th April 2003.
A direct version of Epilogue.
1. 30m 6a. Climb the parallel crack-line right of Karaoke Wall for 20m to a ledge. Make a difficult move to continue up to a bay.
2. 25m 5a. Continue up a corner above to easy ground.

Sail Mhor:
Expanding Universe   100m   VI,5 *. E. Tresidder, G. Robertson. 9th February 2004.
Although short, this route provides two excellent and contrasting pitches, the first on thin ice, the second up steep turfy chimneys. Start at the base of a big obvious groove, some 200m up and on the left wall of Morrison's Gully.
1. 30m. Climb the thinly iced groove, poorly protected, to a good belay below steep chimneys.
2. 50m. Continue directly up the chimneys to easier ground.
3. 20m. A short step leads up on to the shoulder and the end of the difficulties.
Easy ground on Sailing Buttress (about 200m of Grade II) leads to the top, but it should be possible to climb down and right to gain a ledge leading back into the gully.

Note: The following has been written for the forthcoming guide. Mentioned here because bouldering is becoming popular and this is a good venue. Also because T. Rankin has sent the subsequent description:

LIATHACH CRAGS, The Celtic Boulders (NG 909 557):
There are a set of huge boulders behind the gap between two young roadside plantations. After a five-minute boggy walk, they offer some short routes up to 10m, an intriguing cave and some Celtic carvings. A minor venue for a spare couple of hours. The routes include (left to right): a corner (VS 5a), an overhanging leaning corner-crack with some superb holds (VS 4c), a narrow chimney with a chockstone (VS 4b) and a south-facing wall of knobbly rock (two Very Difficult routes with a common start). Also climbed is the impressive arête of the largest

SMC Abroad? – Paul Brian laybacks Paragon at Bosigran, Cornwall. Photo Ed Grindley.

boulder, the arête furthest away from the main wall (6b). Other routes have been done.

Trend Setter   10m   E5 6b/c **. T. Rankin (unsec.). 5th April 2003.
On the right-hand of two obvious south-west facing walls half-way along the crag. Start just left of the tree. Climb a thin crack to the first break, make a desperate move to gain a good hold at the base of a thin crack above. Follow the crack up right, then straight up to finish.

DIABAIG, The Main Cliff:
Botanic Warrior   30m   Severe 4a *. S. Kennedy, A. MacDonald. 31st August 2003.
To the left of The Grunter and close to the lowest point of the Main Cliff lies a short slabby corner leading to the right end of the prominent roof. Climb the corner, then pull out right by a cracked block. Continue up a short corner to a steepening, then move leftwards to the buttress edge. Finish up the edge to finish at the abseil slings at the top of Dead Mouse Crack.

CAIRNGORMS
LOCHNAGAR:
Note: R. Clifton and T. Fox finished the Right Branch of The Black Spout by a right-hand variation in January 2004 at 40m III,4. Break out right on to water ice about 40m from the cornice. This short icefall was followed on to mixed ground towards an obvious wide chimney about 20m right of the cornice. This provided a short and entertaining crux, well protected.

Causeway Rib Direct   130m   VS. S. M. Richardson, J. Ashbridge. 27th July 2003.
A direct version of the original route taking the centre of the buttress.
1. 35m. Climb the first pitch of Causeway Rib to the stance at the head of the V-cleft.
2. 30m 4c. Move left to the centre of the buttress and climb a crack splitting the front face to a stance in a small notch.
3. 45m 4c. Continue up the slab above and climb the wall at its top via shallow cracks to reach the causeway. Move along this to its end.
4. 20m 4a. Finish up the front face of the final tower via steeped shelves as for the original route.

The Stuic:
Shepherd's Warning   70m   III. C. Cartwright, S. M. Richardson. 14th March 2004.
The first feature right of the crest of Stuic Buttress is a shallow left-facing corner. Start just left of the depression of Daybreak Corners and climb mixed ground over steep steps to the corner. Climb the corner for 15m to reach a good platform on the right (45m). Continue up the line of the corner above before exiting left onto the crest (25m). Continue up the crest of The Stuic to the plateau (50m).

The Stuic, Coire Lochan na Feadaige:

Goldie 110m III. B. Findlay, G. Strange. 15th December 2002.
On the larger, most westerly buttress in the corrie, right of Feadaige Buttress.
Start up a slanting depression, passing a pink overhang on the left. Continue by
a groove, then trend right on easy ground to finish by a left-slanting ramp on the
upper rocks.

CREAG AN DUBH LOCH, Central Slabs:
Cerberus 165m E1. S. M. Richardson, J. Ashbridge. 15th June 2003.
A good line up the clean sweep of rock left of Nemesis. Start 5m left of Nemesis
at 'the big obvious boulder at pink rocks.'
1. 45m 5a. Climb a right-facing corner to its top, and continue up a crack in the
slab above to below a steep wall. Move left and climb a crack in the wall to a
ledge.
2. 30m 4a. Step left and climb a grey rib just left of a depression on good holds to
reach a large terrace below the steep upper wall cut by the chimney of Nemesis.
3. 30m 5a. Traverse left along the terrace and climb up awkward slabby walls to
the prominent twin cracks that split the left side of the wall.
4. 40m 5b. Step right on to the subsidiary pillar on the right and climb this to enter
the right-hand crack. Climb this and move left where it joins the left-hand crack.
Continue up the chimney above, passing a loose chokestone, to reach easier ground.
Finish up Central Buttress.

Central Gully Wall:
Gorilla 105m E6 **. G. Robertson, T. Rankin. 24th August, 2003.
An excellent superdirect version of Bombadillo, taking the true crest of the nose
all the way. The first ascent started up grooves to the left of Bombadillo, but it is
probably better to follow that route until where it moves right to the hidden flake
crack.
1. 45m, 5c. Start up Bombadillo, but where it moves right, go up left over a bulge
on to a cracked slabby wall. Trend right across the wall via thin cracks to near the
edge where bold moves up then right gain a good flat hold. Swing right into
Bombadillo and follow this to belay uncomfortably at the left end of the ledge.
2. 30m 6b. From the ledge pull left into a tiny groove and where this ends make
hard moves left across the wall to gain a big side pull. Pull directly into another
groove and follow this to its top, then move up right on to the crest and follow this
in a superb position to ledges at the top of Bombadillo's second pitch.
3. 30m 5c. Bombadillo pitch 3, etc.

The Buff Slabs:
Buffy 55m E6 **. N. Morrison, W. Moir. 24th August 2003.
A fine, but fairly serious, route taking the central line through the steeper red wall
between Stark and Naked, then the slab above finishing via an obvious corner
system. Top-roped prior to lead.
1. 15m. Start as for Naked right of the crevasse feature and follow the initial
cracks of that route until a belay can be taken on the left in an area of more broken
ground below a left-facing corner.
2. 25m 6b. Climb the overlaps left of the left facing corner to the slab below the
steep wall. Follow the crack-line up the centre of the wall (crucial Alien#2 or

Friend#0 equivalent in finger pod, this blocks the hold but the edge is still available), to a good layaway flake at the base of the upper slab. Move up and left via feint cracks to belay on the right below the corner.
3. 15m. Follow the corner to an exit onto the Caterpillar.
Get off the cliff by escaping up the grass and occasional rock into False Gully or descend the Caterpillar a short way to a superb nut placement and abseil.

Bare   40m   E5 6a. W. Moir, N. Morrison (on sight). August 2003.
Start well left of the through-route at a small pink corner. Start awkwardly by the corner, then step left and climb rippled slabs to reach a grass ledge. Continue up to the right side of the bulge above (good protection), and climb the bulge (crux), using a good flange to start. Go up to reach more wires at a green-speckled flake. Continue very boldly by the line of flakes to reach a belay under the steep headwall. Abseil off, or finish via Stark, or its direct finish.

GLEN CALLATER, Coire Kander:
Note: S. Muir thinks that Wee Gem (SMCJ 2003) is the same as Pick Breaker (SMCJ 2002), despite the difference in grades.

Tuircish Delight   55m   III. S. Muir, H. Watson. 7th March 2004.
Climb the icefall on the left of the deep gully which descends from the col between Carn an Tuirc and Cairn of Claise. A good sustained pitch.

BEINN A' BHUIRD, Coire na Ciche:
Note: A free winter ascent of Sandy Crack taking the lower chimney direct (crux), climbed under mixed conditions in February 2003 by B. Findlay and G. Strange. No change of grade (V,6).

Archtemptor   160m   VII,8. C. Cartwright, S. M. Richardson. 7th March 2004.
The unclimbed area of crag between Pigs in the Wing and Hot Toddy is characterised by a prominent arch-shaped feature at mid-height. This prominent winter line takes a right slanting ramp to the arch and continues up the gully above. Start at the foot of Jason's Chimney.
1 and 2. 75m. Climb the ramp, easy at first, passing a thinner section beyond a right-facing corner. Continue for a further 10m and belay just before the ramp narrows on a large flake with the arch visible up and left.
3. 25m. Surmount the flake and move left to under the arch. Climb up via a free-standing flake to under the roof of the arch then move right across a steep wall to gain a groove on the right (crux). Climb the groove to a snow slope.
4. 60m. Move up and left into a shallow gully that leads to the top of the crag.

Coire an Dubh Lochain:
Mortal Coil   70m   III. S. M. Richardson. 15th February 2004.
The corner-chimney between The Vital Spark and Birthday Route. Steep cornice exit.

Big Foot Buttress   80m   E1. C. Cartwright, S. M. Richardson. 12th July 2003.
The well defined buttress on the north side of Coire an Dubh Lochain at NJ 091

994. Start in the centre of the front face just left of 2 metre-long foot-shaped flake below the prominent crack system
1. 40m 5b. Climb the crack for 20m, step right into a parallel crack and follow this passing the capping roof on the left.
2. 40m. Continue up the easier upper ridge to the plateau.

Coire nan Clach:
Nipped in the Bud 100m V,6. S. M. Richardson, C. Cartwright. 22nd February 2004.
A direct line following the crest of the buttress between Crocus Gully and Snowdrop. The upper half of the buttress is split by a vegetated right-facing corner.
1. 30m. Start at the toe of the buttress and climb mixed ground up the crest to where it steepens.
2. 15m. Climb the steep wall on the crest to a good ledge.
3. 15m. Continue up the awkward bulging wall above and climb the vegetated slab to where the angle eases at the foot of the right-facing corner.
4. 50m. Climb the corner to the top.

Narcissus 150m III. S. M. Richardson. 15th February 2004.
Start 50m right of Crocus Gully and climb a short gully and left-facing grooves and easier mixed ground at the top.

Ribeye 70m III,4. S. M. Richardson. 15th February 2004.
The short north-facing rib midway between the Promontory and Summit Buttress. Climb snow to the foot of the steep prow and continue up a right-trending fault-ramp with a difficult section at half height.

Stob an t-Sluichd:
Caprice 100m Severe. C. Cartwright, S. M. Richardson. 7th December 2003.
The clean well defined pillar just the left of Token Groove. Move up and left from the foot of Token Groove and climb up to a steep crack. Climb this on good holds to easier ground and the narrow final arête.

CAIRN TOUL, Coire an Lochan Uaine:
Solitude Rib 250m II. I. Small. 6th March 2003.
This route climbs the most prominent rib directly to the summit. Climb an initial ice pitch then traverse left to gain the rib and follow it to the top.

LOCH ETCHACHAN CRAG:
The squat crag above the head (south-west corner) of the loch.

Bacchus 50m E3/4 5b **. J. Lines (on-sight solo). 13th July 2003.
A beautiful climb on good rock, both balancy and scary. A quartz dyke runs from the bottom right of the crag diagonally leftwards above a steep wall. Follow the dyke until it runs out, step left round the rib into a scoop, toe traverse the scoop (absorbing and precarious) to gain the superb diagonal crack which splits the slab above. Climb the crack (good gear halfway). When crack turns into a runnel, move left to a flake and follow good holds.

STACAN DUBHA:
Observers Buttress 150m II. J. Edwards, D. McGimpsey, A. Nisbet. 19th February 2004.
The triangular buttress between the 1987 gullies. Start on its left side. Climb shallow grooves until a ledge leads right. Climb a narrow chimney with a through route which leads right on to the crest. Follow this ill defined crest to the top.

Ribbon Ridge 150m IV,4. J. Edwards, D. McGimpsey, A. Nisbet. 19th February 2004.
Climb slabby turfy ground to the base of the ridge. Climb a subsidiary buttress on the left, then step right on to the main ridge immediately above a chimney. Climb a steep turfy groove, then the easier crest to a tower. Climb this by a turfy ramp on the left, then follow the sharp crest to the miniature "tower gap". After this is a steep finishing wall. There is an easy escape right here; if used the route becomes grade III. Make a rising traverse left across the wall, then step down and cross a groove before climbing straight up to the top.

CARN ETCHACHAN, Upper Tier:
Malicious Midget 80m E2 5c. I. Small, J. Walker. 2nd August 2003.
This route climbs a series of corners and an arête cutting across Poison Dwarf, then crosses the Rock Window to finish up the wall to the left of Crevasse Route.
1. 35m 5b. Start at the foot of the Equinox gully. Follow a left-slanting ramp-line passing below a perched boulder to gain an obvious corner. Climb to a triangular roof, move right on to an arête, then gain the corner on the right. Follow it past a niche to a ledge, then take the corner above to exit left to a large ledge (this final corner is common with Poison Dwarf).
2. 40m 5c. Arrange a side runner in the wide crack of Poison Dwarf, then traverse rightwards above a roof (exposed) to gain the arête. Climb this on the left side to a short groove leading to ledges by the Rock Window. Gain a standing position on the block that forms the Window and step left on to the wall above. Finish by cracks and ledges.

Dreadlock 90m V,6. J. Edwards, D. McGimpsey, A. Nisbet. 18th February 2004.
Climbs the crest at the right end of the Pagan Slit wall, well marked by a steep area of pink rock. Start 5m right of The Hairpin Loop.
1. 25m. Climb a fault which leads slightly leftwards into a bay at the lower left end of the pink rock. Traverse right past a step with a wide crack to a ledge. This last traverse is shared with The Hairpin Loop, which then goes up to a bigger bay.
2. 15m. Instead, step up and move right to reach a spike in an overlap formed below a left-slanting ramp. Gain and climb the ramp to a large ledge.
3. 20m. Climb a wide crack on the left to a higher ledge and continue up the steep wall on the left. Return right by a blocky groove.
4. 30m. Follow the crest easily to a wide crack; climb this and pull out left. Continue slightly leftwards to finish up a groove with a capping chokestone (as for The Hairpin Loop).

SHELTERSTONE CRAG, Central Slabs:
Icon of Lust 115m E8 ***. J. Lines, P. Thorburn. July 2003.

A monumental voyage up the full height of the Central Slabs, taking a direct line through Realm of the Senses and L'Elisir d'Amore. Start 20m down and left from the initial crack of The Pin.

1. 35m 6a. The serious pitch! Climb a cracked groove to a ledge at 10m. Pull on to a bleached slab and climb it veering right into a vague left-facing corner at it top (good gear). Then go straight up the steep wall on small positive edges to pockets over the top, step left and pull onto the ramp and follow this rightwards to the belay.

2. 25m 6c. A brilliant pitch, desperate and bold. Follow the Realm of the Senses groove to the overlap, step right and pull through the overlap with disbelief, sketch up the slab to a weird pocket (#00 cam), move diagonally leftwards, very thin, to join Missing Link amidst its crux. Gain good holds and gear then traverse down and left above the overlap to gain a flake leading to the Thor belay.

3. 55m 6b. Extremely bold, a cool head required. Climb Thor to the crescent crack, step up into pockets, make thin moves up and left to a jug in the red streak A precarious stretch left enables a #00 cam to be placed blind, the only protection in 25m of climbing. Climb the red streak to a pocket, step right and up the right edge of the red streak past a flat hold into a scoop (frightening). Climb vertical wall past a PR (RP#2 one metre above) to gain flakes in a scoop, move diagonally left along flakes and on to the slab above. Continue up the slab to a grassy ledge and possible belay. Continue up the wall above to the apex of the slabs, peg belay.

GARBH UISGE CRAG:
Feld Spur 100m III. J. Lyall. 3rd January 2004.
The spur right of Quartz Gully.

HELL'S LUM:
The Bats, The Bats 50m HVS 5a*. B. Fyffe, A. Fyffe. 14th August 2003.
Takes the crack-lines in the clean pink slab right of The Vaccum. Descend by traversing left from the top of the pitch. Good climbing on immaculate rock. Climb a clean crack into a short shallow right-facing corner. From the top of the corner, trend left to gain a prominent crack and climb it to where it disappears, then move right to a square nose. From the right side of the nose follow another crack to the fault.

Road to Nowhere 25m HVS 5a. A. Fyffe, B. Fyffe. 14th August 2003.
Takes cracks bordering the left side of the smooth slab. Climb the cracks to where they run into a grassy left-facing corner and move right into a clean open groove. Climb this to ledges, go to a thin crack in the upper slab and then move right to finish up the deeper cracks of Two Little Devils to the glacis.

Omen Direct 35m E3 6a. J. Lines. 15th July 2003.
A direct version of pitches 2 and 3. From the first belay climb the thin slab directly above straight into the corner on pitch 3.

Paranormal 165m E1 **. A. Fyffe, R. D. Barton 24th August 2003.
Some excellent climbing although it uses bits of other routes. Mostly sustained with the hardest move at the top of the last pitch. Start at the crack about 3m right of the obvious pink initial crack of Auld Nick and Devil Dancer.

1. 50m 4c. Start just right of the crack and climb up to join it after the initial mossy section. Where this runs into a left-facing corner, take the diagonal crack going right, then return left to climb the edge overlooking the corner to big ledges below the overlap.

2. 25m 5a. Climb the crack up the next slab via the crack right of Auld Nick's. This starts with a short left-facing corner, gives excellent climbing and is quite well protected. Go right on the horizontal crack of Auld Nick and belay at its end.

3. 50m 5a. Work leftwards through the steep wall above, just right of the jutting nose to reach the glacis (common with Devil's Alternative). Climb up cracks and corners to reach the slot at the right end of the long low roof and belay on the horizontal flake above (as for Big De'il).

4. 40m 5b. From the flake belay go right and work up the wall on rounded flakes to the right edge of a shallow recess. Go back left and up on flakes to a ledge, go up a small corner to an upper ledge then go right to climb a grey flake leading to the upper horizontal fault. Make an awkward move to gain a standing position (as for Devil's Alternative) and then a grassy terrace and easy finish rocks. A surprising pitch.

STAG ROCKS, Cascade Area:
The Red Planet 60m E1 **. A. Fyffe, R. D. Barton. 24th August 2003.
Another good route but slow to dry. It takes the straight crack-line right of Lost in the City. Start at twin cracks just right of that route's initial left-facing corner.

1. 25m 5b. Climb a twin crack then a ramp leading into the cracks. Climb the left-hand cracks to the rock ledge.

2. 15m 4c. Climb the short right-facing corner on the right, then the crack through the headwall. It is possible to scramble off from this point.

3. 20m 4a. Climb the corner system to the top.

COIRE AN LOCHAIN, No.2 Buttress:
Reprieve 50m IV,5 *. M. Bass, S. Yearsley. 18th March 2003.
An icy counter diagonal to the Executioner, sharing the block-capped groove of that route. Start in the Couloir about 5m above the dead end left branch at the foot of a short steep wall adorned with an ice smear. Climb this icy wall, and move up to the foot of the block capped groove. Climb the groove, overcome the blocks and step left. Climb a steep ice bulge to enter a right-facing corner which is followed to the cornice. This may be large; on the first ascent there was an unusual natural tunnel through the cornice which was passable after enlargement.

Lagopus 100m V,6. I. Taylor, N. Carnegie. January 2004.
A direct start to Snow Bunting.

1. 30m. Start 30m right of Central Crack Route at the entrance to The Couloir. Climb a crack-line to a ledge at 5m. Traverse up and left below an overlap to another ledge then follow steps up and right to gain a small gully and belay at the top of this.

2. and 3. 70m. Trend up and rightwards to gain the easy-angled snow bay of Snow Bunting and finish up this.

NORTH EAST OUTCROPS
DEAD MCIVOR GULCH:
Arachnaphobia   10m   E4 6a/b *. W. Moir. October 2003.
The roof and alcove right of Spiders Walk. Lean across from the slab opposite and gain a good flat hold. Monkey up to a good break and move left to the alcove, exit this to easier ground. Essentially a highball boulder problem, best done with spotters.

SOUTER HEAD, Girdle Traverse Wall:
Shoestring   10m   E3 6a *. N. Morrison, P. Allen. May 2003.
Climbs the arête right of Bootlace Crack. Start up Bootlace Crack and reach over the overlap to place a runner. Traverse right to the arête using finger pockets on the lip of the overlap and pull over to the slab. Finish up easier ground directly above.

Jeelyfish   10m   E1 5b *. N. Morrison, P. Allen. May 2003.
Climbs through the overlap left of Black Corner. Start at the foot of that route and climb up left to the overlap. Pull left through this into the corner above. An obvious finish is available but is very grassy at its top so climb the clean right rib.

Overhanging Gully:
The following routes have almost certainly been done before but not recorded.
Yum Yum Bubble Gum   8m   Very Difficult. R. Henderson, P. Randall. 4th September 2003.
One metre right of Scylla, there is a slanting corner then a bulge. Climb over the bulge direct and continue to an obvious large break at the top.

Cunning Linguist   8m   Severe. P. Randall, R. Henderson. 4th September 2003.
One metre right of Yum Yum Bubble Gum there is a flake which slopes from right to left. Below the flake there is an overhanging bulge below which is a sloping ledge. Climb the flake direct and continue to the obvious break at the top, joining Yum Yum Bubble Gum. Or climb the overhanging bulge direct, traverse right and join up with the obvious break.

SOUTH COVE:
Super Cracks in Reality   45m   XXS 6b   S3 ****. J. Lines. 27th May 2003.
The true start to Cracks in Reality provides the best route on the Aberdeen coast. Start just below the starts to Procrastination and Space Rats. Bridge between the slab and the hanging wall, grab a smooth boss hold and traverse the break leftwards. Go left round the rib and move down to a small foot ledge just above the sea. Make a thin move leftwards across a smooth black slab to gain a ledge (awkward rest), climb the vague diagonal crack in the black rock leftwards to gain the original route just after its right traverse on undercuts. Then finish as Cracks in Reality.
Note: This new start is not affected by seeps, but will be unclimbable in heavy seas and damp conditions. The start can be used as a variation start to Procrastination (has been climbed to the Procrastination belay at 20m 6b), which would avoid the seeps on the original first pitch. Thought is definitely required for protecting the second on the initial section (and to reduce rope drag for the leader) if attempting

a lead. Possibly best to back-rope the initial peg of Procrastination to stop a swing! The route was deep water soloed on sight, with two splashdowns on the initial traverse, the day before the successful ascent.

FINDON NESS, Kay Hole, Lesser Kay Hole:
The following three routes are on a very steep little wall at the very eastern end of the Kay Hole inlet. Easily seen and reached on the approach to The Glider. The rock is sound and juggy, similar to Berrymuir Head. Small Friends are essential, including a #00.

Through the Kay Hole   10m   E2 5c *. T. Rankin, M. Scott. April 2003.
The central line. Climb a steep juggy crack to a spike. Rock up left below a roof and use a hidden hold on the lip to gain jugs above. Continue direct over the next roof, then finish up and slightly right.

Kay Holed   10m   E2 5b *. T. Rankin, M. Scott. April 2003.
Start up Through the Kay Hole but continue up and right to below the obvious break in the overhang. Climb through the overhang and finish straight up.
Independent Start: E3 5b. Up the corner to the right, then trending across the wall leftwards to gain the horizontal break below the overhang. Less satisfying.

Kay Hole Surgery   10m   E1 5b *. T. Rankin, M. Scott. April 2003.
The left-hand line. Climb the initial roof at the obvious jug 2m left of Through the Kay Hole. Go straight up to a shelf above; finish left, then right up an easy slab.

The Grey Wall:
No Doubts   35m   E2 5b **. T. Rankin, R. Birkett. 8th July 2003.
An excellent exposed route up the wall right of Gronk on reasonably good rock. Climb Gronk for about 20m (possible belay to avoid rope drag) until an obvious exposed traverse leads out right past a jammed block on to a hanging slab. Move up to take the flake-crack through the roof into a hanging flake-groove above. Climb this to pull out left to finish.

At the back of the dry inlet to the right of The Grey Wall is a shallow cave with an impressive red granite dyke running through the roof.

Fascination Streak   15m   F7c. T. Rankin. May 2003.
Perhaps the most outrageous sport route in Scotland. The route climbs the dyke on jugs to a lower-off at the lip. Prone to dampness; the best chance would be on a sunny morning or with a favourable breeze.

Findon Ness South:
Odin   20m   E3 5c *. T. Rankin, M. Reed. 3rd June 2003.
Right of Halo is a left-slanting crack. Climb the crack to a niche, avoid the temptation to pull out right and continue up left to join Halo below the final wall. Step right and finish up the wall in a fine position above a roof.

PORTLETHEN BOULDERS, Octopus Inlet:
This is the short narrow inlet which cuts back in towards Craigmaroinn beach

from the large bay of Portlethen harbour. The routes are all on the very steep east-facing wall and all but Little Octo require a low tide. The rock in general is excellent. There is a belay stake on the saddle of the ridge well back from the lip. Routes described left to right.

Little Octo 5m E3 5b. T. Rankin (on sight solo). 22nd July 2003.
Before the main wall is a short steep wall above a left-trending groove. Climb the wall direct above the groove on good holds to a horizontal break (possible protection) and use a jammed block above to pull over on to a ramp. Good moves but a bad landing.

Monster of the Deep 12m E5 6a **. T. Rankin, A. Crofton (inspected). July 2003.
The obvious central line. Climb to below a left-trending crack; follow this to pull right to the base of a small triangular niche. Climb stright up to good holds, step left and finish right. Low in the grade.

The Relic 10m E3 6a *. T. Rankin, M. Reed (inspected). 26th July 2003.
Right again is an obvious crack high up. Climb a right-trending ramp to the base of the crack. Climb the crack direct to its top. Pull out right to finish.

Deep Rising 10m VS 4c. T. Rankin. 22nd July 2003.
Climbs directly up shallow grooves to finish up the fine short flake-crack in the upper part of the wall.

Sports Wall Left-Hand:
The steep little left-hand continuation to Sports Wall. It contains one route and some good bouldering, the best being *Razor Rump* (5b+), the sharp steep right-trending ramp. Out to Lunch (6c, Font 7b **), the undercut arête just right of Razor Rump without using holds on that problem. Jump off from the lip (high!).
The Incredible Sulk 7m 7b *. T. Rankin. 2003.
A desperate extended boulder problem taking a little hanging groove and wall above.

CRAIG STIRLING:
Raw Meat, Direct Finish 10m E2 5c. W. Moir, P. Allen. August 2003.
Rather than finishing up Lean Meat, go up the right side of an elongated pocket to gain a horizontal break. Go left along this, then climb flakes, finishing at the pointed block. Climbed this way, the route is perhaps worth **.

Note: Roaring Forties is a fine DWS at XS 6b S0. Raw Meat lower section is XS 6a S2.

Red Meat 20m XS 6a S0/1 **. J. Lines (on sight). 15th May 2003.
A lovely deep-water solo, but not for the liking of vegetarians. Start as for Lean Meat and follow the horizontal traverse right where Lean Meat goes diagonally up. Keep traversing on finger crimps to a final slap for a jug on the arête. Climb the arête to the top.

Sushi 25m XS 6c S1/2 ***. J. Lines. 3rd June 2003.

An outrageous deep-water solo, the climax to DWS developments at Craig Stirling. Start as for Jack Sprat. Follow Jack Sprat on to the wall at good finger pockets, then climb the wall to a roof. Sidle leftwards and then make a powerful move to gain the next break, beneath the huge roof. Using a weird flake in the lip, cut loose and make powerful and technical moves to establish oneself in the overhanging scoop above. Move left to a respite, then move up to join Lean Meat and continue straight up the overhanging wall as for Raw Meat.
Note: Three splashdowns and not even off the crux (some shunt practice at the lip of the big roof). May be nudging E7.

CLASHRODNEY:
Perseus 15m XS 6a S0/1. J. Lines. 6th June 2003.
A short, but fun deep-water solo. Start on the ledges underneath Gorgon, then traverse rightwards to a good hold in a groove in the left side of a hanging prow. Using small finger holds climb the prow head on, utilising a heel hook on the right (don't fall off rightwards). Easier up the slab to finish.

BERRYMUIRHEAD:
Fist Full of Barnacles 12m XS 6a/b S1. J. Lines. 9th June 2003.
A good deep-water solo where high tide is essential. From the start of the niche stretch left and gain a jug, traverse leftwards around the arête just above the water. On the left of the arête a rising set of holds leads to a quartz ledge just right of Quick Draw McGraw. From the ledge, use a small quartz layaway to start a blind sequence of moves up the overhanging wall on good but hidden holds.

A deep water boulder is situated 30m to the south-east of Quick Draw McGraw. It faces north-east and is the shape of a black pyramid with an overhanging face. The face is 5m high at high tide. A calm sea and a high tide are required for these routes. All the routes are crimpy and bouldery and provide a new concept to Scotland, deep-water bouldering. All routes are perfectly safe at high tide and exiting the sea is straight-forward. All routes start at the seaward end where a slab-ramp joins the base of the face.

Majuro 12m 6a/b S1. J. Lines. 9th June 2003.
The traverse from left to right just above the high water mark, gives varied climbing. 6b to on-sight, easier once the holds are chalked.

Enewetak 8m 6a/b S1. J. Lines. 9th June 2003.
Climb along the traverse to gain the good holds at the prow, then climb the prow moving right on huge jugs.

Taongi 8m 6b S1. J. Lines. 9th June 2003.
Climb along the traverse to gain the good holds at the prow, then move up and left past an obvious finger jug to finish at the apex of the wall.

Kwajalein 5m 6a S1. J. Lines. 9th June 2003.
Start as for the traverse, step right and make a blind reach for a good hold, then stretch right to another good hold. Finish straight up just left of the apex of the wall.

THE GRAIP:

Nest Route 15m HVS 5a. B. Duthie, B. McAdam. 6th September 2003.
Start left of Unhinged. Climb straight up until beneath the overhang. Pull over on the right side and follow a left-trending line on easier ground to the top.

The Vineyard 15m Hard Severe *. G. W. M. Allan, K. Wallace. 28th July 2003.
Climb Knee Trembler to where that route goes slightly right, traverse left above the large overhang and climb the wall near its left edge.

ROSEHEARTY, Murcurry South Wall:

Tombstone 15m E5 6a *. N. Morrison, W. Moir. 6th September 2003.
Takes the wall between Heart of Stone and Stone the Crows, giving fine and surprisingly independent climbing. Cleaned on abseil, some snappy rock and shoogly holds remain but are nothing out of the ordinary for this wall. Start up either, the true diagonal crack of Stone the Crows, or the subsidiary crack. Where the two meet step left onto the wall and move up and left to gain a right-slanting crack. Move up this to a niche with a large shaky block (well wedged). Follow the continuation crack up right to a further niche which is exited on its left to a slopey finish.

CLACH NA BEINN:

Glen Dye Slab 25m E4 6b **. J. Lines. 12th March 2003.
A unique all out crystal route taking the slab between Bogendreip Buttress and Crack o' the Mearns. Start up Crack o' the Mearns but after 3m bridge between to vertical cracks to reach holds on Bogendreip, then up to a good hold in the slab (large cams in a diagonal crack on the left). Scratch up the centre of the slab on crystals to better holds and the top.
Note: A good combination is to climb Bogendreip buttress to the big jug at 15m, then make a thin move left to join and finish up Crack o' the Mearns. Possibly E1 5a/b ***.

BENNACHIE, Mither Tap:

Best Forgotten Art 15m E6 6b **. T. Rankin, M. Reed. 23rd August 2003.
The strangely neglected flake-line left of Finger Ficker. Step up Finger Ficker and arrange protection on the left wall. Make hard moves left to a painful jam in the flake and crucial protection. Pull up to a jug, then use the crack on the left to gain a break above. Step right and pull up to an obvious pocket; climb the slab above to the next break. Step left to pull over at a good jug. An excellent route on clean rock.

Reed's Bogey 20m E3 5c *. M. Reed, T. Rankin. 23rd August 2003.
Start below the left arête of the wall. Climb the crack in the crest to its end, then make bold moves up a slab to a break. Go left and up a flake to the next break. Step right and finish as for Best Forgotten Art.

Mither Tap, West Wall Upper Tier:

This fine little wall emanates directly from the summit of the tor. It is directly in front of the trig point when facing west. Gain the base of the wall down a little gully to its south.

Gift of Contentment   10m   E6 6b *. T. Rankin, M. Reed. 30th September 2003.
Start at a low protruding ledge 2m right of an obvious crack. Boulder up to gain
the first break and protection. Move up right to the next break (Friend#half), step
left and climb the upper slab trending slightly leftwards to an easier but serious
finish.

ANGUS, Ley Quarry, The Waterfront:
Ley Jungle   19m   F4. N. Cole (roped solo). 13th July 2003
A further route to the right of The Magic Thumb. Unlike most Ley Quarry routes
it is possible to top out! Poorly protected with loose rock and earth and no bolts.
Start as for Magic Thumb. Gain the mantelshelf, move right across and on to a
narrow ledge to another small ledge with a bush and rotten stump in a corner.
Scramble on to the ledge under a small overhang. Move right and continue upwards
trending left to top out between two overhanging rock piles.

HIGHLAND OUTCROPS
MALLAIG CRAGS, Ardnish Peninsula, Lizard Crag (SMCJ 2000):
Chameleon   12m   Severe *. S. Kennedy, R. Hamilton, T. Hamilton. 8th November
2003.
A large block leans against the right side of the crag forming a cave. Enter the
cave and climb a thin crack up the slabby left wall to a roof. Traverse left to gain
the edge. Finish up a groove.

Gecko   7m   Severe. S. Kennedy, R. Hamilton, T. Hamilton. 8th November 2003.
A short distance left of Lizard Crag, just above the idyllic beach, is a prominent
leaning block. Climb the short seaward face surmounting a small ledge at the
foot.
Note: The lengths of the routes described in SMCJ 2000 seem to be overstated;
15m for The Lizard and 10m for The Snake.

STRATHSPEY, Shillochan Rock (NH 937 217):
The crag is well hidden by trees but marked on the 1:25000 map.
Approach: Park near Boat of Garten sawmill. Follow a forest track north of the
A95, keeping straight on after 500m to pass a shooting lodge after 1.5km. Keep
taking left turns thereafter to reach the end of the road. The crag lies over a ridge
from the road end. The most obvious features are the three corner lines.

Friendly Fire   6m   Severe. B. Sparham. 28th June 2003.
The wall to the right of the rightmost corner.

Tony   10m   VS 4c. B. Sparham, P. Edwards. 5th May 2003.
The right corner, finishing slightly left.

George Junior   10m   HVS 5b. B. Sparham, J. Mason. 28th June 2003.
The central corner, moving into Tony at the top.

Saddam   10m   E1 5b. B. Sparham, P. Edwards, S. Partridge. 15th May 2003.
The left corner gives a good sustained climb.

Colateral Damage 12m HVS 4c. J. Mason, B. Sparham. 28th June 2003.
Go left to the arête from a stump on Saddam. Climb the arête to finish with an exciting run-out.

Old Pulkeney 5m Severe. B. Sparham, S. Partridge. May 2003.
A short wide crack left of the bay left of Saddam.

BINNEIN SHUAS:
Cubist 40m HVS 5a. S. M. Richardson, I. Small. 10th August 2003.
A direct line up the right side of the slab taken by Cube Wall. Climb the initial corner flake of Cube Wall and step left on to the ledge. Continue straight up the slab above to reach the right end of the diagonal fault of Cube Wall. Cross this and climb up the nose above to the top.

ROCK DUST (Pitlochry):
Moulin Rouge 20m 6c **. R. Anderson, C. Anderson. 2002.
A direct line between 21st Century Citizen and Quiet Revolution, sharing the lower-off of those routes.

Cabaret 18m 6b+. R. Anderson, C. Anderson. 2003.
A bit of an eliminate just left of 21st Century Citizen to a lower-off slightly down and left of the lower-off for that route.

Rubrique 18m 5+. R. Anderson, C. Anderson. 2003.
The rib to the right of Ha Ha Tarawangee to reach the lower-off of Cabaret.

DUNKELD, Upper Cave Crag, Sinners Wall:
Sinners Paradise 15m 7a+ *. R. Anderson. 12th October 2003.
Straight up the steepest bit of the crag left of Six Fours-les Plage, noted in the guide as a project.

NEWTYLE QUARRY, The Tube:
Hurlyburly 18m F8b **. D. MacLeod (also soloed after leading). 14th June 2003.
The left hand of the three bolted lines on the roof of The Tube. Starting at the highest point, it is possible reach the rock (further bolts extend downwards into the manky depths). The climbing is totally sustained on completely manufactured slots, finishing at a lower-off at the lip. Excellent and unusual climbing.

Gone in 60 Seconds 15m E7 6c *. D. MacLeod (headpointed). 19th August 2003.
A serious line taking the left arête/lip of The Tube. Start at a cracked block and smear rightwards to a good jug. A hard technical sequence on the lip gains a borehole thread. Continue up the arête (reaching right to clip the belay of Hurlyburly) to finish up the easy wall above.

BEN NEVIS, AONACHS, CREAG MEAGHAIDH

BEN NEVIS, North-East Buttress:

Note: On an ascent of Slingsby's Chimney on 10th March 2004, A. Hughes and M. Stygall climbed the Chockstone Variation at V,5. It may bank out under heavy snow conditions, so perhaps has been climbed before.

Douglas Boulder:

Turf War 250m V,6. G. Hughes, J. Edwards. 21st December 2003.

Based on the summer line of Militant Chimney. Start at the middle of the lower tier.

1. 60m. Climb up into a bay in the middle of the lower tier and head for a short V-groove in the second band. Climb the groove until a slant up right leads to overhangs.

2. 40m. Move round to the right (avoiding the knobbly wall) and back left heading for the line of Militant Chimney. Go up this to a good thread on a ledge.

3. 30m. Climb the Militant Chimney.

4. 50m. Continue up and then teeter rightwards across slabs and go up a turfy right-facing corner to a huge block.

5. 60m. Climb easier ground leftwards to a short overhanging chimney to reach a slab. Go up the corner to gain a ledge on the right. Move delicately left and climb the exposed arête (bold) until it is possible to step right and move up to gain a belay.

6. 10m. Move up to reach easy ground leading to the summit of the Douglas Boulder.

Left-Hand Chimney, Alternate Start 7. G. Hughes, J. Edwards. 22nd December 2003.

A two-pitch start taking a left-trending line heading for an overhanging black wall which was bypassed on its shorter right-hand side. Left-Hand Chimney itself was much harder than IV,4 in the lean conditions.

Jacknife IV,6. J. Baird, A. Turner. 26th November 2003.

By the summer line, but with a start on its left.

Number Three Gully Buttress:

Arthur VIII,8. B. Poll, T. Shepherd. 2nd January 2004.

No description received.

Chinook IV,5. M. Edwards, D. McGimpsey, A. Nisbet. 3rd April 2002.

Described in the guide as a direct finish to Number Three Gully Buttress (route 89a), but was an ascent of Chinook on ice (the initial 5m including the spike were banked out).

Creag Coire na Ciste:

Central Rib Direct 200m VI,7. S. M. Richardson, I. Small. 3rd April 2004.

A direct ascent of the rib avoiding the deviation into Central Gully Right-Hand and finishing directly up the final tower. Excellent climbing.

1 and 2. 100m. Climb the crest of the rib starting up a right to left ramp, to reach the snow terrace where the rib steepens.

Iain Small climbing sunny waterice on the top pitch of Swordfish V, Creag Dubh, Geal Charn, Loch Ericht. Photo: Andy Hume.

3. 35m. Climb a right-trending corner cutting the right edge of the rib and pull onto a huge flat chockstone below the capping roof. Step left onto the overhanging arête on the left and climb this to easier ground. A sensational pitch.
4. 50m. Continue up the rib to below the final tower.
5. 15m. Climb the overhanging chockstoned crack just right of the summer Tower Finish to reach the cornice.

South Trident Buttress:
Poseidon Groove 100m IV,5. S. M. Richardson, I. Small. 3rd April 2004.
The steep groove-line splitting the central part of the south-facing upper tier of South Trident Buttress. Start by climbing easy snowy grooves from the mouth of Number Four Gully to below twin grooves in the centre of the wall.
1. 35m. Move up and right into the right groove and climb this over two steep sections to reach a ledge 5m right of a wide vertical crack.
2. 50m. Step left and climb the left of two corners to reach easier ground. Climb the snow gully above to reach a belay.
3. 15m. Finish up easy ground to the top.

Carn Dearg Buttress:
Note from I. Taylor: The Banana Groove Pitch 3 is 30m, not 45m.

STOB BAN (Mamores):
Overlooked Gully 150m I. J. Lyall, S. Fraser, M. Twomey. 8th February 2004.
The gully between the East Ridge of North Buttress and Foxtrot (which seemed worth III,4 *).

AONACH MOR, Coire an Lochain, North-East Face:
Outer Limits 90m III. R. Hamilton, S. Kennedy. 6th March 2004.
The buttress left of Sprint Gully. Start at the lowest point of the buttress just left of a slabby right-facing wall. Climb up a shallow depression by a series of grooves to reach more open ground (50m). Finish by easier ground close to the left edge of the buttress (40m).

Streamline 90m III *. R. Hamilton, S. Kennedy. 16th February 2004.
Sideline starts up a short gully/groove and then takes a line up the right side of the wide fault-line some distance left of the Prow. This route climbs the left side of the same fault up a corner which is overlooked by a steep rock wall defining the left side of the fault. Start above and left of Sideline and follow a wide ramp leading rightwards to below the steep wall (40m). Climb the corner directly under the steep wall to the steep upper snow slopes. Finish high on the left where the cornice often forms an unusual through route (50m).

Three Kings 70m IV,5 *. R. Hamilton, S. Kennedy, A. MacDonald. 6th March 2004.
This route follows a system of ramps and corners situated close to the crest of the steep rock wall defining the left side of the wide fault-line containing Streamline. Start up the ramp a short distance left of the start of Streamline to reach a prominent

James Maclaurin setting off up the first pitch of Orion Face, Ben Nevis. Photo: Alastair Matthewson.

steep corner with a slabby left wall at 20m. Climb the corner (crux) to a ledge. An exposed move back right just above the corner leads into the upper system of ramps which are followed to a thread belay on the left (50m). The easier upper slopes lead to the cornice (20m).

The Prow:
Pro Libertate   90m   V,6 **. S. Kennedy, R. Hamilton. 6th March 2004.
A fairly sustained mixed route on the buttress between The Guardian and Stirling Bridge following a prominent chimney/corner in the upper reaches. Quite close to The Guardian in the lower section. Start at the foot of The Guardian and climb the buttress just to the right (banks out later in the season) to reach a short wall. Step right under the wall into a slabby corner. Follow the corner then move up rightwards over a jammed block to below a steep corner. Steep moves across the wall on the left lead to a ledge. Move back up rightwards into another corner containing a large booming flake. Make exposed moves out left from the top of the flake to easier ground close to the chimney of The Guardian. Belay at the foot of the prominent chimney on the right (45m). The right wall of the chimney was climbed to a wide ledge below the steep upper corner. Climb the corner to a large block belay on the crest overlooking Stirling Bridge (20m). Finish up the easy upper slopes as per Stirling Bridge (25m).

Homo Buttress:
Ayrton Senna   70m   V,6. R. Durran, O. Samuel. February 2003.
1. 40m. The groove in the left edge of the buttress.
2. 30m. The easier crest above.

The Ribbed Walls:
Note: J. Lyall and J. Preston climbed Nid Arête direct at the start on 24th March 2004, making the route V,5.

An Cul Choire:
The Vice   45m   IV,4 *. S. Kennedy, R. Hamilton. 16th February 2004.
The icy chimney/groove on the right side of the prominent buttress containing Bishop's Rise. Short but often in condition.

Knobbing Madge   130m   III. R. Hamilton, S. Kennedy. 21st February 2004.
The slabby buttress containing The Killing Fields often forms large quantities of ice although it is affected by the sun from mid season. This route starts up a series of left trending icy ramps close to the left defining edge of the buttress. This is about 40m left of The Killing Fields. Climb ramps out left then climb directly by a groove line to more broken ground (50m). Broken ground and the upper snow slopes lead to the top (80m).

Coire an Fhir Dhuibh:
Rib Dubh   100m   III. D. McGimpsey, A. Nisbet. 22nd December 2003.
The rib which forms the right end of the face. The middle section was climbed by grooves right of the crest.

AONACH BEAG, West Face, Skyline Buttress (NN 188 708):
The following routes are situated on Skyline Buttress (p 264 of the current guide) which is well seen from Steall. The buttress presents a cracked right (south) wall and steep bulging left (west) wall split by a left-facing corner. Descend on the right (south).

Zigzag   45m   Severe *. S. Kennedy, A. Nelson. 19th April 2003.
Approximates to the arête between the west and south faces following a system of exposed ramps. Start at the toe of the arête which is climbed for a short distance before stepping left on to a leftwards-trending ramp on the edge. Follow the ramp to a wide ledge running across the face on the left. Step back right on to the arête which is followed a short way then move left on to another left-trending ramp. Climb the ramp and a short wall to finish.

Flake Out   65m   HVS 5a *. S. Kennedy, A. Nelson. 19th April 2003.
Follows a line just left of the left-facing corner on the west face. Start by a small flake and climb steeply into a small depression. A natural line leads back left to below a bulging crack. Climb the crack and trend right to a grassy ledge below the upper corner (35m). Finish up slabby rock left of the corner (30m).

AONACH BEAG, An Ghaidh Garbh, Braxton-Hicks Buttress (SMCJ 2003):
Catabasis   100m   IV,4. I. Small. 16th March 2003.
This takes the left-hand groove (the right one being Braxton-Hicks) to easier snow slopes and a cornice finish.

Inducement   110m   III. I. Small. 16th March 2003.
Start down and right of Catabasis. Climb a slanting gully line to easier snow slopes.
Notes: I. Small also did Goblet of Fire (SMCJ 2003), a great ice line, easy to combine with a route on Braxton-Hicks Buttress. Also thought Anabasis worth a star. Aurora (SMCJ 2003) felt like III but in icy conditions.

STOB COIRE AN LAOIGH (Grey Corries):
Socialist   60m   V,7. D. McGimpsey, A. Nisbet, J. Preston. 2nd March 2004.
Climbs the centre of the left wall of Centrepoint buttress. Start along a ledge about 6m right of Tat Gully (lean conditions).
1. 10m. Climb leftwards through an overhang to gain a ledge above (crux).
2. 25m. Traverse right until possible to climb the wall above and gain the highest ledge below a steep wall.
3. 25m. Move right again and climb a chimney to a ledge. Step right and climb the wall above slightly leftwards to the top.

Note: The obvious corner left of Centrepoint was climbed by J. Edwards and R. Martin in March 2003. This led to the girdling ledge (35m, 6, moss reluctant to freeze).

Jaws   60m   IV,5. A. Nisbet, J. Preston. 24th February 2004.
Climbs the two tiered section of buttress left of The White Streak. Start as for Yee

Ha but soon climb the wall on its right to move into an obvious widening crack. Climb its upper chimney and the corner above to easier ground. Go rightwards and up a step to a smooth V-groove about 20m right of Yee Ha chimney and 10m left of the big groove of The White Streak (35m). Climb the smooth groove past an overhang and up turf to finish (25m).

Switchback 60m IV,5. D. McGimpsey, A. Nisbet. 4th January 2004.
Start at the same point as Jaws/Yee Ha but move up right to a steep flaky corner, the least steep feature in this band. Climb the corner, then go more easily up right to belay as for Jaws below the smooth V-groove (35m). Climb diagonally rightwards up a line of weakness, then traverse left into the top of the groove and pull out of its top. Steep turf leads to the top (25m).

Note: J. Edwards and J. Thacker repeated Sloppy Suzie but climbed the fault direct at V,6.

BEN ALDER, Garbh Coire Beag:
Pat-a-Cake 300m II. A. Nisbet. 8th April 2004.
A shallow gully right of Culra Couloir. An apparently steep section at two-thirds height was breached by an easy hidden diagonal gully, There was a break in the cornice above the rib between this route and Culra Couloir.

GEAL CHARN (Drumochter):
The following routes lie on the Geal Charn crags at NN 593 802, approximately 1km from the main Creag Dhubh Crag. The crag is smaller than Creag Dhubh.

Flight of the Navigator 100m VI,6 ***. I. Rudkin, K. Watson, K. Neal. 29th February 2004.
An obvious piece of ice. Start up easy ground (40m) to belay left under a hanging ice pillar. Turn the pillar on the left to finish on steep ice pulling right and on to the top of the ice pillar (30m). Finish up easy ice above (30m).

Map and Compass 120m III,4 *. K. Neal, I. Rudkin. 28th February, 2004.
About 40m to the right of Flight of the Navigator is a gully which cuts quite deeply into the hillside. Climb on easy ice for about 40m. The second pitch takes a narrow right-trending gully. The final pitch was taken on the right to finish; an easier exit could be taken on the left.

GLEN COE
BUACHAILLE ETIVE MOR, Rannoch Wall:
Glaistig 40m Hard Severe 4b. S. Kennedy, D. Ritchie. 10th August 2003.
Takes a line close to the striking arête forming the right wall of Domino Chimney. Sparsely protected in the middle section. A couple of metres right of foot of the arête is a pinnacle leaning against the wall. Climb the corner forming the left side of the pinnacle. From the top of the pinnacle step on to the wall above and move diagonally left to the edge overlooking Domino Chimney. Follow the arête to the top.

Cuneiform Buttress Note:
C. Cartwright and I. Small thought The Mighty Atom deserving of E3 5c.

STOB COIRE NAN LOCHAIN, North Buttress:
Tuberculosis 50m VI,6. D. Hollinger, G. Willett. 7th February 2004.
Right of Crest Route is a steep groove leading to an impending corner. Begin at the top of a snow bay beneath a short chimney. Make a few moves up the chimney before a difficult swing left gains the groove proper. Follow the groove (sustained) and continue up the steep corner to a snow ramp which leads to the top of the buttress. Excellent climbing but a little rattly in places – well frozen conditions helpful.

Diamond Buttress:
Crazy Diamond 110m III. J. Lyall. 27th January 2004.
Start at the beginning of the narrows in Central Gully. Move left along a ledge and up over a bulge to gain a turfy fault which is followed to easier ground and the top.

Choker 100m III. J. Lyall. 27th January 2004.
Start 15m higher up Central Gully and climb the first narrow gully in its left wall.

Collie's Pinnacle:
North Chimney IV,5. S. Taylor, J. Danson. 31st January, 2004.
A good short route.

West Face (maybe?) 50m IV,6. R. Cross, D. Hollinger. 30th January 2004.
This is the obvious cracked corner-line at the bottom of the right branch of Easy Gully. Climb the corner past some loose blocks and make a tricky move right into an off-width slot. Squirm up this exiting left and climb easier walls and ledges to the top of the pinnacle. Entertaining!

Fever Pitch 60m V,7. D. Hollinger, R. Cross. 30th January 2004.
Good climbing up the steep groove-line on the left side of the west face of the pinnacle. Begin at an overhung slot. A tricky move out of the slot leads steeply to gain a rest beneath the turfy groove. Another hard move gains the groove which is followed to easier ground and a huge boulder. An easier pitch leads to the top of the pinnacle.

West Top of Bidean, Bishop's Buttress:
Under the Weather 60m VII,7. G. Hughes, J. Edwards. 28th December 2003.
Climbs a right-facing corner to an overhang about 5m left of the arête on the left section of the upper tier of Bishop's Buttress. Start 50m along a widening terrace left of the Fang at an open V-slot below the obvious right-facing corner on the left-hand side of the arête.
1. 45m. Climb the corner slot to reach a platform at 10m (possible belay). Go up to the right-facing corner and climb it until possible to surmount the overhang and reach cracks. Continue in the same line via ledges and steep grooves (bold) to a large ledge.

2. 15m. Climb the right-slanting crack behind to reach easy ground.

The Crook   VI,7. D. King, A. Nelson. 28th December 2003.
By the summer line. The crux was well protected but some bold moves thereafter.

Note: J. Lyall climbed The Gallery on 27th January 2004 and thought it grade III.

AONACH DUBH, Terrace Face:
Note from I.Taylor: De Vreemde Stap is 30m rather than 40m and best climbed in one pitch, one star. Hesitation first pitch is 35m and should read "….move up and right to a ledge at 25m….". E1 and one star.

STOB COIRE NAM BEITH, No.4 Buttress:
Tarbh Uisge   65m   E1/2 5b *. A. Nelson, S. Kennedy. 7th September 2003.
A thin crack-line runs up the steep wall about 5m right of Isis. The crack-line leads to a corner which eventually leads into the final corner of Isis. From the foot of Isis, traverse horizontally right on to the initial wall just left of the crack-line. Follow the wall and crack-line (peg runner) before pulling out right to better holds. Continue up easier ground into a corner leading to a grassy bay at the junction with Isis (45m). Finish up the corner (20m).

CREAG DOIRE-BHEITH:
The tree filled amphitheatre up right of the Aristocrack area has a black corner in its top left side.
Jist Hingin' Thegither   35m   HVS 4c. J. Lyall, H. Burrows-Smith. 12th April 2003.
Climb the corner and slab on the left, before moving boldly back into the corner, which is followed to finish up a narrow right-slanting wall.

The Rowling Stones   30m   HVS 5a. H. Burrows-Smith, J. Lyall. 12th April 2003.
The wall right of the tree filled amphitheatre has an obvious right-slanting wide crack. Just left of this is a thin crack which is climbed, moving out right at its top to finishing up the edge above. Either abseil off from the tree belay or follow heather and easy rocks to the top.

CREISE:
Note: C. Moody notes that the obvious line left of Inglis Clark Ridge, finishing up a gully/chimney, has been climbed at grade III **.

GLEN ETIVE, Trilleachan Slabs:
Note: J. and L. Biggar think that pitch 4 of The Pause is more than 4c, more like 5b.
C. Moody notes that the peg runner on pitch 4 of Hammer is long gone.

GLEN GOUR, Indian Slab Crag:
Note: C. Moody does not agree with G. Latter's times (SMCJ 2003) but is willing to split the difference.

SOUTHERN HIGHLANDS

THE COBBLER, Centre Peak Buttress:

The Cathedral X,11 ***. D. MacLeod (unseconded). 28th Jan 2004.

A wild and strenuous line through the roof of the large cave/recess feature which defines the lower half of the Centre Peak Buttress (just left of Lobby Dosser). Although short, the climb features 6m of horizontal climbing through the roof section. Start directly below the cave. Move up to the right-hand corner and torque up this until it is possible to swing left and mantel on to a turf ledge (harder than it looks). Now climb directly to a tight niche in the back of the cave roof, from where the central thin roof-crack emerges. Launch across the roof-crack using overhead heel-toe jams to aid progress (Friend protection extremely strenuous to place and dubious if ice is present), the crux being about 4m out. The climbing eases just above the lip with good turf eventually leading to a thread belay. Descend by abseil or continue up easy (Grade II) ground if desired. FA ground up/on sight at the second attempt.

Buzzard Crag (NN 247 061):

This crag is high up on the west side of the Cobbler. It is visible from the top of the Rest and be Thankful, directly above the forestry plantation. Park in the layby on the A83 for the path up the back of the Cobbler, then head up the path. When the forestry starts curving up to the right, break away from the path and follow the edge of the plantation. At the highest point of the trees strike up the hillside to the crag. 40 minutes. The crag is in three sections with the highest on the right. This starts as a steep slab, then rears up to a leaning headwall. To the left is a corner, then a large boulder at the base of the cliff. This section is bulging, with an overhanging bouldering wall on the left. Left again is a smaller section above a grassy terrace. There are two routes on this.

Alzheimer Arête 15m VS 4c. R. Wallace, A. Wallace July 1993.
Climb a curving arête at the left end of this section.

Eye to Eye 15m E2 5c. A. Wallace, R. Wallace July 1993.
Walk along the terrace to the right-hand end. Struggle up an off-width crack in a corner.

BEINN UDLAIDH, Coire Ghamhnain:

Tinkerbell, Left Hand Variation 9m III. M. Karatay, G. North. 7th March 2004.
After the main difficulties climb the collection of hanging icicles on the left wall of the gully to escape.

CRUACH ARDRAIN, Creagan Dubha (NN 420 214):

This crag lies on the south-east flank of Cruach Ardrain, and is approached from Inverlochlarig.

Hard Rain 240m III/IV. W. Jeffrey, D. Barry. 11th February 2001.
The main stream draining over the crag gives a good climb when frozen.

BEN CRUACHAN, Stob Garbh, Coire Chreachainn (NN 096 302):

This crag lies in the North-east corrie of Stob Garbh. The corrie consists of two buttresses, Summit Buttress and East Buttress which are separated by two gullies which in turn are separated by an impressive fin of rock.

East Buttress:
This is the long tapering north-facing buttress on the left side of the corrie. The following two climbs are located on the steep upper gully wall of the buttress, opposite the prominent fin of rock. Although short, the climbs provide interesting technical climbing in a fine setting.

Great White Groove 60m III,4. E. Brunskill, G. Macfie. 22nd February 2004.
Start at a prominent V-groove at the bottom left side of the upper buttress and level with the start of the fin. Climb the groove and continue in the same line except for a minor deviation right, then back left along turfy ledges to avoid a cracked roof. Belay above the roof (30m). Continue up and right and follow a right-trending chimney line formed by a large block. Continue straight up over large blocks to easy ground and the top (30m).

Riddles 55m IV,7 *. E. Brunskill, G. Macfie. 22nd February 2004.
Start at a steep corner-line 10m up and right of Great White Groove. Climb the perplexing but well protected corner (crux) and continue in the same line avoiding a steep blank slab by a flake-crack on the right. Climb up and left to a ledge (30m). Finish as for Great White Groove (25m).

Shark Gully 100m I. E. Brunskill, G. Macfie. 22nd February 2004.
The narrow gully on the left side of the fin.

Coire Chat:
The buttress is situated at the head of Coire Chat on the north side of the ridge running west from Cruachan's summit.

East Gully 40m I.
A descent gully that can cornice up quite quickly; abseil possible to the base of Chatter Rib.

Chatter Rib 50m III. S. M. Richardson, C. Cartwright. 23rd November 2003.
The obvious rib defining the left-hand side of the buttress. Start at the left-hand toe of the buttress.
1. 25m. Climb the left edge of the buttress for 15m, then trend slightly right to an obvious recess.
2. 25m. Step right and surmount large blocks. Continue up grooves to the top.

Quickfire 45m III. I. Small, C. Cartwright. 25th January 2004.
The obvious left to right ramp-line starting in the recess immediately right of Chatter Rib. Climb the ramp with one awkward step, pull out into the gully and continue to the top.

Toxic Brew 60m IV,4. C. Cartwright, S. M. Richardson. 23rd November 2003.
Follow a line of shallow icy chimneys and grooves starting 20m right of Quickfire.
1. 30m. Climb the initial groove to a steep wall barring access to the continuation chimney. Surmount the wall and bridge the chimney to a belay on the left.
2. 30m. Follow the right-trending groove to the top.

Tainted Elixir 65m V,6 **. C. Cartwright, S. M. Richardson. 14th December 2003.

Right of Toxic Brew there is a right-facing corner.
1. 25m. Climb up between the corner and a large perched block. Surmount the bulging corner and continue up to belay on the left.
2. 25m. Climb the cracked wall above and continue with interest to an overhanging barrier wall split by a tapered slot. Pull up and into the slot, then exit and go left to overlook Toxic Brew. An excellent pitch.
3. 20m. Step into Toxic Brew groove and follow it to the top.

Double Chaser 65m V,6 *. I. Small, C. Cartwright. 25th January 2004.
Climbs the intermittent double crack system starting 3m right of Tainted Elixir.
1. 30m. Climb the crack system by a series of ever-steepening steps to a bulging crux. Contemplate the left and right options, choose the right and step awkwardly up on to a small ledge. Reach high for a right tool placement, then make a committing pull up and left to easier ground.
2. 35m. Immediately above is wide overhanging chimney. Bridge spectacularly up this to easier ground. Step left to a short right-facing corner and crack and follow this to the top.

In the Knoe 85m VI,6 **. I. Small, C. Cartwright. 12th February 2003.
This climbs the left-facing corner come fault-line dividing this section of the buttress in two. The route requires some build-up of ice.
1. 30m. The fault-line starts up an overhanging left-facing corner. Climb the steep right wall of the corner via a turfy crack and continue straight up to a good ledge below and to the right of the continuation chimney.
2. 40m. Step left 2m, surmount a short wall and slab to enter the chimney. Climb the chimney to an impasse, make hard moves to exit out right and continue up the steep groove come left-facing corner to below a deep, wide crack/corner (visible from the ground). Spectacular bridging leads to a good belay.
3. 15m. Easy ground leads to the top.

Goldfinger 85m VII,7 ***. C. Cartwright, S. M. Richardson. 29th December 2003.
A surprisingly steep route that climbs the third section of the buttress, starting down and right of In The Knoe. The primary feature is an apparent off-width crack splitting the clean wall high on the buttress. Start at a slightly raised platform 3m right of the left edge.
1. 30m. Above is a short wall with twin cracks. Climb this into a small niche, then step higher before moving rightwards to a short left-facing corner. Surmount this, then step right on to a sloping ledge and into a fault-line. Climb the bulging wall above via the fault and work up and slightly left to a ledge with a recess on the left. On the right is a right-trending, off-width groove. Climb this and so to the ledge shared with In The Knoe.
2. 35m. From the left end of the ledge, climb the left-facing corner directly above and pull right on to a ledge (possible belay). Continue up the cracked corner come groove until it runs into the headwall. Make a hard move up to a horizontal break, then commit rightwards and step up into the apparent off-width, a short shallow right-facing corner. Climb the corner, then a bulge to easier ground. Continue to a belay on the left overlooking In The Knoe.

3. 20m. Continue above trending right, then back left to a final steep bulge. Pull through this bulge to the top.

Dr Noe   85m   VI,6 ***. S. M. Richardson, C. Cartwright. 4th January 2004.
Right of Goldfinger there is a stepped ramp-line running left to right up to a point overlooking Noe Gully. This is best seen by standing well over to the right and down from Noe Gully. Belay as for Goldfinger.
1. 35m. Move off right from the belay over to the base of an obvious stepped fault-line taken higher up by Goldfinger. Climb up and right into the start of the ramp-line. Step right, then up and left to then follow the ramp-line via a series of steps to an obvious ledge.
2. 35m. Continue along the ramp-line by a series of ever steepening steps to the crux step, an awkward right-facing corner with an off-width crack. Pull out right from the top of this and continue until a final pull on to a ledge overlooking Noe Gully.
3. 15m. Step down and right on to the left-hand wall of Noe Gully. Make a couple of steep moves directly up the wall to easier ground before a final awkward move to the top.

Noe Gully   70m   I/II. D. Ritchie, M. Shaw. 9th February 2002.
An impressive, free-standing square-cut fin of rock, the Noe Fin, marks the right-hand end of this section of buttress. The fin is defined by a distinct gully on the left-hand side, Noe Gully and a deep chimney, Thunderbolt Chimney, on the right. Climb the gully via a narrowing to the base of the fin then continue up the left hand easy gully.

Thunderbolt Chimney   70m   IV,5 *. R. Webb, C. Cartwright. 11th January 2004.
The right-hand side of the Noe Fin is defined by a deep chimney.
1. 35m. Climb to the base of the fin as for Noe Gully and belay on the right at the base of the chimney.
2. 20m. Climb the chimney via three large chockstones, the second being the most awkward.
3. 15m. Continue up easy ground to the top.

Noe Buttress   100m   IV,4. D. Ritchie, M. Shaw. 9th February 2002.
This route climbs the left wall of the next buttress, down from the Noe Fin. Start some 30m up from the lowest toe of the buttress in Noe Gully.
1. 50m. Move on to the left-hand edge of the buttress, climbing mixed ground above to gain a shallow right slanting chimney. At its top turn the rock nose on its right side, climbing a groove, then a right-slanting fault to easier ground.
2. 50m. Follow the buttress crest more easily to finish.

Noe Buttress Direct   120m   VI,6. I. Small, A. Hume. 27th January 2004.
A direct version of Noe Buttress up the front face. Start at the lowest point of the buttress.
1. 40m. Climb slabs to a right-facing corner, go up this to top and pull out left on to a ledge. Take a small icy corner and strenuously pass a small flake to an overlap and ledge above. Move left up a flake, then back right across a steep wall to gain a slabby recess. Exit this to an easier groove and up rightwards to a huge flake.
2. 50m. From the flake climb a left-slanting ramp to below a monstrous perched

block. Swing right to gain the wide crack behind it and climb to the top and the crest of the buttress. At this point the original route joins from the left. Continue up the buttress crest by the original route.
3. 30m. Finish easily to the top.

Yes Gully (left-hand)   50m   II. S. M. Richardson, C. Cartwright. 14th December 2003.
The right-hand side of the buttress is bounded by a double gully system divided by a rock fin, similar to, though less impressive than the Noe Fin. Climb the left-hand of the two gullies.

MEALL NAN TARMACHAN, Cam Chreag, Forgotten Buttress:
Something Grooves Direct   100m   III,4 *. G. E. Little. 15th February, 2003.
Climb the groove without deviation to make exposed moves out right where it ends at an overhang. Finish straight up on easier ground.

Fan Buttress:
Bunting Rib   80m   II. G. E. Little. 15th February, 2003.
Start at the foot of the rib just to the right of the open icy scoop of Knuckleduster Corner. Climb the rib and progressively easier ground above.

Lozenge Buttress:
Lozenge Buttress Right-Hand   120m   III,5 *. G. E. Little. 15th February, 2003.
This is a short and meaty start to the normal route. Start just right of the overhung toe of the buttress. Climb very steep ice or a rippled wall farther right to gain a recess, then go straight up to join the normal route.

BEINN GHLAS (near Ben Lawers):
The shallow corrie to the north of the summit of Beinn Ghlas contains a short steep escarpment below the summit ridge. The route was climbed in lean conditions.
Pint Size   70m   II. S. Muir. 6th March 2004.
Climb a short gully in the centre of the escarpment and then trend right up a shallow scoop on turfy ledges to the ridge. The summit of Beinn Ghlas is just to the west.

ARRAN
CIR MHOR:
The pitch grades for Incus (SMCJ 2002) should be 5a 6b 5c.

BEINN A' CHLIABHAIN:
Haakon's Highway   75m   IV,6 **. C. Schaschke, G. E. Little (alt.). 4th January 2003.
The north-facing buttress holding Haakon's Highway lies at NR 967 411, and is the slim buttress lying to the east of a more sprawling mass of slabby rock and separated from it by a shallow boulder-choked gully. This fine winter line follows the somewhat neglected summer route. The chimney on the last pitch provides a well protected, but very troublesome, crux.

LOWLAND OUTCROPS
With a new guide imminent, no descriptions are published.

MISCELLANEOUS NOTES

The W. H. Murray Literary Prize.

As a tribute to the late Bill Murray, whose mountain and environment writings have been an inspiration to many a budding mountaineer, the SMC have set up a modest writing prize, to be run through the pages of the Journal. The basic rules are set out below, and will be re-printed each year. The prize is run with a deadline, as is normal, of the end of January each year. So assuming you are reading this in early July, you have, for the next issue, six months in which to set the pencil, pen or word processor on fire.

The Rules:

1. There shall be a competition for the best entry on Scottish Mountaineering published in the *Scottish Mountaineering Club Journal*. The competition shall be called the 'W. H. Murray Literary Prize', hereafter called the 'Prize.'

2. The judging panel shall consist of, in the first instance, the following: The current Editor of the *SMC Journal;* The current President of the SMC; and two or three lay members, who may be drawn from the membership of the SMC. The lay members of the panel will sit for three years after which they will be replaced.

3. If, in the view of the panel, there is in any year no entries suitable for the Prize, then there shall be no award that year.

4. Entries shall be writing on the general theme of 'Scottish Mountaineering', and may be prose articles of up to approximately 5000 words in length, or shorter verse. Entries may be fictional.

5. Panel members may not enter for the competition during the period of their membership.

6. Entries must be of original, previously unpublished material. Entries should be submitted to the Editor of the *SMC Journal* before the end of January for consideration that year. Lengthy contributions are preferably word-processed and submitted either on 3.5" PC disk or sent via e-mail. (See Office Bearers page at end of this Journal for address etc.) Any contributor to the SMC Journal is entitled to exclude their material from consideration of the Prize and should so notify the Editor of this wish in advance.

7. The prize will be a cheque for the amount £250.

8. Contributors may make different submissions in different years.

9. The decision of the panel is final.

10. Any winning entry will be announced in the *SMC Journal* and will be published in the *SMC Journal* and on the SMC Web site. Thereafter, authors retain copyright.

The W. H. Murray Literary Prize 2004

THE winner of this year's W. H. Murray literary Prize is Robin Campbell for his essay, *Climbing And Writing The Victorian Way*. It is usual form in the judging of this competition to remove the author's name from the article in order to minimise the possibility of personal bias creeping in to the judgment but, given Robin's well known penchant for things Victorian, the judges would have been hard-pushed to fail to ascribe authorship in this case. What I find amazing is, that even with this weighty handicap, Robin managed to win through.

Right from the opening lines: "Since my taste in literature is irredeemably lowbrow, I address my chosen topic as an imposter," one realises that satire is on the menu. However, this is a humorous, but at the same time, serious look at Scottish mountaineering writing. Robin introduces a number of historical vignettes from the pages of the Journal, ranging from Norman Collie's *Divine Mysteries of the Oromaniacal Quest* to an article by one Fraser Campbell "about bouldering. It proposed the formation of a 'Boulder Society' and was illustrated by minutely tedious drawings of boulders". One can't help but wonder if Binor Pellcambus has the recent plethora of bouldering guides in his sights here. The merits of this essay was summed up concisely by our President in his capacity as one of the judges: "An erudite and interesting analysis of writing styles – should be compulsory reading for all Journal contributors."

Other articles which came in for favourable comment from the judges – Peter Biggar, last year's winner was co-opted onto the panel and nailed his colours firmly to the mast with this comment on Julian Lines's *Skye Is The Limit*. "This has a freshness I like. In places almost a Robin Smith-like quality – a well unified piece." Praise indeed.

In spite of Campbell's adage, given in his winning essay, that: "The poetic impulse is the product of a debilitating condition, in its effects resembling malaria, which seizes hold of its victims at moments of weakness and reduces them to gibbering wrecks." There was praise also for Hamish Brown's poem *Life's Day* as "having some wonderfully evocative lines". I very much liked the piece with its wonderful imagery as in "Gear rucksacked in a robber's rush" to mention but one. I have often thought that dissecting a poem line for line is a rather questionable pursuit so I will only ask that you cast aside any pre-conceived ideas you may have of the genre and read it – more than once – I'm sure you won't be disappointed, this particular poet is no Rodney Spelvin!

I would also like to make mention of Mike Jacob for his excellent short story *A Hard Rain*. This is a well structured piece that attempts to examine the motivations behind his protagonist's climbing and where it fits, or indeed fails to fit, into the lives of those around him.

Congratulations again to Robin Campbell, and to the other contributors and all the other budding authors out there – there's always next year. The winning article, as well as appearing in this year's Journal, can also be read in full on the SMC Website.

Charlie Orr.

Naismith's Rule Overhauled

By Dr W. G. Rees.

Scott Polar Research Institute,Cambridge)

Introduction:

For more than 100 years, estimates of the time taken to walk in hilly terrain have mostly been essentially based on Naismith's Rule (Naismith 1892). This, in its metricated form, states that the time is 12 minutes per horizontal kilometre, plus one minute for each six metres of height ascended, descents being ignored. (Naismith's original formulation, to which this is virtually identical, was three miles per hour, plus one hour per 2000ft. of ascent.) Various refinements have subsequently been proposed, as discussed by Carver and Fritz (2000), including allowances for fitness, fatigue, altitude, weather and ground conditions and so on.

However, most of these refinements have ignored the common experience that steep downhill slopes are *not* covered as quickly as the corresponding distance over level terrain. Thus Naismith's rule, and simple variants on it, tend to be more optimistic for steep downhill slopes relative to uphill slopes.

Langmuir (1984) adapted Naismith's rule by introducing a slope-dependent correction to recognise that while gentle downhill slopes can be covered more rapidly than the same distance over level ground, steeper downslopes will be slower. Langmuir's approach offers an improvement over the standard Naismith rule, although it can still be criticised on the grounds that it does not 'penalise' steep uphill slopes sufficiently. For example, consider an ascent of 200m. over a distance of one kilometre. The Langmuir formula, like Naismith's original rule, gives a time of 32 minutes regardless of whether the climb is a steady one at a slope of about 11°, or a short, steep pitch at 45° over a horizontal distance of 200m., followed by a level walk of 800m. This is certainly contrary to the author's experience, and probably to that of most other walkers.

A much more complicated procedure has been adopted by the Schweizer Wanderwege SAW (1999), in which the walking speed is calculated from the slope using an equation with 16 coefficients. This can certainly provide more realistic estimates of walking times, as indeed can the Langmuir formula, but neither of them is easy to use in practice. (The Swiss formula is, in fact, made available as a computer spreadsheet, which is convenient if one has a computer handy.) The aim of this paper is to introduce a simple but realistic formula.

Basis of the new method:

It is assumed that the walking speed v (measured with respect to the horizontal) is some function of the slope m, where the slope is defined as the height gain per unit horizontal distance. (For example, if one descends a height of 15m. over a horizontal distance of 100m., $m = -0.15$). It is, in fact, more convenient to model the *reciprocal* of the speed. What is needed is a simple function that recognises the fact that speed on both steep uphill slopes and steep downhill slopes will tend to be lower than on level ground, with an increasing time penalty for increasingly steep slopes. The simplest candidate is a quadratic function, in which $1/v = a+bm+cm^2$. In this equation, the term a just determines the (reciprocal of the) speed over level ground, while the term c represents the extent to which very steep slopes are 'penalised'. If the slope m exceeds some critical value that is determined by c, the formula implies that it will be quicker to proceed by making zig-zags rather than along a direct route. This seems realistic. The term b introduces a difference between uphill and downhill slopes of the same steepness.

Testing the new method:

Data to test the new formula were collected by the author, usually accompanied by wife and dogs, over five walks in the English Lake District and five walks in Snowdonia. The author and his wife are moderately fit and in their early Forties (the dogs are fitter and younger), so the times ought to be roughly typical of average walkers. The walks ranged in length from five to 20km. and involved total height gains (defined in Naismith's sense, i.e. ignoring descents) from about 300m. to 1000m. All the walks were on reasonably well-defined paths, reasonably familiar to the walkers, although route-finding was occasionally an issue. The terrain ranged from tarmac roads to occasional straightforward scrambling (Jack's Rake on Pavey Ark, Striding Edge, and the Crib Goch ridge), although most was on typical unimproved mountain footpaths.

Data from the walks were collected using a GPS receiver, in a manner similar to that employed by Carver and Fritz (2000). The GPS receiver was set to record the walker's horizontal location (i.e. the Eastings and Northings values in the Ordnance Survey grid system) at one-minute intervals. The data were subsequently downloaded to a computer, and compared with a digital map of the area to determine the height. Analysis of these data then allowed the actual distances and times of ascent and descent to be calculated (stops for such purposes as refreshment, photography and so on were subtracted from the times).

The data were analysed mathematically to find the most suitable values of the coefficients a, b and c, and to test whether the formula did, in fact, represent an improvement compared with Naismith's rule and variations on it. Two interesting facts emerged from this analysis. Firstly, the new method was clearly *much* superior to Naismith-type rules for estimating the time. Secondly, the coefficient b could be ignored without any significant loss of accuracy in the method. The implication of this second fact is that it is simply the *steepness* of a slope, and not whether it is an ascent or descent, that is the major factor in determining how slowly it will be traversed.

Practical application of the new method:

The most accurate way to apply the new method involves measuring distances and heights from a map. It is only slightly more complicated than the procedure needed to implement the Naismith rule. The route of the walk is first divided into segments, in each of which the slope is (more or less) constant. (This can easily be established by looking at the spacing between the contours.) Thus, adjacent segments are separated by significant changes in slope. For each segment, the distance d and height gain h (which may be positive or negative) are measured from the map. If d and h are both measured in metres, the time for the segment is estimated as $(0.75d + 14.6h^2/d)$ seconds. By adding the results of this calculation for all the segments of the walk, the total time can be estimated.

There is a simpler, but less accurate, way of applying the new method. This only works if the start and end points of the walk are at the same height (for example, in the case of any walk that returns to its starting point), but it requires only knowledge of the total distance D and the total ascent H defined in the Naismith sense, i.e. ignoring descents. It is based on some statistical assumptions about the manner in which the slope varies along the walk, which appear to be valid unless there is an exceptionally long walk in. If D is measured in kilometres and H in metres, the formula for the total time T (in minutes) becomes $T = 12.5D + 0.00153H^2/D$.

Examples:
First, I will give two examples of the calculation for single segments of a walk. The first is the descent from the summit of Glyder Fawr to the pass between it and Glyder Fach, in Snowdonia. The horizontal distance d is almost exactly one km and the height gain h is –72m. Naismith's rule would predict a time of 12 minutes for this walk. The calculation using the new formula is 0.75¥1000 + 14.6¥(-72)¥(-72)/1000 seconds = 826 seconds or about 14 minutes. My own actual time for this walk is about 14 minutes. The second example is a steep section on the ascent of Glyder Fawr. This section has a horizontal distance d of about 400m. and a height gain h of 190m. Naismith's rule predicts a walking time of 36 minutes while the new formula predicts a time of 27 minutes. My own actual time is about 20 minutes, which is closer to the prediction of the new rule than to Naismith's rule, though perhaps not by much.

Secondly, I give examples of calculations for entire walks. The times are in minutes.

	Actual	Naismith	New	New (round trip rule)
Scafell ascent	148	228	132	
Scafell descent	133	89	129	
Scafell round trip	281	317	261	263
Grasmoor ascent	104	187	102	
Grasmoor descent	127	112	150	
Grasmoor round trip	231	299	252	243
Helvellyn ascent	128	209	125	
Helvellyn descent	161	141	169	
Helvellyn round trip	289	350	294	289
Langdale Pikes acsent	97	151	112	
Langdale Pikes descent	229	187	205	
Langdale round trip	326	338	317	276
Glyders ascent	106	168	168	
Glyders descent	99	63	112	
Glyders round trip	205	231	233	211
Cadair Idris ascent	123	179	118	
Cadair Idris descent	81	53	90	
Cadair Idris round trip	204	232	208	206
Tryfan ascent	134	144	121	
Tryfan descent	77	30	71	
Tryfan round trip	211	174	192	202
Snowdon ascent	134	205	135	
Snowdon descent	156	107	160	
Snowdon round trip	290	312	295	281

The Old Man of Stoer. Photo: Niall Ritchie.

The results show that Naismith's rule generally over-estimates the time of ascent by around 50%, and understimates the time of descent by about 30%. These errors partially cancel each other for round trips, so that Naismith's rule over-estimates by only about 10% in these cases. The new formula, on the other hand, seems to give much more realistic estimates of the times of both ascent and descent. For round trips, the simpler version of the new formula generally works well too. It only failed in the case of the Langdale Pikes walk, which had an unusually long walk in by comparison with the others.

Conclusions:

To summarise, the results of this analysis of a rather limited set of personal data suggest that Naismith's rule is fundamentally mistaken, and that it should be replaced by a rule such as the one proposed here that recognises the increasing importance of steeper slopes. Naismith's rule tends to over-estimate the time of ascent and underestimate the time of descent. The reason that Naismith's rule works as well as it does in practice is probably because it is mostly applied to walks in which the heights of the starting and ending points are not very different, but even so it can under-estimate the total time by up to about 50%. The new rule, proposed in this article, focuses on steepness rather than height gain *per se*, and, interestingly, does not differentiate between steep uphill and steep downhill slopes.

It should be emphasised that this proposed rule has been calibrated using my personal data, and only for a limited number of short-to-middling length walks. It may well be that the author is significantly more or (probably) less fit than the 'average' mountain walker, so the coefficients may need to be adjusted slightly. Also, the usual restrictions to the Naismith rule apply – it assumes that the walk includes no serious and sustained scrambling, and ignores possible effects from weather, fatigue, altitude, ground cover (e.g. snow or boot-grabbing heather) and so on. It also makes no allowance for halts. My own personal estimate is to add between 15% and 20% to the total time to take these into account.

References:

Carver, S. and Fritz, S. (2000). Munro-bagging with a computer…? Naismith's rule and the long walk in. Scottish Mountaineering Club Journal **191**, 317-322.
Langmuir, E. (1984). Mountaincraft and Leadership. The Scottish Sports Council/MLTB. Cordee, Leicester.
Naismith, W.W. (1892). Scottish Mountaineering Club Journal, **2**, 136.
Schweizer Wanderwege SAW (1999).
Dr W. G. Rees. **(Scott Polar Research Institute,Cambridge)**

Easter Meet 2003. Photo: Peter MacDonald.

Easter Meet 2004. Photo: Peter MacDonald.

SCOTTISH WINTER NOTES

OPINIONS differ on the 2004 winter season. For some it was a good winter with long settled spells in the West. The air was clear and the sky blue for many days through February and March, and if you wanted to front-point classic gullies on squeaky neve this was the season for you. On the other hand, lack of any significant snowfalls until late March (when it was too late), meant that there was never enough build up for the likes of Orion Face to form on the Ben. Few of the classic Grade V climbs were in condition, and many Grade III climbers became unwitting grade IV leaders as routes were typically at least one notch harder than their advertised grade. For the technical mixed climber it was a frustrating time too, for the infrequent snowfalls were swiftly followed by deep thaws that stripped even the highest crags.

Despite this, the 2004 winter saw some outstanding achievements. Arguably the finest example was the first winter ascent of *Marathon Corner Direct* (VIII,8) on Ben Loyal by Guy Robertson and Pete Benson. With a summit elevation of only 764m, Ben Loyal is not an obvious winter climbing venue, especially in a lean season, but when bitterly cold strong North-West winds swept southwards across the country in late January, the Aberdeen based pair took the gamble and made the long journey north up to Sutherland to visit the little known 300m-high cliff on Sgor a'Chleirich, Ben Loyal's westerly top. Marathon Corner is an E1 summer climb that was first climbed by Les Brown and A.Turnbull in 1969. The guidebook description of the cliff is particularly enticing for a winter climber, mentioning that several summer parties have been repulsed by extraordinarily steep vegetation, loose rock and a distinct lack of protection. All this made for a superb seven-pitch winter route climbed on a mixture of turf, snowed-up rock and icy smears. For many climbers, climbing a new route of this length and quality on a cliff that was previously untouched in winter is close to the ultimate, and *Marathon Corner* joins the likes of *Magic Bow Wall* and *The Godfather* as one of the most significant ascents in the Northern Highlands in recent years.

By contrast, the other major new route of the season was made three days earlier at the other end of the Highlands. Over the last couple of seasons Dave MacLeod has been pushing the winter envelope with a series of difficult ascents such as his on sight repeat of *The Demon Direct* in the Northern Corries. During the cold snap near the end of January, Dave pushed the technical limit yet further when he succeeded on his long-standing roof project on the Cobbler. *The Cathedral* (X,11) climbs up to a tight niche at the back of the cave on the front face of the Centre Peak, and then traverses a six metre horizontal roof crack across the middle of the cave to gain turf at the lip and easy ground above. The 30m-long line is not taken by a summer route and is an ideal winter only line as it features wet, dirty rock with lots of turf.

The Cathedral is the largest continuous roof ever climbed in Scottish winter and was climbed ground up at the second attempt. Dave had tried to on sight the route in January 2003 but had failed due to lack of physical endurance. This time he was full of confidence having just returned from a very successful visit to Uschinen in Switzerland where he had climbed several of continental Europe's hardest mixed routes including the M12 test piece *Vertical Limit*. One only has to imagine a route that combines the technical difficulty of *The Cathedral* with the stature of a route like *Marathon Corner* to see that the long-hoped for quantum leap in traditional mixed climbing standards is not far away.

Big news on Ben Nevis was the first winter ascent of *Arthur* (VIII,8) by Bruce Poll and Tony Shepherd. This steep four-pitch HVS runs up the centre of the front face of Number Three Gully Buttress and was first climbed by Klaus Schwartz and Gordon Webster in 1971. They used a point of aid on the third pitch and it is possible their route has never been repeated. Lying high on the mountain *Arthur* was a likely candidate for a winter ascent, but recent mild winters have thwarted several hopefuls as the line has failed to carry much snow or hoar frost. Bruce and Tony timed their climb to perfection and nipped in to make a very smooth ascent just after New Year when the cliff was white with frost and the cracks free of ice. *Arthur* is only the third Grade VIII to be climbed on Ben Nevis, and along with *Marathon Corner*, joins a very small number of Grade VIIIs that have had on sight first winter ascents.

The Ben also saw some new additions to the Douglas Boulder. Gareth Hughes and James Edwards climbed *Turf War* (V,6) based on the summer line *Militant Chimney* and also climbed an alternative start to *Left-Hand Chimney*. Further right Jonny Baird and Andy Turner made a winter ascent of *Jacknife* (IV,6). A new winter route on the Ben always feels extra special, and it was particularly fitting that Nevis regular Jonny should at long last have a Nevis climb to his name. Iain Small and I took advantage of a heavy early April snowfall to climb *Central Rib Direct* (VI,7) on Creag Coire na Ciste. The original line climbed by Jimmy Marshall and Robin Campbell avoided the steep central section by taking a line close to *Central Gully Right-Hand*, but an improbable line of holds led up the outside edge of the impending right arête to give a spectacular and unique pitch.

Aonach Mor saw heavy traffic and many climbers enjoyed the easier gullies that held good ice and neve throughout much of the season. Steve Kennedy and Bob Hamilton showed that Coire an Lochain still has new routes to yield with a handful of good new lines including *Pro Libertate* (V,6), a sustained mixed route on the buttress between *The Guardian* and *Stirling Bridge*. Further north, Andy Nisbet and Dave McGimpsey visited their old haunt of Stob Coire an Laoigh in the Grey Corries and added a clutch of new routes including *Socialist* (V,7) which climbs the centre of the left wall of Centrepoint buttress. Further east Kevin Neal and Iain Rudkin made a productive visit to Geal Charn above Loch Ericht near Drumochter. Their first addition was called *Map and Compass* (III,4) and implies that they were a little unsure of their location on the mountain but they capitalised on this with the fine steep ice line of *Flight of the Navigator* (VI,6) when they returned with Kirk Watson the following day.

The high crags in Glen Coe saw some action in the cold snowy snaps in late December and January. Of note was the first ascent of the short but good *Tuberculosis* (VI,6) in Stob Coire nan Lochan by Dave Hollinger and Guy Willett. This takes the impending groove right of *Crest Route* and gave excellent climbing, although well-frozen conditions are recommenced to cement everything in place. Bishops' Buttress on the West Top of Bidean saw a couple of technical additions on the same day in late December. Donald King and Andy Nelson made a winter ascent of *The Crook* (VI,7) and Gareth Hughes and James Edwards found *Under The Weather* (VII,7) a difficult climb on the upper tier of the buttress.

James Edwards had a very good season with new routes across the Highlands. If you're serious about seeking out unclimbed lines, you have to be prepared to put in the groundwork and James made a productive visit to Coire nam Fhamhair on Beinn Bhan last summer. The intention was to scope out the wall right of *Die Riesenwand* for a possible repeat of *The Godfather*, but James noticed a couple of lines left of *Genesis* on the left side of the crag. He returned at the end of December with Sam Barron and climbed *Revelations* (VI,6), a superb natural line of weakness near the left end of the cliff. Three weeks later James was back with Gareth Hughes to climb *Biblical Knowledge* (VI,5), the second line he had spotted, which takes the left edge of the fault-line taken by *Genesis*.

The other major addition on Beinn Bhan was the steep buttress between Mad Hatter's and March Hare's gullies by Malcolm Bass and Simon Yearsley. This was a well-known objective and is mentioned in Cold Climbs as a new route objective, but nobody had stepped up to the challenge of a direct ascent of the wall. Malcolm and Simon were concerned about how much weaving around they would have to do to find a way through the succession of rock tiers, but they managed to find a logical direct line. Conditions were good with a thin covering of good neve, hard frozen turf and bits of ice but not enough to choke the cracks. The seven-pitch *Realisation* (VI,6) is a major addition to the mountain and deserves further repeats as it has good belays and protection.

Other notable new route activity in the North West included the first ascent of *Aquila* (VI,7) on Ben Damph by Andy Nisbet and Jonathan Preston, *Expanding Universe* (VI,5), on Sail Mhor by Guy Robertson and Es Tressider, *Avalanche Goose* (VI,7) on Slioch by Iain Small and Neil Wilson, and the excellent sounding *Underground Resistance* (V,6) on Stac Pollaidh by Erik Brunskill and Daffyd Morris. All these climbs show that even on relatively well known cliffs there are still good new routes to discover.

Farther west, John Mackenzie continued to develop the Stratchconon and Ben Wyvis crags with an astonishing 11 new routes. With the increased focus on climbing new winter lines across Scotland, it is difficult to believe that John will retain a monopoly on his home turf for much longer, but his unrivalled knowledge of the these crags gives him a head start over the competition. The finest additions this season were *Oh Dearie Me* (III,4) that takes thin discontinuous turf streaks on the 250m-high East Buttress of Creag Ghlas, and the superb *Temptress* (V,5) in Coire Mor on Ben Wyvis. Both routes were climbed with Alan Dennis.

The Cairngorms were particularly quiet this winter. Beinn a'Bhuird held snow well and saw the most activity with a handful of new routes. Chris Cartwright and I were particularly pleased with the first ascent of *Archtempter* (VII,8) in Coire na Ciche, a good winter line based on the prominent arch in the unclimbed section of crag right of *Jason's Chimney*. This one had been on the list a long time but went without a struggle at the first attempt. *Nipped in the Bud* (V,6) in Coire nan Clach was a different story and only succumbed on the fifth visit with all previous attempts being stymied by horrific weather or lack of conditions. Persistence pays in the Scottish winter game! The Nisbet-McGimpsey team joined forces with James Edwards for a good weekend in February when they made the first winter ascent of the all-too obvious *Ribbon Ridge* (IV,4) on Stacan Dubha and *Dreadlock* (V,6) a new addition on the Upper Tier of Carn Etchachan. Those that thought the Northern Corries are worked out will be surprised by the addition of *Lagopus* (V,6), a direct start to *Snow Bunting* in Coire an Lochain by Ian Taylor and Neil Carnegie.

The finest winter climb in the Cairngorms however was Guy Robertson and Jason Currie's ascent of *The Winter Needle* (VIII,8) on the Shelter Stone. The route was first climbed by Andy Nisbet and Colin MacLean in February 1985. They used a point of aid and spent two days on the route with a bivouac, but the route was so far ahead of its time that it took thirteen years before it was repeated by Alan Mullin and Steve Paget in October 1998 with a major variation in the lower section. The second ascent created a storm of controversy, because many climbers believed it was climbed too early in the season to be a valid winter climb. This was rectified by Alasdair Coull and Sam Chinnery who made a free ascent of the Nisbet-MacLean line over two days in February 2000. The next logical step was a one-day free ascent and this was achieved by Guy and Jason on a perfect day at the end of February in a swift eleven hours to give a powerful demonstration of the continual progression of Scottish winter standards.

For many, the exploratory nature of Scottish winter climbing is the big attraction, and this year revealed a number of new venues. I was particularly intrigued by the climbing on Creag an Lochan Ulbha on Meall Horn and the fine crop of routes that Andy Nisbet, Dave McGimpsey and Dave Allan pioneered one superb day at the end of February. Two days later Dave Allan was out again with Davie Moy to add *Eas a' Chual Allan* (IV,5) on Glas Bhein. Tongue firmly in cheek, Dave notes that unlike its illustrious neighbour, this is one of the shorter waterfalls in Britain!

I am surely biased, but in my view some of the finest exploratory winter climbing this season was high up on the north side of Ben Cruachan. The superbly steep granite cliff above Coire Chat is seamed by cracks and grooves. It was first climbed by Dave Ritchie and Mark Shaw in February 2002 when they added *Noe Buttress* (IV,4) and the Grade II gully to its left. Chris Cartwright and Iain Small visited the cliff last winter and were immediately struck by the climbing potential of the unclimbed wall to the left of Noe Gully. They left their mark with the first ascent of *In the Knoe*, a fine VI,6 that cleaves a central line up the wall.

The cliff proved to be an ideal location in the variable weather early this season for it faces north, lies above the 1000m contour and comes into condition very quickly. Although the routes are relatively short, typically between 80 and 100m high, they are continuously sustained from the first move to the very top of the crag. Chris methodically set about developing the cliff adding a dozen routes along with Iain Small, Andy Hume, Roger Webb and myself. The finest additions were *Goldfinger* (VII,7), the impressive central line that takes the impending crack splitting the clean wall high on the buttress, and *Dr Noe* (VI,6), the stepped ramp-line running left to right up to a point overlooking Noe Gully.

New winter crags are developed every winter in Scotland, but what is remarkable about this discovery is that the quality of the climbing is so good and it lies on a relatively accessible mountain. One of my abiding memories of this winter will be climbing the superb corner line of *Tainted Elixir* (V,6). As I pulled through bulge after bulge on good solid hooks and torques, the cloud cleared behind us to reveal a magnificent view down Loch Etive across to Glen Coe with Ben Nevis standing regally behind. It was the very essence of Scottish winter climbing, and it makes me wonder just how many other great winter crags are out there still waiting to be discovered.

Simon Richardson.

100 YEARS AGO...

THE year began with the Annual Meeting and Dinner in St Enoch's Hotel, Glasgow on Friday 4, December,1903. President William C. Smith was in the Chair; Treasurer Robert Napier reported a balance of £185 2s. $2^1/_2$d.; Secretary Inglis Clark announced 10 new members, two deaths and four resignations – a balance of 152 members; and Librarian Goggs (300) and Slide Custodian Robertson (900) enumerated their treasures. A motion, proposed by James Maclay – useful if chaos is to be prevented at AGM and Dinner – was passed: "The election of the President shall not take effect till the day after the General Meeting at which he has been elected." Finally, a motion put by Alexander Frazer, that Volumes I and II of the Journal be reprinted was ungenerously vetoed by Hugh Munro, who claimed copyright in *Munro's Tables*. Forty-two members and 26 guests then enjoyed a French menu of oysters, soup, sole, sweetbreads, haggis, roast meats, pheasant, dessert and cheese – only nine courses, a belt-tightening deficiency of four from the previous year.

New Year was celebrated at the Alexandra Hotel, Fort William, and a muster of 30 enjoyed fine weather for four days. There was little snow below 3000ft. *Tower Ridge* was climbed by Maclay, Parr, Unna and MacHarg; Bell, Napier, Raeburn and Rennie made a frosty ascent of the *South Ridge* of Garbh Bheinn; and new routes were made by Maclay, Raeburn and the Walkers (North Trident Buttress), and Maclay and Parr (North Face of Stob Ban). Maclay's Stob Ban route, *Gendarme Ridge*, enjoys a current grade of IV, and although he pointed out various other possible lines on the crags, 44 years would pass before these were explored.

On March 5, Willie Douglas, the entire Inglis Clark family, and Raeburn climbed Ben Lui's *Central Gully* – an unremarkable feat, except that Raeburn and the younger Clarks did it as a Day Excursion, catching the 4.30am train from Edinburgh to Tyndrum, and returning by the 5.22pm train.

Forty-two members and guests gathered for the Easter Meet at the Aviemore Hotel (March 31–April 4). This was the Club's second visit to the Cairngorms. Just as in the first Meet in 1902, severe weather in the form of blizzards affected the Meet, but high winds blew most of the snow away and better conditions for climbing were available. Two parties visited Coire an t'Sneachda (carriages to Old Glenmore) on Good Friday and made the first climbs there: William Garden, Raeburn, George Almond and Roth climbed what is now called *Pygmy Ridge*, and Goodeve, Arthur Russell and Archie Robertson climbed *Central Gully* then descended somehow to visit Aladdin's Seat. Raeburn then fled the Meet – perhaps the Temperance Hotel did not agree with him – to climb his Buttress on Sgorr Ruadh along with Ewen Robertson. In Glen Einich a large party, equipped with two crowbars and a five-foot length of pipe, removed a three-ton boulder from the road just below the Lower Bothy. This facilitated an attack on the Sgoran Dubh cliffs on Saturday. Bad weather prevented any interesting ascents, but Inglis Clark, Parker and Robertson explored the Fan Corrie. On Tuesday, however, Robertson returned to Sgoran Dubh along with Solly, James Rose and Sandy Moncrieff. Solly led the party up a fine ridge forming part of No. 2 Buttress – *Rose Ridge* – but had to give up, due to the late hour, below the last pitch. Robertson returned at the end of the month with Wm. Morrison and Wm. Newbigging to complete the climb. Following the Meet, the Clarks and Raeburn moved to Fort William to join the rest of the Clark family and various others 'enjoying' ski instruction under the tutelage of Willy Rickmers. Raeburn, and Charles and Jane Clark took time off to climb *Central Buttress* of the Trident by a devious route, beginning in *Central Gully.*

This ascent was described by Jane Clark in the *Journal* – the first article contributed by a lady. Describing her approach to the mountain, she wrote: "The rock scenery from this point [the Lunching Boulder] is at all times unspeakably grand, but, seen by the writer for the first time in regal winter garb, it made an impression never to be forgotten. Those wondrous cliffs, plastered and moulded with snow and ice, every crevice filled with glistening white, soared upwards cornice-crowned to the sky. To such a noble and sublime scene the following words of Ruskin are especially applicable: 'The feeding of the rivers and the purifying of the winds are the least of the services appointed to the hills. To fill the thirst of the human heart for the beauty of God's working – to startle its lethargy with the deep and pure agitation of astonishment – are their higher missions.' I claim for this view-point a very high place in Alpine scenery, and maintain that with winter's snowy mantle Ben Nevis from the centre of the Allt a' Mhuilinn Glen can proudly hold its own." Perhaps it was this epiphany which was responsible, 25 years later, for the endowment of the Clark Hut.

In June, the Dundee Walker cousins, Charles and Harry, climbed their eponymous buttress on Carn Dearg.

In the Alps, numerous parties of members enjoyed successful seasons. Douglas explored the eastern peaks, climbing the Disgrazia and Ortler. Goggs and C. W. Nettleton climbed the Finsteraarhorn and traversed the Aletschorn (finding a better variant of the Hasler route) to Bel Alp, before moving to Saas Fee to climb the usual peaks there, finishing their holiday with the Weisshorn. Goodeve packed Zinal Rothorn, Matterhorn, Obergabelhorn and Weisshorn plus two training climbs into an 11-day holiday in Zermatt (guided). Raeburn, lacking his usual partner, Ling, due to a year-long illness, visited the Dauphiné with Charles Walker. They were caught in an electric storm below the Grand Muraille on the Meije, "the ice-axes singing le chanson du Piolet, while every rocky spike on the steep narrow arête buzzed and crackled, and even Walker's rucksack had something to say for itself", but returned later to make a successful ascent. Moving to Pralognan in the Vanoise, they climbed the North Face of the Grande Casse. On Mont Blanc, they climbed the Aiguille Noire, presumably by the newly-discovered East Ridge route. Parker and Gilbert Thomson spent two weeks in the Eastern Graians, based at Cogne, and enjoyed several good climbs, including the taxing East Face of the Paradiso from the Tribulazione glacier.

Farther afield, Stair Gillon climbed the Romsdalhorn, and John H. Wigner and Thomas S. Muir made a month-long traverse of the Vatna Jökull in Iceland, from north-east to south-west, on ski and pulling sledges. This 80-mile traverse was only the second crossing of the Jökull, the first crossing in 1875 being a much shorter south-north route of 30 miles. They also climbed four peaks along the way.

On home ground, Maclay and MacHarg visited Arran in August and found a direct route from Upper Glen Sannox to Cir Mhor, climbing the ridge between *Shelf Gully* and *Maclay's Chimney*, then a trap-dyke to reach *Pinnacle Ridge* and the summit – an expedition that seems to have escaped the notice of Arran editors. Also in August, Ben Nevis was visited by a strong party comprising James Burns, Wm. Morrison, Wm. Newbigging and Archie Robertson. They found the easiest way up the Douglas Boulder (South-West Ridge) before climbing *Tower Ridge* by the *Recess Route*. On the following day, the lower tier of the South Trident Buttress was prospected in vain, then *Pinnacle Arête* was climbed. Burns then left, and the remaining three climbed the *Staircase Route* and descended *Observatory Ridge*, an undertaking aptly described by Robertson as "difficult and tedious...it is really a thing to ascend, not to descend". Finally, in a thin year for new ascents, in September Francis Greig, A. E. Mackenzie and A. N. Other climbed *North Castle Gully* of Carn Dearg, probably "a thing to avoid, not to ascend".

The *Journals* for the year published guidebook articles for Arran (by Goggs), the Eastern Cairngorms (Hinxman and Garden), the Lochnagar Group (George Duncan), the Braes of Angus and Glenshee to Gaick (mostly Munro). Several pieces about the new craze of ski-ing also featured: John Wigner's traverse of Ben Chonzie, and Willy Rickmers' well-known witty piece *Aquatic Sport on Ben Nevis*. Rickmers, who had organised the successful German expedition to Ushba in 1903, joined the Club in 1904 and maintained his membership from Germany, despite an interruption of five years caused by the Great War, until the Second War, when he finally gave it up. A note on p.121 by the Librarian thanks him for the donation "of six pairs of ski, to be lent free of charge to any SMC.men who desire to make themselves acquainted with the art of ski-ing". Where are they now, I wonder?

Finally, the Journal recorded on p.121 and again on p.137 the gift, by Mrs Sharp on leaving Sligachan Inn of the Climbers' Book. A type-written copy was made by the Club, with the inclusion of all pertinent Journal articles, a map, and photographs, this "to be lent to the present manager of the Hotel for the use of all mountaineers".

Robin N. Campbell.

The International Festival Of Mountaineering Literature 2004

Andy Kirkpatrick admitted to being nervous before he read a piece commissioned especially for the Festival which was held at Bretton Hall. He had a slide show running alongside, a changing sequence of snow runnels, winter buttresses and swathed climbers in snowstorms, interleaved with Andy's children, random public signs and interminable valley doses waiting for the right weather. His writing is quirky, direct yet thoughtful.

He says: "Alpine climbing is like having your heart broken repeatedly."

He had an extended metaphor about climbing being like getting off with Madonna, but the key issue was the dilemma of balancing being an obsessive climber with being a father. He was honest, self-questioning, scary and funny.

Katherine Bridge came from British Columbia to tell how she had pieced together the story of Phyliss Munday, Canadian mountain woman extraordinaire. As an archivist in Vancouver, Kathryn had come across 30 boxes of uncaptioned pictures. Unassuming about the part she had played in subsequently working out the story these pictures told, she related an absorbing tale of a woman driven to make a life in the outdoors in the early 20th century, stopped neither by the expectations of the day nor by the arrival of her baby, Edith. The decade -long obsession Phyll Munday shared with her husband, Don, to climb the elusive Mount Waddington was only part of the story. The black-and-white pictures were beautifully evocative and a heartfelt request was added: "If you are a mountaineer and a photographer, caption your pictures before you forget where they were taken."

To mark the publication of his *Collected Short Stories,* Dermot Somers read *Patrick And The Freney Pillar* confidently and strongly, direct to the audience. His writing is assured and real, it's believable fiction grounded in real lives. If you know his work, it's worth seeking out.

By now it was apparent that the International Festival Of Mountaineering Literature had come home. For 15 years the Festival was held in November then, due to building work at its normal venue, it was relocated, not entirely successfully to Leeds. Festival Director Terry Gifford decided to move it to a spring date so that, after 28 months, it was back, successfully at Bretton.

The day had begun with Royal Robbins who considered Brad Washburn and David Bower in his overview of American climbing writing before 1950, but had excluded them from his top three. James Ramsay Ullman was in third place on the basis of his history of climbing *High Conquest.* Clarence King he placed second despite "his tendency to hyperbole", for his *Mountaineering In The Sierra Nevada.* Top Dog was John Muir, not known primarily as a climber but as a "Prophet of Preservation". Muir, says Robbins, was "gifted and eloquent", he "spoke to climbers about how to think about mountains and how to treat them".

After Robbins, Joe Fitschen pursued the theme, pondering on post-1950 American climbing writers. He had clearly researched widely and thought hard but he was not always easy to hear and his delivery was, at times, pedestrian. On his long list were Jon Krakauer, Dave Roberts, Rick Ridgeway, Lito Tejada-Flores, Steve Roper, Yvon Chouinard and the man who had been on stage a few minutes earlier, Royal Robbins. Fitschen's short list, which turned out to be anything but short, featured Jeff Long, mentioned particularly for *Angels of Light,* John Sherman, Doug Robinson, Pete Sinclair for *We Aspired,* Mark Jenkins, Joe Kelsey and Chuck Pratt. There were brief quotes but no real explanation as to why these writers made the higher echelons. Put on the spot by a questioner at the end of his talk as to why he had mentioned no woman, Fitschen seemed momentarily nonplussed until others contributed the names of Alison Osius, Miriam Underhill and Lynn Hill as possible contenders.

Jamie Andrew's *Life And Limb (see Reviews Ed.) will* no doubt be a strong contender for the 2004 Boardman Tasker Award. He set the scene for three extracts from his book which describes his survival, albeit at the cost of his hands and feet, and his rehabilitation, after being pinned down in the Alps for five days by a terrible storm which took the life of his climbing partner Jamie Fisher. And what a tale – Jamie Andrew has climbed again, been snowboarding and paragliding, is a better skier than he was before the accident and has even completed the London Marathon.

David Hopkin, chair of the 2003 Boardman Tasker judges gave a re-adjudication speech from October last year. Something of a historical item by now, it was nevertheless interesting to hear why the judges had chosen Simon Mawer's novel, *The Fall,* as the winner.

Lindsay Griffin announced the winner of this year's High/Festival writing competition. Stephen Venables had been his fellow judge, assessing entries on the theme of people extricating themselves from tricky situations. The winner, Tom Sinclair's story, *The Great Escape* was read with characteristic verve by Ian Smith.

Ken 'Daffodils' Wilson and Geoffrey Chaucer, cunningly disguised as Gordon Stainforth, made unscheduled appearances on stage, reading effective spoofs from the previously undiscovered and newly-published classic *The Owl And The Cragrat.*

Matching her careful delivery to an astonishing sequence of pictures, white and hand coloured, from the archive of her father Captain John Noel, Sandra Noel gave a fascinating presentation linked to her new book *Everest Pioneer (See Reviews Ed.)*

The finale of the Festival saw the reappearance of Royal Robbins talking on *A Golden Age In The Range Of Light* this, of course, was Yosemite in the 1950s and 1960s. Robbins was on home territory, his talk sprinkled with insight and humour. For example, John Salathe was his role model regarding style. The first reason that put Robbins off climbing the face of Half Dome for some years was awe, the second was dread. His tale was peppered with legendary names, Chuck Pratt, Tom Frost, Yvon Chouinard and Warren Harding, with whom he had differences of opinion regarding climbing style.

"Mountains are an anvil on which a climber forges his character," he said, musing on his 10-day solo of the *John Muir Route* on El Capitan when, after seven days out and with 1000ft. still to go, he felt finished. The "five feet at a time" method got him near enough the top in the next days that he knew he would make it. "I was reaching into the rucsack of my soul."

Legendary climbers, stunning scenery, well known stories brought alive again, it was a fitting climax to an excellent day.

Kevin Borman.

Sex Changes on Ben Nevis

THE intrepid Jane Inglis Clark, whose husband was William Inglis Clark, took part in many interesting ascents on Ben Nevis in the early years of the Club, some new and some old. For example, in 1902 she took part in the ascent of Tower Gap West Chimney, now known as *Glover's Chimney*, accompanied by Glover, of course, and her husband William. Again, in 1904, she climbed the *Central Buttress of the Trident*, accompanied by Raeburn and her 16-year-old son, Charles.

Her part in these bold ascents was recorded accurately in the Journal, and in our guidebooks from MacRobert's (1920) through Marshall's (1969). One might complain about the fact that she was described there as Mrs W. Inglis Clark rather than as Jane, but that was the custom of those times. However, since 1969, she has been grossly mistreated. My copy of Simon Richardson's guide (1994) gives *Glover's Chimney* to Glover, C. Inglis Clark and W. Inglis Clark, substituting son for mother, and the *Central Buttress of the Trident* is credited to Raeburn, C. Inglis Clark and W. Inglis Clark, substituting husband for wife. It is surely deplorable that the modern SMC member, having striven to admit women to membership, should then proceed to eradicate them from our guidebooks!

I suspect, however, that these errors – and the very many others like them, arose because of the recent practice of separating details of first ascent from the description of climbs, which inevitably damages the historical record. I tried to change this practice on two occasions during, and just after, my service as President, failing narrowly in each attempt. Indeed, on the second occasion, I failed only because of the casting vote of the Chairman – the aforementioned Simon Richardson…

Robin N Campbell.

Mama Mia – (The latest edition of this most painful of diversions the Huts Run – in the footsteps of Richardson and Keith. Ed.)

It must have been in a moment of boredom that I first thought of running between the SMC huts. The idea came from reading Alec Keith's article in the SMCJ, so I must have been bored. He'd started at the Raeburn and ended at the Ling stopping a night in each hut as well as spending a more comfortable night in the Cluanie Inn. A very impressive achievement, but I did wonder if the hotel stop-over could be eliminated. It would require a very long day to get to the Ling hut. However, all this was mere conjecture. It would be worth seeing if I could manage such distances first.

As training I built up to running round the five FRCC huts in the Lake District. I stashed some food in each and, despite having some of my clearly-marked food scavenged by club members and receiving a reprimand for turning up late at my final hut, I completed the 50 miles in about 20 hours.

The following year was the Bob Graham Round, a circular 72-mile tour of the Lake District taking in 42 of its summits. Having had two years of watching my toe nails turn black and fall off I was fed up with fell running but the Bob Graham had been a serious test and close to the kind of effort I thought would be required to complete an SMC Huts Run. I would also have to keep up that kind of effort for several days and I wasn't sure I could manage that. The final nail in the coffin was hammered home when the Huts Committee bought another hut at Elphin, thus increasing the distance even more!

A few years later while gazing at a map of Fort Augustus, a bridleway running from Cannich to Laggan caught my eye, a good 40 miles and in exactly the direction I would want to take if travelling between the Ling and the Raeburn huts. It followed the line of a road constructed by General Wade and my thinking was, that if I couldn't run between the huts, then maybe I could do them on a mountain bike. I'd just got one, well I'd pulled it out of a skip actually, but it had those knobbly tires, so to me it was a mountain bike.

I poured over the maps and chose my route. I'd start at Elphin heading for the Ling and onto the Raeburn the second day, that would get the two longest days out of the way. Then past Ben Alder Lodge and over to Glencoe and finally to the CIC. As this wasn't going to be a circular route I decided to leave my car at the Raeburn, it being a convenient place to drive to. It would also mean I could restock with food after two days.

After attending a guidebook committee meeting in October I continued north to start my Huts Cycle. The first part of the route was on the road as I'd not been able to find any suitable off road route between Elphin and Ullapool that was fairly direct and I was too anxious about what lay ahead to waste too much energy tramping over peat bogs. The rain started as I left the road to head along the shores of Loch a' Bhraoin and the run down bothy at Lochivraon offered a welcome rest before I pushed the bike over Bealach Gorm. Somehow it all seemed worth it when I reached a good track and shot down to Kinlochewe just in time to miss the shop! Never mind I was carrying sufficient supplies with me, anything bought on the route was simply an added bonus.

The next morning I left the Ling at 6am in the dark as predicted and in the rain as expected. Progress over the Coulin Pass was slower than I'd anticipated and slowed even further once I left the road after Glenuaig Lodge and headed through Gleann Fhiodhaig. I'd intended to cross over to the shores of Loch Monar but my off-road cycling, or rather pushing, meant time was slipping by. A brief glance at the road map I was navigating by made me decide to continue on down the glen I was in. This would get me onto a road sooner and would, I hoped, facilitate quicker progress to Fort Augustus – even if it did lengthen the journey considerably. After several hours of bum numbing cycling I was heading up to join another Wade road above Fort Augustus, racing against time to find the track before the onset of darkness. Climbing over deer fences with a mountain bike on your back makes you really appreciate how cumbersome they are.

In the last rays of the sun, I thanked General Wade for his road and cycled on. By now it was dark and I was tired so, cycling uphill was completely out. After nearly 18 hours in the saddle and more than 140 miles of cycling and pushing (half off road, half on) I eventually reached the Raeburn hut. When I went to bed, my right hand was numb from the vibration of the handlebars and I still had no feeling in the fingers next morning. Somewhat worried by this, I decided that I'd have to give up on the off-road cycling if I was to finish the route round the huts. Cycling along the A86 wasn't really a satisfactory end to the journey, but it did get me to Glencoe.

It was to take an operation and over eight months recovery before I regained the feeling in my fingers but, looking on the bright side, you wouldn't suffer from hot aches in winter!

Convalescing and unable to use my hand after the operation I started to run again. Someone had told me that fell running was virtually as quick as mountain biking. So, now that I knew at least some of the route, I decided I may as well try it while I couldn't climb. At the end of May I was dropped off at the Naismith hut. I first ran the uninteresting road section in the dark so that I swapped the road for the shores of Loch a' Bhraoin just after dawn. Having pushed a bike up Bealach Gorm I decided to try Bealach na h-Imrich to the east. The undulating peat hags were far worse, but at least I wasn't dragging a bike over them and so I made the Ling around mid-morning. This gave me all day to eat and rest. A midnight departure saw me heading across the hillside south of Glenuaig Lodge just after daybreak. As I headed down Glen Strathfarrar I had a blister blow-out. A few miles farther down the road I suffered further blow-outs. The delays and pain slowed me down and cost me several hours as I struggled on to the forests above Cannich. As I came to the end of my chosen path through the forest I realised that the roads had changed somewhat since the map had been printed. Pushing through the forest to open moorland I gave thanks to Scottish Power as I glanced round to locate the electricity pylons that followed Wade's road along this section. A call to my partner from Dundreggan assured her I was OK and we arranged a rendezvous at Fort Augustus. Running downhill through the forest to Fort Augustus I realised things were wrong as I passed under the pylons yet again, I was lost. After several extra miles and demoralised by this latest navigational error, I finally made the car. That, and the opportunity to stopping running after 110 miles in two days were too strong. Charlie Orr was resident in the Raeburn hut when we arrived and as I recounted what I'd been doing and that I wouldn't be having another go, I knew deep down I would. (And so did I! Ed.) My legs were still strong, my feet were blistered but that could be sorted and now I knew the OS maps errors.

With padded road shoes rather than fell running shoes and a month of recovery my feet were ready to try again. Andy Nisbet dropped me off on the A9 as I started my hitch to Elphin. On arrival I got out of the car and thanked my lift before promptly turning round and running back to Ullapool along the road I'd just been driven along. The rain returned as I passed over Bealach Gorm but didn't last long and there was a spring in my step as I called into the shop at Kinlochewe. I had the supplies I needed until my re-supply at the Raeburn hut, but it was nice to get some fresh milk and bread.

A few hours rest at the Ling hut then it was a 10pm start. The route over the Coulin Pass to Craig went well but I was feeling tired as I left the bright lights of Craig behind me. Suddenly I came to a stop. "Mamma Mia, here I go again," I don't know how long I'd been humming the tune. My brain was obviously trying to stay awake and active but there are limits you can't sink to. I tried to keep myself mentally alert calculating the distance I'd come and still had to travel, anything other than Abba.

Spurred on, I was soon crossing Maoile Lunndaidh and running along Loch Monar and, with my route sorted out through the forest, I was in Fort Augustus by mid-afternoon. My first stop in 65 miles. Sitting on a bench with a cup of tea and some soup from a local shop, I started tending to my blisters as the tourists wandered by and stared. The more-padded running shoes and new socks had kept blistering to a minimum. In the afternoon sun I walked along the banks of the River Tarff keeping in the shade and enjoying the soft grass under my feet, knowing I would eventually have to exchange them for the harsh sunshine and stony path of Wade's Road over the Corrieyairack Pass. At Melgarve I popped into the bothy to top up my Elastoplasts and then ran on, ticking off the waymarkers, happy as I realised I was keeping up 6mph. Not too bad after over 70 miles. However, It wasn't to last long and I ground to a halt as a blister popped and I stopped for roadside repairs. I decided to walk to the hut and save my feet for the next day, so after 24 hours on the move I finally got to the Raeburn and my sleeping bag. With only 40 miles to the CIC, I decided I could have a lie in as it was a short day. By lunchtime I was ambling along past Ben Alder Lodge. I'd opted to save my feet so resisted the urge to start running until I could get onto soft grass.

The track was generally good but time was ticking by as I passed Corrour and by the time I reached the old ruin of the Steall the sun had been set for over an hour. In fading light I wandered along the side of the stream into Allt Coire Eoghainn and, forsaking the boggy glen floor, headed west onto a drier ridge. I was too tired to refill my drinks bottle and wandered on with the CIC the only thing in my mind. I looked down in surprise when I reached the top of Meall Cumhann and on consulting my map discovered that this hummock stood to the south of Ben Nevis. I was too tired to be annoyed and just plodded on wishing I could find some water.

Wandering through the cloud on the summit I reached the top of the abseil posts. In winter I've often wondered why people abseil down the posts into Coire Leis, if there'd been ropes there that night I'd certainly have been using them, as I scrambled down into the rocky basin. Stubbing my bruised toes I let out a scream, something I'd been used to doing for the last few days without any worry of being heard. As I listened to its echo returning from the walls of the Ben and considered its popularity I knew I'd have to curb my cursing. As I picked myself up I came across a stick which was to prove useful as a staff as I teetered across the boulders. The cloud lifted as I reached the hut to reveal several tents and open shutters. As I crept into the main hut a female voice cried out in surprise but was silenced by a male friend. Not wanting to wake the residents with cooking I settled myself with several cups of tea and after a fruitless search for blankets I curled up with my feet in my rucsac and shivered the remainder of the night away.

By 7am I felt it was a respectable hour to get up and the residents didn't mind. They turned out to be Andy Fraser and his wife. Over breakfast, my uneaten meal from the night before, Andy gave me some pointers about the way over the Mamores and also informed me that Robin (the hut custodian) had burned the hut blankets which had become somewhat fetid. After gaffer-taping my feet - I'd run out of plasters, I set off. There was no attempt at running on the final stage to Lagangarbh, I had a leisurely stroll staff in hand across An Garbhanach to Kinlochleven where I rejoined another of General Wade's roads to take me to Glencoe and the end of my Huts Run. Over four days I'd travelled approximately 200 miles.

I stopped at Lagangarbh long enough for a brew then headed out, thumb in the air, to start my hitch back to the Raeburn. I sat on the crash barrier by the road to give my legs some welcome relief and woke up as I hit the bank but wasn't quick enough to avoid the fall into the burn. I was obviously tired! Invigorated from my dip I climbed back up to the road, thumb aloft and smiled at every car as it drove past, this could take some time.

I finally made my own bed in Lancaster at 7am the following morning an hour before my alarm went off reminding me that I had a meeting at work that morning.

"Mama Mia here I go again…"

Stages:

Naismith Hut to Ling Hut approximately 60 miles.

Ling Hut to Raeburn Hut approximately 85 miles.

Raeburn Hut to CIC approximately 40 miles.

CIC to Lagangarbh approximately 15 miles.

Brian Davison.

SCOTTISH MOUNTAINEERING TRUST – 2003-2004

THE Trustees met on June 19 and October 3, 2003 and April 2, 2004.

During the course of these meetings support was given to the JMCS for the Coruisk Hut; the Jonathan Conville Mountaineering Trust Scottish Winter Courses 2003-2004; Rev. B. Shepton, Greenland Challenge Expedition; A. L. Stewart, Dundee Mountain Film Festival 2004; Nevis Partnership for path work on the Allt A' Mhuillinn, and purchase of new Avalanche Transceivers for the Scottish Mountaineering Trust.

Gillian Irvine and Grahame Nicoll retired as Trustees by rotation having each served four years. Richard Bott retired as a Trustee by rotation in December 2003, and is the Chairman of the Publications Co. The contributions of Gillian Irvine, Grahame Nicoll and Richard Bott are much appreciated.

The Trust, through the Publications Co., is presently producing a leaflet on the Trust's activities for the purpose of encouraging grant applications to the Trust from charitable organisations.

The present directors of the Publications Co. are R. K. Bott (Chairman), K. V. Crocket, W. C. Runciman, M. G. D. Shaw and T. Prentice (Publications Manager).

The present Trustees are K. V. Crocket (Chairman), P. Macdonald, R. W. Milne, C. J. Orr, M. G. D. Shaw, W. C. Runciman, A. Tibbs, R. J. Archbold, D. A. Bearhop and D. J. Broadhead. W. C. Runciman and M. G. D. Shaw are Trustees/Directors and provide liaison between the Publications Co. and the Trust. J. Morton Shaw is the Trust Treasurer.

The following grants have been committed by the Trustees:

General Grant Fund:

JMCS Couisk Hut	£1535
Jonathan Conville Winter Courses 2003/2004	£1000
Reverend B Shepton Greenland Challenge Expedition	£1500
Purchase of new Avalanche Transceivers	£1800
Dundee Mountain Film Festival 2004	£1000
Nevis Partnership Allt A' Mhuillinn	£20,000

James D. Hotchkis,
Trust Secretary.

MUNRO MATTERS

By David Kirk (Clerk of the List)

ONCE again, I have very much enjoyed receiving Compleation and Amendment letters this year and I thank everyone who has written to me to register. This year's new Compleat Munroist total is 235, up a bit on last year's lowly 192. The main statistical highlight of the year was reaching the 3000th recorded Munroist mark – more of this anon.

Last year, the Munro Society was at the embryonic stage and has now begun to consolidate. Rather than describe its progress myself, Iain Robertson, the Society Secretary has again produced a report, which I've appended here.

Please remember the photograph section in the SMC Website, I would urge everyone on the List to dig out an old final summit photograph of yourself and send a copy (or the original along with a SAE) to Ken Crocket.

This year's Compleatists follow. As before, columns are number, name, then Munro, Top and Furth Compleation years.

2885	Sheila Jefferies	2003			2922	Colin Baird	1999	
2886	Elspeth M. Graham	2003			2923	Ronnie Robertson	2003	
2887	Michael O'Hara	2003			2924	Keith R. Jeffrey	2003	
2888	Steve Marsh	2003			2925	Michael P. Ryan	2003	
2889	Leslie J. Anderson	2003			2926	Graham A. Fielding	2003	
2890	John Wright	2003			2927	Irene Leckie	2003	
2891	Jim Sime	2002			2928	Val Machin	2003	
2892	Brian Shanks	2003			2929	Alexander G. Thow	2000	
2893	Tommy Hunter	2003			2930	Paul Harradine	2003	
2894	Ken Slater	2003			2931	Polly Harrison	2003	
2895	Tom Fox	2003			2932	Colin Robert Semple	2003	
2896	Trevor John Williams	2003			2933	Tony Roberts	2003	
2897	Barry Parker	2003	1995		2934	Kim Ciaran Collis	2003	
2898	Howard Taylor	2003			2935	Martin Dand	2003	
2899	Gillian Taylor	2003			2936	Nigel Hewlett	2003	
2900	Richard Baker	2003			2937	Ian McIntosh	2003	
2901	Nicholas A. Hunt	2003			2938	Sarah Trueman	2003	
2902	Dianne Mary Williams	2003			2939	Scott Wigglesworth	2003	
2903	Michael J. Gibbons	2003			2940	Neil Fullwood	2003	
2904	Jonathon M. Smith	2003	2003		2941	Jerzy Czyzewski	2003	
2905	Miriam Dodd	2003			2942	Mr R. N. Redwood	2003	
2906	Phillip Dodd	2003			2943	Donald R. Sutherland	2003	
2907	Angus M. Buchanan	2000			2944	Timothy P. Johnson	1993	
2908	Dugald B. MacNeill	2002			2945	Jane Logan	2003	
2909	John Penny	2003			2946	David Logan	2003	
2910	Anthony Loftus	2003			2947	John Rhodes	2003	
2911	Howard Marsden	2003			2948	Liz Rhodes	2003	
2912	Fraser Smith	2003			2949	Peter Burgess	2003	
2913	Ewan G. McDonald	2003			2950	Liz Hayhurst	2003	
2914	James Bryson	2003			2951	Dave Hayhurst	2003	
2915	Arnold Foster	2003			2952	Sandy Farmer	2003	
2916	Nick Bowyer	2003			2953	Joan Finnie	2003	
2917	Iain Morrice	2003			2954	Peter Wightman	2003	
2918	Martin D. Knott	2003			2955	Paul Brooks	2003	
2919	Alison Sangster	2003			2956	Roger Reeves	1993	2003
2920	Jonathan C. C. Pyman	2003			2957	John G Harvey	2003	
2921	Kenneth E. Pirie	2003			2958	Charlie Muir	2003	

2959	Roger Squires	2003
2960	Allison Johnston	2003
2961	Joyce Whitton	1996
2962	Jim Whitton	1996
2963	David Joynes	2003
2964	Simon Maltby	2003
2965	Donald McLean	2003
2966	Edith Moran	2003
2967	Geoff Smith	2003
2968	David Paterson	2003
2969	Patricia Elsdon Redhead	2003
2970	Kenneth Redhead	2003
2971	Elizabeth Maitland	2003
2972	Geoff Walker	1992
2973	Peter Clegg	2003
2974	Carolyn Clegg	2003
2975	Donald A. R. Gordon	2003
2976	Fiona C. S. Gordon	2003
2977	David Wallace Young	2003
2978	Andy Gray	2003
2979	Ken Adamson	2003
2980	Jon Barnes	2003
2981	Tony Gribben	2003
2982	George Gallacher	2003
2983	John J. Knight	2003
2984	Rosemary I. Knight	2003
2985	Ewen David Lamont	2003
2986	Patrick Lonergan	2003
2987	Jacqui Turnbull	2003
2988	William Douglas Murray	2003
2989	George Smart	2003
2990	Stewart Gardiner	2003
2991	Ewan James Lyons	2003
2992	Winifred Thomson	2003
2993	Iain Wilson	2003
2994	Iain Walton	2003
2995	Colin Mumford	2003
2996	John D. Fowler	1998
2997	Peter J. Kerry	2003
2998	Iain MacDonald	2003
2999	Arthur McKenzie	2003
3000	Michael Urquhart	2003
3001	David J. Webster	2003
3002	Don Silversides	2003
3003	David Anderson	2003
3004	James D. Upton	2003
3005	Alan Palin	2003
3006	Tom McKay	2003
3007	Chris Low	2003
3008	Roger J. Killick	2003
3009	Keith Gordon	2003
3010	Isabel C. Munro	2003
3011	Nigel Sutton	2003
3012	Tony Hendry	2003
3013	Danus Skene	2003
3014	Peter J. Kerry	2003
3015	John R. Dawson	2003

3016	James Fuller	2003
3017	Gill Eatough	2003
3018	Matthew Linning	2003
3019	John Standaloft	2003
3020	Robert Anthony Lees	2003
3021	Rohan Beyts	2003
3022	Alan J. Murray	2003
3023	*Alan J. Scott	2003
3024	Paul Phillips	2003
3025	Martin Holt	2003
3026	Janet Price	2003
3027	John Bush	2003
3028	Jill Scott	2003
3029	Alex Phillips	2003
3030	Fiona Phillips	2003
3031	Bill McCartney	2003
3032	Gary Clare	2003 2003
3033	Malcolm William Blake	2003
3034	Patrick Green	2002
3035	Bill Howie	2003
3036	Norman Smithers	2003
3037	Gordon C. Stalker	2003
3038	Selwyn C. A. Fernandes	2003
3039	Michael Venables	2003
3040	Leslie Watt	2003
3041	Rebecca Trengove	2003
3042	Alan Needham	2003
3043	Malcolm Proctor	2003
3044	Brian McWilliam	2003
3045	Roger Broad	2003
3046	Peter Ellwood	2003
3047	Susan Primrose	2003
3048	Dan Parker	2003
3049	Sheila West	2003
3050	Fiona Borland	2003
3051	Helen Johnson	2003
3052	Alan McQuiston	2003
3053	Christopher H. Henshall	2003
3054	Geoff Sutton	2003
3055	Isabel Wilson	2003
3056	Tom Noon	2003
3057	David Tyler	2003
3058	Chris Low	2003
3059	Alex MacKenzie	2003
3060	Alan K. Robertson	1995
3061	Nigel G. Thackray	2003
3062	Manoj Patel	2003
3063	Martin Davidson	2003
3064	Ian McAdam	2003
3065	David Jinks	2003
3066	Roger D. Hodgson	1999
3067	Owain Pedgley	2003
3068	Andrew Pedgley	2003
3069	Jane Allan	2003
3070	David Young	2002 2002
3071	George Cairns	2003
3072	Ritchie M. McCrae	2003

3073	Ian G. McCrae	2003		
3074	Ros Adams	2003		
3075	Phil Hardy	2003		
3076	Nick Barr	2003		
3077	Elizabeth Steel	2003		
3078	Rodger Neilson	2003		
3079	Alison Neilson	2003		
3080	Martin Gillespie	2003		
3081	Charles W. K. Morrison	2003 2003		
3082	R John Reavy	2003		
3083	Patricia A. O. Sinclair	2003		
3084	Kenneth S. Jeffrey	2003		
3085	David Neil Sandilands	2003		
3086	David W. Wilkie	2003		
3087	Graham Thomson	2003		
3088	Graham Brown	2003		
3089	Sarah Wingrove	2003		
3090	John A. Smith	2003		
3091	*John M. Shaw	2003		
3092	Tony Stoddart	2003		
3093	Leslie Shore	2003		
3094	Chris Wood	2003		
3095	Ally Anderson	2003		
3096	Rab Cunningham	2003		
3097	Michael Shuttleworth	2003		
3098	Simon D. Templeman	2003		
3099	David Reading	2003		
3100	Collette Coll	2003		
3101	Charlie McCartney	1986		
3102	Charles McCartney	1988		
3103	Michael McCartney	2003		
3104	Peter Ramage	2003		
3105	Fiona Elizabeth Kean	2003		
3106	Morag Anderson	2003		
3107	Steve Kew	2003		
3108	Steven Petrie	2003		
3109	Carolann Petrie	2003		
3110	Michael Saint	2003		
3111	Morag Mitchell	2003		
3112	Bert Barnett	2001	2002	2002
3113	Andrew Lazenby	1994		
3114	Stephen Perry	2003		
3115	Hamish McBride	2004		
3116	Charlie Burgess	2002		
3117	Norman McNab	2003		
3118	Dan Carroll	2001		
3119	David Brown	2001		

In the letters I have received this year, Munro bagging for charity has been mentioned quite often. Stephen Perry (3114) did an epic Lands End to John O'Groats walk between February and September 2003, taking in the major Welsh and English 3000ers and all the Munros. He was the first person to complete such a walk, and raised money for Cancer Research.

Martin Knott (2918) only began his round after taking part in a charity event, The Great Scottish Hill Climb, for Cancer Awareness. David Wilkie (3086) also raised money for Cancer Research. His personal challenge was to compleat in a single calendar year, while continuing his day job at RAF Lossiemouth. Based just along the road at RAF Kinloss, Dan Carroll (3118) utilised the RAF Rescue Team inflatable boat to reach Barrisdale for his last two Munros. Having summited on Mount Everest during an RAF expedition only a month earlier, Dan says that his final summit, Ladhar Bheinn, still meant more to him.

Compleating from abroad is not uncommon, however Kenneth Pirie (2921) did well to compleat while based throughout in British Columbia. Peter Burgess (2949) managed nearly two-thirds of his round while living in New Zealand. He currently doesn't plan to do the Corbetts!

Last year, I received a lot of anecdotes about Ben More – one of the most common final summits. Again, a few stand out, including this year's largest multiple compleation. It was by Jane and David Logan (2945/2946) and John and Liz Rhodes (2947/2948). David had had a triple by-pass only a year earlier. Also on Ben More, friends of Iain Wilson (2993) organised a 'Black Tie' champagne reception for him. Typically, he'd picked the only misty, windy day for weeks.

Elizabeth Maitland (2971) managed to arrange for five separate groups to converge from different directions on her final summit, Carn nan Gobhar (Loch Mullardoch). This also involved organising a boat and various 'car ferries'. The assembled group gave her the classic Ice Axe 'Guard of Honour' on the summit.

Re-taking the island in the middle of Loch Quoich 'in the name of England' was a major event during Colin Mumford's (2995) round. The island also provided Colin and his three friends with an ideal starting point for Sgurr Mor and Gairich, giving them canoe access to the infrequently visited, but more impressive north sides of these hills.

Ben Lomond seems to have been a more popular finishing hill than usual this year (it's usually more of a starting hill). Val Machin (2928) managed to merge her finishing celebrations on May 25, with a summit wedding they came upon, and someone else's compleation too.

David Joynes and Simon Maltby (2963/2964) escaped by the seats of their pants on Seana Bhraigh. Having noted with some distaste, a pair of discarded underpants during their ascent, they were mighty glad to see them again during poor visibility on the descent. More underpants were revealed when Tom Noon (3056) was bitten on the bum by a dog on the summit of his 200th Munro, Beinn A' Choarainn. He had to 'drop them' to prove to the dog's owners what had happened!

Hearing again from old friends and acquaintances I've met over the years is a definite plus point to my job as Clerk. It was good to hear from Colin Baird (2922) who completed in a large party of Ochil MC members. It must have been some party – it took him four years to remember to register.

The Cuillin Ridge has always provided some of the most memorable days of any round. Paul and Polly Harrison (2930/2931) were guided along it in the worst weather their guide, Martin Moran (383), had guided on it. Taking 28 hours, this was also his slowest traverse. Donald Sutherland (2943) got round the common problem of the Inn Pinn looming large, as one approaches the end of one's round. He did it within his first handful: "Just to make sure he could do them all." Phil Hardy (3075) tried to do the ridge in one trip with an overnight bivvy in the middle. Although he and his companion bedded down in fine weather, they were awakened by cold and driving rain. At 3.30am they abandoned the ridge and set off down.

Michael Urquhart (3000) from Bo'ness knew nothing of what awaited him when he completed on An Socach (Glen Cannich). He was, however, delighted to be our No. 3000. Since then, he's been an honoured guest at a Munro Society dinner and presented with a plaque. Allegedly, the paparazzi have been after him too.

A current general policy with entries into the List is the avoidance of titles and letters. Were it not for this, we may have seen a whole host of various things. In the last three years alone we could have had MP, MSP, several military titles, and more academic/professional letters than I can remember. This year, Clan Chief Danus Skene of Skene (3013) compleated. Although I couldn't put his full title on the List, I did of course enter it onto his certificate as requested.

Most hillwalkers reading this article will have heard of Naismith's Rule, and many will have heard of Philip Tranter's (45) modifications to this. Norman Smither (3036) helped him compile them and was with him on his most memorable Munro – The Saddle, in winter conditions, at night, by moonlight. That was February 1966, six months before Philip's death.

We've heard of people hitting golf balls up their last Munro, or even of climbing in fancy dress, however Sarah Wingrove (3089) had to pull a concrete ball and chain up Beinn Sgritheal to compleat. Fortunately, a friend had hidden a sledgehammer in the summit cairn to smash it up – what a way to celebrate what was also her final day in her Twenties.

Most people who register with myself will record a single compleation of the

Munros. A few may also have included the Tops. Bert Barnett (3112) however registered a full compliment of Munros, Tops, Furths and Corbetts, plus a second Munro round. His first Munro round was completed only in 2001, but he had a 17-year gap between his penultimate and his final. Bert has also completed the Grahams and Scottish mainland Marilyns for good measure.

The esoteric pastime of camping in full winter conditions, on or near Munro summits is what Norman McNab (3117) has, for the last 40 years, engaged in. An undoubtedly serious hobby, but one with many rewards, which the substantial article and photographs he supplied me showed. Sunsets have never looked so good.

Finally, I can't finish without using some 'Bad Latin'. Peter Kerry (2997) compleated this year, on Aonach Mor, and his brother, Bob (1152), informed me that the brothers were now *Munrosis Fraternalis* (sic). His other brother, John, is No. 1740.

AMENDMENTS

The following have added to their entries on the List. Each Munroist's record is shown in full. The columns refer to Number, Name, Munros, Tops, Furths and Corbetts.

Number	Name	Munros	Tops	Furths	Corbetts
332	Stephen Bateson	1983	1994	1983	1996
		1995			
2871	Peter Hamilton	1992		2002	1997
		2000			
1074	M. J. Poznanski	1992	2003		1995
924	Alan Fyfe	1991		2003	
2330	Tony Tideswell	2000	2003		
1939	James Leslie	1998	2003		
		2003			
1045	Steve Fallon	1992	1993		
		1994			
		1995			
		1996			
		1997			
		1998			
		1999			
		2000			
		2001			
		2002			
		2003			
2929	Alexander G. Thow	2000			2002
480	Andrew Finnimore	1986	1086	1986	2003
1178	Christine E. Tulloch	1993	2003		2003
		2003			
1179	David I. Hill	1993			
		2003			
635	Maggi Miller	1987			2003
2727	Colin H. Campbell	2002	2002	2003	
460	Chris Pringle	1986			
		2003			
809	David Jones	1990		2000	2003
1162	Sandra Stead	1993	2003		
1164	Brian D. Panton	1993	2003		
358	Michael B. Slater	1984	1987	1987	

		1988			
		1990			
		1993			
		1996			
		1999			
		2003			
592	David F. Geddes	1988	1989	1991	1996
1125	John Hendry	1992	2003		
		2003			
1126	Margaret Hendry	1992	2003		
		2003			
1137	Mike Weedon	1989	2003		
1203	Jean M. Gayton	1993	1993		2003
1204	Robert J. Tait	1993	1993		2003
2161	Donald Brown	1999			
		2003			
2019	Norman Veitch	1998	2000	2003	
1397	Douglas R. MacLeod	1995	1997	1988	
		2000	2002	2003	
1793	Davie Hamill	1997			2003
262	*Roger J. C. Robb	1981	2003		
		2000			
1746	James King	1997			2003
2897	Barry Parker	2003		1995	
2346	David Allison	2000	2003	2002	

As ever, people who wish to register a Compleation or an Amendment, or make any necessary correction to the List, should send a letter with a stamped addressed envelope to me at:

Greenhowe Farmhouse,
Banchory Devenick,
Aberdeenshire,
AB12 5YJ.

If you wish a certificate (for either a Munro or Corbett compleation), please make sure you enclose an A4 SAE. If a certificate is not required, and an e-mail address is given on a received letter, I can speed up return of information, by e-mailing back. My e-mail address is: dave.kirk@greenhowefarm.fsnet.co.uk.

Have a great day on the hill.

David Kirk,
Clerkius Listius.

Iain Robertson reports: The Munro Society is about to enter its third year of existence in good heart. Subscription renewals by the majority of members suggest that the endeavours of the executive committee are consistent with the expectations of members. In addition, there continues to be a steady trickle of new members made up of recent, and not-so-recent, compleaters.

Among the past year's events, the arrival of the 3000th recorded Munroist, Michael Urquhart, was acknowledged by the Society which presented him with a wooden plaque – part of Sir Hugh T. Munro's mansion at Lindertis. The presentation took place during the Annual Dinner held in Grasmere this year, in deference to the large number of Society members living south of the Border.

The speaker was Maggie Body, former editor with Hodder and Stoughton, who specialised in editing climbing publications. The gently humorous description of the literary and other foibles of some of our most famous mountaineers made a most entertaining talk.

An innovation this year has been Munro Re-visits, an additional excuse for members to come together and enjoy a day on the hills. The first of these, based in Glen Etive, was to Beinn Dorain, and further re-visits during 2004 are planned for the Loch Earn hills and Torridon.

The *Society* has sponsored a video, *Mountain Paths,* produced by Jim Closs. In view of the ever-increasing number of walkers of all descriptions going to the hills, the video sets out the case for hill paths and their maintenance being essential to conservation of the mountain environment. The Society has donated copies of the video to the Mountaineering Council of Scotland and the British Mountaineering Council. Member clubs may borrow a copy with only the cost of postage.

Perhaps the Society's most ambitious project to date is the concept of the Mountain Quality Indicator (MQI). This is an ongoing project which reflects one of the Society's principle concerns – the extent to which Munros, and other Scottish mountains, are being degraded by various forms of human activity. What degradation amounts to is, however, too often a subjective matter, dependent upon the viewpoint of the commentator. The Society takes the view that it would be in everyone's interests if objective criteria setting out the 'quality' of a mountain could be established. Clearly, if this were the case, then it would be much easier for a critical but, nonetheless, more comprehensive view of mountain developments to emerge. This would be to the benefit of all mountain-users and, more importantly, to the benefit of the mountains themselves. To this end, the Society has drawn on the considerable experience of its members to develop the MQIs. Work over the last year has now reached the stage at which the comments of other interested parties are being sought. To this end, it is the intention to launch the MQIs as one of the events subsequent to the Annual Meeting in April.

Other events held in conjunction with the Annual Meeting will be talks by Ian R. Mitchell, on the Rev. A. E. Robertson, and Dave Hewitt, on the first 100 Munroists. This year's Munro Lecture will be given by Jim Curran.

The Society's archivist is being kept busy with additional deposits, but he is always happy to receive more. Anything concerning Munros or Munroists will be welcome and not just from members of Society. A considerable addition to the archive this year has been all the material gathered by Irvine Butterfield for his exhaustive, six-year study of Scotland's mountain bothies. This is a monumental piece of work involving maps, locations, photographs and plans of more than 600 buildings in wild places in Scotland. The contents of the archive are available for inspection by the public, and it is housed in the A. K. Bell Library in Perth.

All communications should addressed to: Iain Robertson, 8 King's Place, Perth, PH2 8AA.

IN MEMORIAM

BILL YOUNG j.1953

BILL and I climbed together from the early Sixties and had many memorable climbs. However, there is one which stands out above all – a moonlight winter traverse of the Aonach Eagach in 1966.

Bill Murray in *Undiscovered Scotland* describes the traverse, and cautions: "The root of the problem is to combine leisure with a full moon, a hard frost and a clear sky. Success needs patience."

He could also have added the necessity to react quickly to suitable conditions.

I was returning home from Glasgow on a Saturday evening train and as it left the city behind, I realised I was looking at a full moon in a clear sky and it was cold. The penny dropped. As soon as I got home, I phoned Bill, and about an hour later he picked me up. First stop was Glencoe police station to let them know what we were doing in case any lights were seen on the ridge.

We set off from near Alt-na-reigh at 10.30pm. and were on the summit of Am Bodach at 1am. Conditions were perfect, not a sound, not a breath of wind, perfect visibility and Nevis gleaming. We continued unroped and were on top of the pinnacles by 2am. At no time did we need a torch, even in the moon shadow on the north side of the ridge there was always enough reflected light to see.

As we started on the last lap, we could see high cloud approaching from the south and, as we reached the end of the ridge at 3.20am. the cloud began to move across the face of the moon. Light levels dropped a little but we could still see well enough to descend the steep snow slopes towards the glen. The snow line was at about 1000ft. and we now had to use torches. A solitary car came down the glen and stopped beneath us. A voice called up: "Are you alright?" We shouted back that we were and he continued on his way. A memorable night, as clear in my memory now as it was then.

Bill was Huts Convener from 1972 to 1976 and during these four years he was responsible for a quite remarkable programme of renovation at all three huts. Lagangarbh, CIC and Ling.

These changes were to have far reaching effects not apparent at the time.

Lagangarbh was first, in 1973. The hut was gutted internally down to the bare walls and redesigned with a proper stairway in place of the old 80° ladder access to the upper floor. The old wooden toilet annexe was replaced by a harled concrete block structure. All work, with the exception of the shell of the toilet block, being done with volunteer labour

1974 saw Bill's most difficult project, the CIC extension. The weekend that work started Bill and I had the Friday off and drove up from Glasgow with a load of timber. The hut book records this:

21.6.74. W. B. Young and G. S. Peet spent a long day transporting 50x200lb. gas bottles, several tons of timber in and out of lorries and vans up to the dam. Retired for the night at the dam absolutely knackered.

Plenty of support arrived overnight and early, (am) Helicopter arrived 8am. By 4pm we had finished uplifting 25-30 tons of sand, gravel, cement, building blocks, timber gas etc. (another group was digging out the foundations.) By 8pm work had ceased and memories of penal labour conditions dissipated in a haze of alcoholic euphoria.

Bill was a hard worker as well as a good organiser.

The final project, at Ling, was comparatively simple. The now standard sleep-shelf replaced the old squeaky uncomfortable two-tired iron bunks.

The much-improved facilities and better equipment allowed hut fees to be raised. The resulting increased use began to generate sizeable surpluses which enabled the club to give its members free beds at all three huts, and eventually, gave the club its first new purpose-designed hut – Raeburn.

The club owes this quiet man a considerable debt of gratitude. For me, everything I did with Bill, climbing, camping, huts, journeys, was always fun.

G. S. Peet.

COLIN M. STEVEN j.1938

COLIN STEVEN died in Newton Stewart Hospital on February 20, 2003. He was a member of the Scottish Mountaineering Club for 67 years and with his elder brother, Campbell, who predeceased him by less than a year, was an enthusiastic climber and walker in the pre-war years.

After initial hikes in the Cairngorms while on family holidays in Speyside, the brothers started exploring the hills and crags around Arrochar from the family home in Helensburgh. They later tackled some of the Perthshire Munros before discovering rock and winter climbing in Glencoe and Skye. Weekends and holidays would find them regularly heading north by Loch Lomond in the company of a small group of enthusiasts. The adventures often began immediately, as a variety of vehicles either broke down or succumbed to punctures *en route*. Undaunted the party would press on and pitch camp no matter the weather or the delay, before exploring ever more adventurous routes.

Although walking and climbing widely in Scotland and later in Wales, Skye remained a firm favourite and the campsite at Glen Brittle features often in a comprehensive diary and photographic record of climbs, routes and companions. The weather was often inclement and local cattle regularly raided the campsite and tents but Mrs Chisholm at Glen Brittle Post Office often provided sanctuary and fodder if spirits were ever low.

Campbell and Colin joined the JMCS in the early Thirties and climbed regularly at meets in Glencoe and Skye before graduating to the SMC in 1938. Colin climbed mostly in twos or threes with Campbell, his elder brother often taking the lead. Other notables included Ian Jack, Wilf Coates, George Arthur and their cousin, Freer Rodger. Colin was on Ben Nevis in 1934 when Kirkus and Linnell were avalanched. Linnell died but amazingly Kirkus survived to be avalanched a second time in 1936. By a quirk of fate Colin was again on the mountain that day and assisted with the rescue from the CIC hut the following day of Kirkus's injured companion, using a pony from Achintee for transport.

He continued climbing while a student at Glasgow University Medical School, mainly with colleagues and friends from the SMC covering a variety of Munros in Perthshire, Skye and Sutherland and a number of rock climbs and winter routes. A detailed stores list for a three-day stay for five at the CIC hut at Ben Nevis was costed at 35 shillings!

Colin participated in a number of adventurous routes including, in April 1936, the second ascent of Zero Gully on the Ben, with Graham Macphee and George Hemmings. They followed the initial pitches of Slav Route and the week-old footsteps of Bell and Allan. Colin made trips to North Wales in 1934 and 1935 and tackled a variety of routes with different groups, including a couple of ladies who were impressed with their skills by leading on a number of tricky pitches. They fitted in a stopover in the Lake District on the way home and tackled a number of standards including Amen Corner.

With Tom Mackinnon, Graham Macphee, and John Brown the brothers formed an SMC contingent on a trip to the Swiss Alps in 1938, whither they travelled, not by jet but with third-class tickets on wooden railway benches, providing a lifelong memory and the additional difficulties and hardships cemented their achievements. Their exploits are documented in Campbell's recently published autobiography *Eye to the Hills*.

Colin's last recorded climb was in 1940 while a resident at the Western Infirmary, Glasgow. The party of four climbed the Spearhead Arête and Jam Block Chimney on Ben Narnain. Shortly thereafter, war service broke up the group and while Campbell's skills were put to good use in the Commandos, where he taught colleagues the skills of cliff climbing in Iceland and Cornwall, with a view to the forthcoming invasion of Europe, Colin's posting in the RAMC and subsequent career effectively ended his climbing days. Although he honeymooned with Grace at the Sligachan Hotel in June 1945 and took his new wife up a couple of adjacent Munros, Colin's subsequent move to a single-handed general practice in Wigtown in 1947 and burgeoning family, left little time for the hills and he pursued other outdoor activities – fly fishing and shooting. Apart from occasional days in the Galloway hills with his family, Colin was content to retire from climbing but retained his lifelong love of the Scottish hills and countryside and enjoyed reading of the ever more adventurous climbs and routes by the new generation of post-war climbers.

Bill McKerrow.

PROCEEDINGS OF THE CLUB

The following new members have been admitted and welcomed to the Club in 2003-2004.

VICTORIA CHELTON (26), Outdoor Activities Instructor, Aviemore.

ERIC CHRISTISON (45), Design Engineer, Edinburgh.

HOWARD CRUMPTON (48), Engineer, Arbroath.

JAMES EDWARDS (27), Teacher, Edinburgh.

ALAN FOX (45), Maintenance Engineer, Dundee.

EDWARD GILLESPIE (57), Retired bank official, Edinburgh.

MARK J. HUDSON (41), Commercial Artist, London.

GARETH W. HUGHES (24), Research Assistant, Glasgow.

ALLAN C. PETTIT (58), Dentist, Bridge of Allan.

EWEN M. RIDDELL (37), Outdoor Activities Instructor, Ballater.

MUNGO ROSS (52), Teacher, Law, Lanarkshire.

The One-Hundreth-and-Fourteenth AGM and Dinner

AND we returned to Pitlochry and the Atholl Palace – your Committee could do no better and the price was right. The afternoon sessions become ever better attended, and this year comprised Simon Richardson talking about Scottish winter developments and Hamish Irvine describing the latest Club outing to Greenland.

The AGM by contrast was a domestic affair. The Treasurer's decision to change the Club's bankers and the consequent need for everyone to complete a new Standing Order mandate seemed beyond the comprehension of many, and remains so to date. Dick Allen led a spirited discussion on the ban of skis in the huts as stipulated in the recently revised Hut Rules, but CIC devotees seemed pleased at the proposal for warm slippers being available to greet them on arrival off the hill. The vexed issue of toilets at the CIC again came up, but Robin Campbell was advised that matters were at a very early stage and no action would be taken without formal approval of the Club.

We repaired to the vast spaces of the dining room where 150 members and guests attended table, and a meal very much more filling than past occasions, following which our President, Peter Macdonald, gave a graceful address and Alec Keith toasted the guests with wit and not a little politics.

Our principal guest was Dick Balharry of the John Muir Trust and we also entertained Andrew Thin of the Cairngorm Partnership, Peter Biggar as winner of the W. H. Murray Prize, Sarah McKay of the Ladies Scottish Climbing Club, our own Quintin Crichton representing the Grampian Club, Alan Rowland of the Fell & Rock, Rupert Hoare of the Alpine Club and representing the JMCS, Helen Forde, whose father W. E. Forde, a former member, made the first Greater Traverse with Ian Charleson.

Dick Balharry offered a wonderful reply, as Malcolm Slesser noted, speaking without notes or hesitation for more than 20 minutes.

The problems over musical accompaniment appear at last to have been solved with the President hiring a cathedral quality organ for the occasion. Gordon Ross was in great voice with the Club song and *Dark Lochnagar,* with further socialising continuing, for some, well into the small hours. In a return to tradition, the President managed to lead a small party to the top of Ben Vrackie on the Sunday.

There has been much debate over the timing of the Dinner and by popular request, this year will see a return to our traditional date of December 4, in the refurbished Ben Wyvis Hotel at Strathpeffer.

J.R.R.F.

Easter Meet 2003 – Loch Maree

THE meet was held at the Loch Maree Hotel with clear but windy and cool days. The interest was enhanced by the generosity of Paul van Vlissingen, the owner of the Letterewe Estate, who arranged transport for the members across the Loch on the Saturday. With this additional attraction there was a very good attendance.

Notable achievements were the numerous climbs on Ben Lair – David Jenkins, Colin Stead, Dougie Lang and Quentin Crichton on *Wisdom Buttress*; Malcolm Slesser and Bill Wallace on *The Tooth* and two ropes on *Bat's Gash* (Peter Macdonald, Roger Robb), (Paul Brian, David Stone and John Fowler). The Buttress and the Tooth were fine but various curses and crashes of falling rock indicated that Bat's Gash, which has two stars in the Northern Highlands guide, was more challenging.

There were mutters about those people who write guidebooks and allocate the stars! Everyone managed to get back to the pier before the appointed hour with several members running to catch the boat. Noel Williams and Robin Chalmers did a route on the north face of Martha's Peak on Beinn Airigh Charr originally climbed by Bell, Burt and Matheson in 1928 (on the Easter meet at Kinlochewe). Hills ascended included: An Teallach, Liathach, Slioch, Beinn Eighe and Beinn Alligin. Several members climbed in Stone Valley on Sunday before going home.

Those present: President Peter Macdonald, Robin Campbell, Brian Fleming, Malcolm Slesser, Iain Smart, Bill Wallace, Dick Allen, Peter Biggar, Paul Brian and guest David Stone, Robin Chalmers, Quintin Crichton, Mike Fleming, John Fowler and guest Helen Forde, Phil Gribbon, John Hay, David Jenkins, Dougie Lang, Rob Milne and guest Bill Taylor, Roger Robb, Nigel Suess, Douglas and Audrey Scott, Colin Stead, Noel Williams.

Dick Allen.

Easter Meet 2004 – Kintail

THE meet was held at Kintail Lodge Hotel with mixed weather, rain showers and low cloud. The highlight was the enforced candlelight meal served during a power failure on the Saturday night.

The poor weather did not deter members. John Hay came with Bill McKerrow from his 'stalking lodge' by boat up Loch Mullardoch and then walked via the Falls of Glomach to Dorusduain returning to his boat the next day along Glen Elchaig. Rob Milne and Yvonne Thomson climbed Ben Nevis on their way to the meet and then went on to climb Glamaig on their way home. Nigel Suess cycled to Iron Lodge then went on to climb Mullach na Dheiragain. Other hills ascended included: A' Ghlas Bheinn, Ciste Dubh, Aonach Meadhoin, Am Bathach, Mullach Fraoch-choire, A' Chralaig, Carn Ghluasaid, Sgurr nan Conbhairean, Sail Chaorainn, Meall Dubh, Creag a' Mhaim ,Druim Shionnach, Aonach air Chrith, Maol Chinn-dearg, Sgurr an Doire Leathain, Sgurr an Lochain, Sgurr Mhic Bharraich, Beinn a' Chapuill and The Quirang.

Members attending included the President Peter Macdonald, Robin Campbell, Brian Fleming, Malcolm Slesser, Iain Smart, Bill Wallace, John Fowler and guest Helen Forde, Dick Allen, Paul Brian and guest David Stone, Robin Chalmers, Mike Fleming, Phil Gribbon, John Hay, Bill McKerrow, Rob Milne and guest Yvonne Thomson, Roger Robb and Nigel Suess.

Dick Allen,

Ski Mountaineering Meet 2004

THOSE present: Members – Donald Ballance, James Hotchkis, Colwyn Jones, Ann MacDonald, Peter Macdonald, Chris Ravey and Brian Shackleton. Guests: Paul Hammond, John Porter, Bill Shaw and Nick Walmsley.

The meet was held at Milehouse, Feshiebridge – the excellent Ladies Scottish Climbing Club hut on the weekend of March 12-13.

On Friday evening the hut gradually filled up and we all enjoyed the glow from the stove, and from the wine. In short, the hut became less vacant while the opposite effect was evident among the occupants!

Saturday saw the club President lead from the front, accompanied by Donald, Brian, Paul and James.The group ascended Carn Ban Mor on ski (after carrying gear to a point well above the second deer fence). They then descended in poor visibility towards Tom Dubh and eventually, Monadh Mor. Difficult visibility restricted the speed of ascent and descent such that the sole pedestrian among the party, John Porter, was able to maintain contact throughout the day despite the many large, unintended detours enjoyed on the plateau.

The descent back to Glen Feshie was less eventful, excepting the final section along a narrowing icy bank of snow, which was a bit too exciting for some of the party. GPS, altimeters, maps and compasses kept the party on track all day, and eventually, deposited them back at the cars after 1270m of ascent and 9.5 hours of effort.

Nick and Chris started with the main body of the meet, again skinning up the final 200m to the Feshie plateau. However, they then turned left, apparently by design, and followed their compass to Sgor Gaoith. They endured a pleasant lunch in the cloud and then set off to Mullach Clach a Bhlar via a few dog legs and much pacing/timing. Skis remained on for the whole day (on the feet we mean) – a rarity for an SMC ski meet. On contouring back onto the top of Allt Fhearnagan their timing was immaculate (or not depending on ones point of view) in that they met the Presidential party descending back to the cars.

Ann (SMC stalwart and currently the first non-male President of the Glasgow Section of the JMCS) accompanied by Bill and Colwyn skied from the busy Cairngorm carpark up to the deserted rime iced summit of Ben Macdui. Eschewing the psychological comfort of a GPS, they navigated with altimeter, map and compass the whole day. It was windy and very claggy. On many occasions the visibility deteriorated to a state where it was impossible to know whether you were up, down, or somewhere in between, as they often proved to be. Late in the day, on the final descent, when the empty piste was reached, they pondered why people pay for the experience of skiing thin ribbons of rutted ice and prominent boulders.

Other members of the Glasgow Section of the JMCS who were sharing the hut had a splendid day climbing *Raeburn's Gully* and *Centre Post Direct* on Creag Mheagaidh.

After a good night of chat, haute cuisine and wine etc. in front of a not so glowing stove (a result of confusing domestic coal with anthracite) Sunday dawned, but they slept on.

Blustery, wet weather meant that there wasn't the same enthusiasm as the previous morning. Many chose that well known classic route, Home superdirect. Without skis, some ventured up Corbetts (Geal Carn Mor, the highest point in the Kinveachy Forest and Ben Rinnes farther east), some up a unidentified Monadhliath Graham. Others drove up to the carpark at Cairngorm but didn't leave the car.

All were agreed that the LSCC hut at Milehouse was an excellent venue.

Colwyn Jones.

JMCS REPORTS

Edinburgh Section: Membership is currently 79, including one aspirant and seven associate members. Rock climbing, winter climbing and hill walking are the main activities, with ski-mountaineering and mountain biking also popular.

The section holds mid-week meets at the Heriot-Watt climbing wall during winter and various crags around Edinburgh in summer. Traprain and Aberdour are the most popular outdoor venues, but there are also visits to crags farther afield such as Dunkeld, Kyloe and Bowden Doors. This year, the wet weather alternative is the Ratho Adventure Centre.

Members gather at Alien Rock on a Monday night, and there is also a pub meet on the first Thursday of the month at Kay's Bar in Jamaica Street from 9pm onwards.

The highpoint of the summer 2003 weekend meets was the annual visit to the Shelter Stone in August. Teams were out on Shelterstone crag, Coire Sputan Dearg and Creagan A'Choire Etchachan, climbing *The Steeple*, *Djibangi* and *Dagger* among others. Other well-attended meets were held at Caer Fran Hut in North Wales and Salving House in Borrowdale.

The winter meets began with hill walking at Inbhirfhaolain in Glen Etive in December. January's meet at Muir of Inverey cottage was affected by bad weather and turnout was poor. The weather brightened up by the end of the month with eight members spending a memorable weekend at the Ling Hut.

The Blackrock Cottage meet in Glen Coe proved popular with a settled high pressure system meaning steady wind from the north. Climbing conditions were good if a little thin. Teams were out on Ben Nevis and Aonach Mor, enjoying *Tower Scoop*, *Hesperides Ledge* and *Jet Stream*.

Ben Nevis was the venue for the last meet of the winter season, our annual trip to the CIC Hut at the end of March. Climbing conditions were poor due to a thaw, but teams made the best of it with ascents of *North East Buttress*, *Glover's Chimney* and *Tower Ridge*. The Sunday was windy and wet, so a number of members paid a visit to the Ice Factor in Kinlochleven to sample some of the climbing there. The ice climbing was reported as being "highly enjoyable if somewhat sanitised".

Abroad, club members visited a number of different destinations. Hot rock continues to be popular, with visits to Sardinia and Mallorca. Members continue to visit the Alps in winter for ice climbing and skiing, taking advantage of the new direct flights from Edinburgh to Geneva. Members were active in the regular alpine venues of Chamonix, Zermatt and the Dolomites during the summer. Outside of Europe, New Zealand saw a number of visits for skiing and climbing.

The Annual Dinner once again took place at the Atholl Arms Hotel in Blair Atholl. An excellent meal was followed by an entertaining and amusing speech from Paul Brian of the SMC. Paul regaled those present with many anecdotes from his long climbing career including his involvement with Lochaber Mountain Rescue in the TV show *Rock Face*. There was much laughter and warm applause at the end of his contribution to the evening.

The section's huts continue to be popular with both members and other clubs. The traditional Hogmanay at the Smiddy was well-attended this year. Committee members have been kept busy with discussions regarding the continuation of the lease at Jock Spot's cottage, but it is hoped this will be resolved in the not too distant future.

The Joint Eastern Section SMC/JMCS slide nights have continued to be interesting events with speakers on a wide-range of subjects associated with climbing and mountaineering. The slide nights take place at 7:30pm on the second Tuesday of the month from October to March at Pollock Halls, Edinburgh.

George McEwan started the slide nights off with an interesting lecture on life an as instructor at Glenmore Lodge. Other speakers have included Robin Campbell, Malcolm Slesser and Dave MacLeod. In February Mike Dales of the MC of S gave an update on current access and conservation issues.

These gatherings have a social aspect as well, with dinner beforehand at the New Bell Inn Restaurant. Thanks go to Des Rubens for all his efforts in organising these evenings.

Next year marks the 80th anniversary of the founding of the JMCS and plans are afoot to mark this occasion with an event later in the year. Former members interested in taking part should contact the Secretary.

Officials elected: *Hon. President*, John Fowler; *Hon. Vice-President*, Euan Scott; *President*, Helen Forde; *Vice-President*, Sally Dipple; *Treasurer*, Bryan Rynne; *Secretary*, Neil Cuthbert, 25 Plewlands Gardens, Edinburgh (secretary@edinburghjmcs.org.uk); *Web Master*, Davy Virdee; *Smiddy Custodian*, Alec Dunn, 4 King's Cramond, Edinburgh; *Jock Spot's Custodian*, Ali Borthwick, 2 Aytoun Grove, Dunfermline. *Ordinary Members:* Patrick Winter (Meets Secretary), Stewart Bauchop

Perth Mountaineering Club (JMCS Perth Section)

The Perth Mountaineering Club has had another busy year with 13 weekend meets and seven day meets. The Club is looking forward to celebrating its 75th anniversary in 2004.

Attendance at meets has been inexplicably variable. The July meet to the CIC hut had no takers and was dropped from the programme. Other meets have, however, been well attended. Seventeen people braved less-than-perfect weather conditions for a weekend camping meet at Glen Brittle. The now annual family meet in June was also very well supported. This year it was based at the camp site at Scourie where 16 adults and seven children made the most of the Sutherland beaches, as well as a more energetic traverse of Foinaven.

The traditional Milehouse meet in November was also very well attended with 21 members taking part.

A new venue was ventured in December – Clashgour Hut by Loch Tulla. A select group of seven members attended and found the accommodation rather more basic than the Club has become accustomed to. This did not prevent them from having an enjoyable weekend's hill walking and comradeship.

Other highlights of the year included: a night and day of hard frost at Blackrock Cottage in January; a weekend spent at scenic Strawberry Cottage in April, with many hills climbed; a traverse of Liathach from the Ling Hut at the end of May; an August weekend on Arran where several members tackled the A'Chir ridge; and a round of the Ring of Steel from Steall Hut in October.

The Wednesday evening rock climbing fared much better than the previous year with lots of dry sunny evenings. The Club has now transferred from Falkirk to the new Dundee climbing wall for its winter sessions.

Three Club members completed their Munros during the course of the year. Tom Barnard finished on Fionn Bheinn in May, and then husband-and-wife team,

Carolann and Steve Petrie, had a joint celebration on the Loch Lomondside Ben Vorlich in October.

Several members furthered their mountaineering exploits overseas. A group of five visited the Ordessa area of the Pyrenees and two others the Dolomites. Grahame Nicoll took a week's break in Norway for some seriously cold ice climbing, and Willie Jeffrey took a warmer option, climbing in Colorado.

The Club also proved its worth as a useful way of meeting prospective partners. Donald Barrie and Sue Adams met through the Club and celebrated their marriage in March. A number of Club members attended the wedding in the Lake District.

The Club provides a speaker for an annual joint meeting with the Perth Society of Natural Science. This January Pete Hemmings gave a most enjoyable presentation on his climbing expedition to Greenland during the summer of 2002.

Another social event took place in March when the Club, as recompense for winning last year, hosted the 2003 Mountainmind Quiz at the Dewar Centre, Perth.

The 2002 Annual Dinner was held at the Cultoquhey Hotel at Gilmerton in November.

Officials elected: *President:* Karen Campbell; *Vice-President:* Mike Aldridge; *Secretary:* Sue Barrie; Glensaugh Lodge, Laurencekirk, Aberdeenshire, AB30 1HB. Tel: 01561 340673; *Treasurer:* Pam Dutton; *Newsletter Editor:* Des Bassett; *Meets Convener:* Beverly Robertson; *Committee Members:* Julia Banks, Carolann Petrie, Willie Jeffrey and Chris Hine.

Sue Barrie.

London Section: Our new year resolution for 2003 was to improve the cottage and try to gain some new members from the 'introductory' weekend events we ran in 2002 – no change there then.

Formal membership remains in the mid-40s though the secretary's distribution list of has-beens and hangers on seems to be about double this!

We continue to slowly improve the fabric of our cottage in Bethesda as funds permit. This year, we have embarked upon providing an additional shower room which should make the place much more usable for mixed groups – work is still in progress. The improvements from last year mean that the cottage is structurally sound, with a new roof and repairs to the exterior which generally contribute to keeping it clean and tidy.

As for new members, we have had a clutch of keen young tigers join us and they have helped bring the climbing standard back up to where it has traditionally been (before middle-age spread set in) and provide a 'core' of enthusiasm for proper climbing weekends.

Interestingly, we have had very little (i.e. none) take-up of membership from the introductory weekend events we ran last year. Enjoyable though the events were, and successful in attracting interest, they did not translate into membership – perhaps it says something about us!

With well-attended meets (monthly) across the UK and a keen core of climbers, the club is returning to its traditional style of camping and climbing. Meets are mostly well attended (subject to the weather forecast) and a broad range of activities takes place including mountain biking, walking/scrambling, skiing and of course climbing at various standards up to about E2.

Particularly successful, for the number of routes completed, was Pembroke at Easter. We also have a Munroist – John Steele compleated this year –

congratulations to him. Other extra-curricular highlights included a two-week sailing/walking trip to the Outer Hebrides and St Kilda by an intrepid party of seven chartering a yacht. They had mixed weather but all the more spectacular sailing for that. As usual, members organised some skiing trips to France taking on the traditional downhill style as well as ski-mountaineering and cross-country. Overall, reflecting our broad interests in all activities mountain and wilderness and a healthy appetite for adventure.

The finale to the year is the AGM and dinner, and this year we moved back to a favourite haunt – the Tyn-y-Coed in Capel Curig.

Apart from the usual proceedings we also hosted Jerry Gore who was kind enough to entertain us after dinner with an illustrated lecture on the climatic changes to the Alps and his recommendations on how to make the most of the new conditions to be encountered there. Again a return to an old format that has served us well.

Officials elected: President, Marcus Harvey; Treasurer, Dave Hughes; Hut Custodian, Rod Kleckham; Secretary, Chris Bashforth; Vice-president, John Firmin, and Geoff Deady. Meets responsibility is shared among the committee.

Club contacts and details can be found at our web-site www.jmcs.freewire.co.uk

Chris Bashforth.

SMC AND JMCS ABROAD

Europe

Colwyn M. Jones reports: Four club members, Colwyn Jones, Mark Litterick, Ann MacDonald and Brian Shackleton spent a week in April ski-mountaineering in the Italian Gran Paradiso National Park and the adjacent area of Switzerland north of the Grand Combin. The group had an international flavour with German and Swiss friends Anja Von Werden and Hans-Jakob Schuhmacher (Kobi).

The Scottish contingent travelled by a scheduled Ryanair flight from Prestwick (not very near Glasgow) to Bergamo (not very near Milan) on April 17. The party met Mark at Bergamo airport and we then drove up the Aosta Valley turning left up the Val Saverenche to spend the evening at the roadhead in the comfortable Gran Paradiso Hotel in the village of Pont. This is in a fabulous National Park with chamois and ibex in abundance. As planned there was snow down to the road and next day all six of us skied up through the trees to the comfortable Rifugio Vittorio Emanuele at 2732m.

After a relaxing afternoon in the warm sunshine, but with the barometric pressure falling, some cloud came over and the morning of April 19 was a white out with falling snow and poor visibility. The light snow continued to fall until lunchtime. Thereafter it slowly cleared allowing an escape from contagious cabin fever at about 3pm to slowly reinstate the ski trail up to the 3200m contour. The late afternoon descent back down to the hut in superb powder snow was ample reward for the arduous trail breaking.

Breakfasting at 5am next day, the team left the hut in excellent weather and achieved the summit of the Gran Paradiso by late morning. There were two guided parties who broke trail from 3200m to the summit at 4061m. The view was superb in all directions but the now gathering cloud precluded a long stay and the descent was again excellent in untracked powder snow.

After a beer at the hut the descent to the valley floor in very soft snow was

Bill Young on The Cobbler in 1956. Photo: A. McKenzie.

Colin Steven climbing Zero Gully/Slav Route, April 1936. Photo: Colin Steven collection.

tiresome. There, the four Scots departed from Anja and Kobi, who had to get back to work, and drove across the Aosta Valley, through the Grand St Bernard tunnel to Bourg St. Pierre. As Mark had a significant birthday, it was necessary to book into a hotel for an excellent meal with accompanying wine and liqueurs. An appropriate celebration which may well influence the future date of these Spring ski-mountaineering trips!

The news from the hut wardens in the area was that the "Le Grand Combin n'est pas bon." Therefore we drove to Fionnay to ascend to the Panossiere Hut which might allow an attempt on the main peak if conditions improved. The hut is now confusingly named the Francois Xavier-Bagnoud hut (2671m) in memory of a helicopter pilot. The late start, relentless sunshine and long approach did not help to concentrate attention on the technical difficulties of the climb to the hut. Nor did the large numbers of young heliskiers skiing recklessly down the narrow track of icy moguls. The final danger was the crumbling slushy filthy moraine which had to be crossed to finally reach this excellent, modern hut. The wardens have been working there for 36 years and their welcome and care was super. We particularly commend the drying facilities and excellent food, unless you are vegetarian.

Next morning on April 22, the weather was again excellent and we elected to ski up the Tournelon Blanc (3707m). The ascent started at dawn (6am) up the main Glacier de Corbassiere. Heading west there was then the steep ascent up to the ridge, which was excellent, and the final narrow arête to the summit giving a super little peak with an excellent view across the Alps. It also confirmed the poor condition of the corridor route on the Grand Combin.

The regular freeze-thaw cycle of the last couple of days had resulted in a deep crust over the wide snow cover. This dictated either energetic jump turns on the descent or more sedate step turns and terminal traverses. Hence, it was an exhausted but triumphant team who arrived back at the hut just after midday for an excellent lunch. There were only two other guests in the hut that night and the resulting portion control at another excellent dinner was rather poor!

Next day, we set out to scale both the Combin de Corbassiere and the Petit Combin. It was a long approach and the late morning sun proved to be a testing companion. However, leaving skis a bare 100m below the top and climbing the final steep mixed slopes, we finally achieved the first summit at just after 11am (Combin de Corbassiere, 3715m). The short descent between the two peaks was in excellent powder but again the sun-drenched, south-facing climb to the summit of the Petit Combin (3672m) baked us alive. For those favouring the long approach and the peace of the mountains, the Petit Combin has a designated helicopter landing site on the summit and a large flat adjacent glacier for ski planes to land. Nevertheless, the view is excellent. That morning only Mont Blanc and Monte Rosa had a veil of cloud. The descent back down the glacier, passing teetering seracs was exciting enough and we were soon safely back at the hut for some afternoon sunbathing and another excellent evening meal.

We descended from the Panossiere Hut early on Saturday, April 24, experiencing variable conditions as we lost height. There was a small avalanche which carried one member down off the path. A tree, which he managed to grab en *passant*, proved to be his salvation. Thereafter, we skied with exaggerated gaps between us while, on the sunlit side of the valley, the avalanches crashed down with monotonous regularity.

Fiftieth anniversary of the first routes on the Trilleachan Slabs by Eric Langmuir, Mike O'Hara and John Mallinson. Bob Downes, Langmuir and Mallinson display equipment – June 13, 1964 (Sickle). Photo: John Mallinson.

Andy Tibbs and Eric Langmuir's daughter, Moira, at a belay on Spartan Slab. Photo: Alastair Matthewson.

That afternoon, we drove back to Lake Como in Northern Italy for an excellent evening by the waterside and, returning to Bergamo airport early next day, we flew home after an excellent trip.

We had skins on our skis on seven successive days and recorded a total ascent of 6,500 metres (21,300 ft). The most ascent in any one day was 1380m (4,500ft) on the Friday during ascents of the Petit Combin and Combin de Corbassiere. The least ascent was 120m on the last day when leaving the lower Corbassiere Glacier basin during the descent to Fionnay.

Apart from snow late Monday lasting through into the Tuesday, during our visit to the Rifugio Vittorio Emanuele, the weather was generally sunny and clear although some afternoon cloud also occurred. On the final Saturday, the party started their day in still mountain air well below freezing and finished it in sultry warm air around 28 degrees Centigrade in Lecco on the shores of Lake Como!

ADAM KASSYK REPORTS: In early June 2003 I had a very short ski touring trip with Matthew Priestman (Alpine Club) on Monte Rosa in the Pennine Alps. We enjoyed perfect weather and snow conditions. From the Monte Rosa Hut we climbed the Grenz Glacier to the Lisjoch (4256m) on our second day, and descended to the Rifugio Gnifetti in Italy to recover.

After a day's rest we spent the night in the Balmenhorn bivouac hut, and from there we traversed Ludwigshohe (4341m), Parrotspitze (4432m) and Zumsteinspitze (4563m) on our fourth day. My partner went on to the main summit (Dufourspitze 4634m), having also managed to collect nearly all the other minor summits on the Italian side. All that remained was a serious, but exhilarating, ski down the Grenz Glacier the following morning – carefully avoiding the crevasses. At this time of the year we had the mountain virtually to ourselves.

In June of the previous year (2002) I went to Chamonix with Keith Anderson for a week. Unfortunately, the weather was poor. We climbed most of the SE Spur of the Minaret (TD) on the one good day, followed by an ascent of the Aiguille d'Argentiere by the South-east (Fleche Rousse) Ridge (AD) in very mixed conditions, piles of powder snow and rock pitches well iced – somewhat reminiscent of Lochnagar in winter. After that a metre of snow fell so we gave up any hope of ice climbing and descended from the Argentiere Refuge. The Cosmiques Arête on the Midi was just about the only route possible in the massif in these conditions, so we ploughed a deep trench up this to complete a week with a rather uniquely Scottish feel to it.

The previous autumn I had a very successful alpine week in October with Matthew Priestman. After heavy snowfall we climbed the Obergabelhorn by the Arbengrat (AD) in wintry conditions, and this classic ridge gave entertaining rock climbing in crampons, followed by the traverse over the Wellenkuppe and a night-time descent in deep snow – another typically Scottish experience. We then decamped to the Oberland for the classic South Ridge of the Stockhorn (TD), this time on dry and sun warmed rock, followed by the South Rib of the Aletschorn (PD) to round off the trip. On all three trips we were almost always the only people on the mountain, and we generally had the refuges to ourselves as well – luxury.

Greenland

Stephen Reid reports: Two excellent alpine ridges received first ascents from the SMC East Greenland Expedition 2003 – Stephen Reid (Leader), Colwyn Jones (Medical Officer), Jonathan Preston, and Hamish Irvine.

They visited the Staunings Alps – a large range of mainly granite and gneiss glaciated peaks in the North-East Greenland National Park, from mid-July to mid-August. The objectives of the expedition were the first ascents of the South and South-West Ridges of Dansketinde (2930m), the highest peak in the range.

Having been helicoptered in to a base on Col Major (2010m), the team acclimatised by ascending Dansketinde via the Original Route and climbing a lower more or less independent part of the South Ridge. An attempt was then made by all four climbers on the main part of the South Ridge, but, after some 18 hours of increasingly difficult climbing (long sections of sustained VS in places) on mainly excellent rock, this petered out under a steep verglas and snow covered wall. A long abseil retreat was organised.

After several days of bad weather and a brief reconnaissance, the team had more success on its secondary objective, the unclimbed South-West Ridge of Dansketinde. This gave a great natural line of sustained difficulty with numerous pitches of Scottish Grade IV and V ice and mixed climbing. In all, 19 pitches (including one moving together for 150m) were climbed to reach the Western Summit. A snow arête joins this to the Main Summit from where the Original Route was descended to base camp. The overall grade was felt to be TD+.

At the end of the expedition, two days of good weather allowed Reid, Preston and Irvine a second attempt on the South Ridge. Conditions were perfect and, climbing through the night, rapid progress was made to reach the foot of the 'Impossible Wall' which was now free of verglas and the party were astounded to find it went at only Hard Severe. Higher up an interesting chimney through-route at Scottish V provided a gateway through the headwall to the summit, which was reached at 5pm, but a particularly unpleasant descent meant it was 10.30pm by the time base camp was reached – a round trip of 30 hours. Twenty-eight pitches (1545m) were climbed in total (not including the preliminary section of 500m) with one moving together pitch of 300m, and several more of 100m. With pitches of VS and Scottish V, and the difficulties high on the route, it was felt a grade of TD+ was appropriate.

The team was airlifted out by pre-arranged helicopter 12 hours later. The expedition was supported by the BMC, the Gino Watkins Trust and the MEF.

Africa

JAMIE ANDREW reports: In January 2004, I was part of an all-disabled expedition to Kilimanjaro in Tanzania. The other team members were David Lim from Singapore who has partial paralysis of the lower legs after suffering the rare nervous disorder Guillain-Barre Syndrome; Pete Steane from Tasmania who also has partial lower leg paralysis due to a spinal injury, and Paul Pritchard – well known British climber who sustained a serious head injury on the Totem Pole and has severe paralysis of the whole right side of his body.

The objective of the 'Voltaren Kilimanjaro Challenge' was to make a rare ascent of one of Kili's Northern Glaciers, either the Little Penck or the Credner, unsupported from the Shira Plateau. However, on reaching Lava Tower camp

(4600m) it became apparent that the Little Penck Glacier is now little more than a patch of dangerous looking seracs, sitting perched over a band of cliffs and moraine.

The team turned its efforts to the Credner Glacier, also considerably receded, but promising a climb of gentler angle. Further setbacks occurred when Paul began to develop pulmonary oedema, forcing a retreat back to Shira Camp at 3800m, then three days of bad weather dumped over a foot of snow on the mountain. Two attempted recces during the bad weather failed to find a route to the start of the Credner and then, to cap it all, two of our Tanzanian guides became snow blind and were forced to descend.

Faced with these setbacks, and running out of time, the team decided to focus their efforts on the much more well-known Western Breach, or Arrow Glacier Route. They also made a further compromise by taking two Tanzanian guides along on the final climb.

A start was made at 1am on January 18. The Western Breach Route gave a superb climb of about Scottish II under snow and the team reached the crater rim at about 11am. At 3pm the team reached Uhuru Peak (5895m) which basked in glorious sunshine while the whole of the rest of Africa was hidden beneath cloud.The descent to Barranco (3900m) took until midnight, giving an exhausting 23-hour day.

'The Voltaren Kilimanjaro Challenge' was in aid of the Upendo Leprosy Centre, a Rotary Club project on the slopes of Kilimanjaro, and more than £5000 was raised for this worthwhile cause.

SOUTH RIDGE DIRECT

Finger ends curl like a cat's cold claws
Chasing mouse-grey granite's crystal flaws
 But miss…to trace the spikeful scrapes
That a cruel and clumsy crampon drapes
Upon the rock.

The quartzy cast eludes my reach,
Slips silently away, unlike the screech
Of pecking picks and their whacking ring
Slamming in the crack. They call it torqueing
To the rock.

Be reassured, the first fiddles play,
We lead – and this is The Way.
The scars will heal and our star will shine.
We wait. All we need is a frosty line
Up the rock.

"Don't do this," the Code of Conduct says, but it's just a guide,
And rule seven states that discretion should be exercised
"Classic climbs often have little vegetation or even snow,"
So it's up to you. Now, who'll be the first to crow
To have raped the rock?

Mike Jacob.

REVIEWS

With Friends in High Places:- Malcolm Slesser. Mainstream Publishing, 2004. 256pp. £15.99.

SOME would say that to be a Friend of Malcolm Slesser is a heavy burden, and In High Places heavier still. You would have to guard your spoon and other goods such as whisky, prepare the morning porridge to his rigid (but vague) specification (see Appendix 4), eat semolina (Appendix 3), endure his detailed (but inconclusive) opinions about energy, environment, and risk (Chapters 10, 15, Appendix 1), and praise his piping – unless you are Geoff Dutton "What's a finger or two to a piper like you?" (p. 81). Your name would also be either mispronounced, forgotten or mis-spelled. Bonington, for example, is always 'Bonnington' here, but perhaps this an understandable reaction to Slesser so often becoming 'Slessor', or 'Sleazer' as Carlos Ziebell preferred to call him (p. 166). The number of Malcolm Slesser's friends was easily counted in Loch Scresort in 1997 on the occasion of the Club's Yachting Meet. Although it was common knowledge among the flotilla gathered there that the Slesser boat was anchored in shallow water, and would lie on her beam ends at the coming low water in the dead of night, all were so anxious that he should enjoy this experience that no-one passed on this information until substantial seas began to roll into the loch – surely an excellent example of 'the camaraderie' of the SMC celebrated on p. 7!

Like Bill Murray's autobiography *The Evidence of Things Not Seen*, Slesser's autobiography applies the wisdom of long years to retrospection of achievements already described in detail in previous works (*Red Peak, The Andes are Prickly* – see parts of Chapter 5 and all of Chapters 6 through 9). Perhaps new insights are available now to justify covering old ground, but the earlier accounts had the benefit of the freshness of experience and the security of recent memory. For example, the tussle with Robin Smith in the Lake of Communist Youth at Dushanbe is recalled as a grievous assault here, instead of as 'a horse-fight' in *Red Peak*. A new story about Smith appears here, in which he stands at the door of Slesser's (occupied) tent, 'penis hanging out' (p. 84) and urinates into it. Of course, one would not say that Slesser has invented this story, since (unlike Smith) he is still alive, and able to sue. So it must be true, or true-ish. But I knew Smith pretty well. He was polite, shy, and sexually inexperienced. He was not the sort to expose himself, still less to urinate into a tent. If he did so, then the provocation must have been extreme. The climbing side of the Russian visit to Scotland in 1960 was largely taken care of by Smith and his Edinburgh friends, whose advantageous position was then supplanted (or perceived to be) by Slesser 'sheathed in smiles' (*J.* 1961, 174). Smith surely resented Slesser's leadership of the Scottish group in the Pamirs, and the exclusion of his friends. At the very least, there is more to these stories about Smith than we are told here. Certainly, Slesser has succeeded in leaving a stain on the reputation of this peerless and beloved climber more durable than any left by him on the floor of that tent.

The section assessing the character of Robin Smith is one of a series of interesting vignettes in the book. Dougal Haston and Tom Patey are described in the same chapter. Chapter 12 – 'Two Sides of a Coin' – deals with Ernest Henley (the familiar Dedo de Deus story), Norman Tennent and Iain Smart. A recurring theme of the book is Slesser's view of safety: that safe climbing depends not on avoidance of danger but on awareness of risk and the adoption of a calculated approach to the management of it. So those who perish have failed to attend to risk, or have calculated wrongly. Thus the deaths of Haston, Patey and Smith, are attributed (p. 76) to 'trivial errors of judgment'. I think we need to know a great deal more about these accidents to justify such a sweeping and comfortable diagnosis. If Malcolm Slesser (inattentive to risk, and miscalculating it) had moved an inch or two on his stance of the Bonnaidh Donn (p. 25) he would have been obliterated by a falling stone. 'Bad luck', we would have said, and so should we say for Haston, Patey and Smith. I prefer the theory of Iain Smart, in which mountaineering is represented as an addictive and dangerous drug, which kills a good proportion of those hooked by it.

Other chapters are concerned with exploratory trips to Greenland. Our Club's involvement with Greenland has been constant, and considerable, since the 1950s, and Slesser has been a prime mover in advocacy of that once pristine land, and in organising (or persuading others to organise) expeditions there. For a reader like me, who has never been there, the accounts are hard to follow in the absence of illustrations and adequate maps, but there is a serious attempt made to describe the beauty of land and sea, and the predicaments faced by those who travel there.

Safety gets a chapter, as do expedition food, ski-mountaineering and use of mountain land. Although Slesser is keen on his analysis of safety, I don't feel that he is as comfortable with this topic as the others. The measurement of risk is a technically tricky business – much trickier than the ridiculous Scale of Risk (Appendix 1) would suggest. When considering all forms of mountaineering, a rate of death per annum may make some sense, since approximately the same collective risks are taken each year, but when considering climbing K2, the rate of death by altitude attained curve is a better indicator: choosing bases for risk calculation is never straightforward, and is hotly debated even in well-trodden areas like transport risk. And whereas the costs of taking a risk are perhaps sometimes calculable, the benefits seldom are. On the other hand, Slesser's comments about food, ski-mountaineering and the use of mountains seem perspicacious and wise. I found the latter chapter 'The Mountaineer's Footprint' particularly engrossing, insightful and witty: 'If you want to save energy the best way is to be poor' (p. 224); 'Nuclear energy [is] the match [which] will always be there when we get tired of rubbing two sticks together' (p. 225). His expertise in this area of energy/environmental costs and benefits is evident, and reading his views made me thirst for more. And there is more: the endpapers list six other books on this topic.

Considered merely as a book *With Friends* is a reasonable cheapish job by the publisher: illustrations are only the author's (free), the excellent poetry is cadged, the sparse footnotes are not located where they should be at the bottom of the page, and – despite the 'meticulous editing' of Deborah Warner – there are several mistakes. But there is an Index, and the book is attractively laid out. Considered as an autobiography, despite its miscellaneous contents, it hangs together well and is well-written in a breezy and humorous manner. I was left with the impression of a life lived most vigorously, the hook of mountaineering firmly set, with no opportunity for adventure spurned, and with little account taken of personal hardship. This is most evident on the Peak of Communism (now the Peak of Ismail Samani), which Slesser and Graeme Nicol struggled up despite severe illness, but it is plainly a necessary virtue for every Arctic mountaineer too. The mark of toughness is borne by many distinguished Scottish mountaineers: Raeburn, Bell, MacInnes, Ritchie, Haston, and Patey come to mind, and it is evident too in the hawk-nosed gimlet-eyed Slesser.

Robin N. Campbell.

Everest Pioneer – The Photographs of Captain John Noel:- Sandra Noel, (Sutton Publishing, 2003, hardback, 176pp. ISBN 0-7509-3278-3, £25).

In 1919, Captain John Noel, a 29-year-old Army Officer, suggested, during a presentation of his expeditions to Tibet, that an attempt should be made to climb Mount Everest. The mountain lay in a country rarely seen by westerners and had never before been climbed. Hidden behind the barrier of the Himalayas, it had retained an almost medieval character.

Taking up his suggestion, the Mount Everest Committee was formed under the leadership of Francis Younghusband. Due to Army commitments, Noel was unable to accompany the first Reconnaissance Expedition in 1921 but, on the two pioneering expeditions of 1922 and 1924, Noel was the official photographer.

Watching the climbers' brave attempts in hazardous conditions to achieve the summit of the mountain the Tibetans knew as Chomolungma – Goddess Mother of the World, he was also witness to Mallory and Irvine's doomed ascent along the northern precipice and captured the last haunting images of the two men.

Battling against extreme weather conditions, the complex technical demands of high altitudes, cold and fatigue – and sending his photographs to the other side of the world via packhorse and local runner – Noel made a unique collection of still images and film. This book draws together his work for the first time. Stunning images capture the drama and tragedy of the expeditions – the first to venture upon the highest mountain on earth – the landscape's extraordinary beauty and the life of the people who inhabited one of the remotest regions on earth. Mothers coat their children in butter to protect them from the cold; men are shown in traditional dress, their pendant earrings defining their rank; nomad shepherds stand beside their yak-hair encampment. On the world's highest mountain climbers are seen edging along a dangerous precipice, relaxing at camp, sitting triumphant on their way to the roof of the world and searching in vain for lost companions.

Written and compiled by Noel's daughter and including the first pictures of mountaineering expeditions by westerners, many previously unpublished, *Everest Pioneer* will appeal to anyone intrigued by exploration, history or mountaineering.

Charles J. Orr.

Yosemite – Half a Century of Dynamic Rock Climbing:- Alexander Huber and Heinz Zak (Baton Wicks, 2003, hardback 176pp. ISBN 1898573573). £30.

The publication of this splendid book covering the history of modern climbing in Yosemite Valley could hardly be more timely. 'The Valley' is undoubtedly the most spectacular arena for rock climbers to pursue their dreams and ambitions. As such, it has always been the forcing ground of some of climbing's greatest adventurers and athletes. Over the last decade Alex Huber has placed himself among this band of legendary figures with his free ascents of *Salathe Wall* and other climbs on Yosemite's massive granite walls. Together with the world class climbing photographer Heinz Zak, Huber has attempted to capture the spirit of Yosemite climbing by combining stunning images of the valley and its landmark climbs, and historical accounts by the climbers who pioneered them.

This is a large format coffee-table book which is very well produced, providing a chronicle of key stages in the progressive development of climbing in the valley. This concise history has been compiled by Huber, interspersed with some brilliant articles by a good selection of leading climbers in these periods, such as Warren

Harding, Royal Robbins, Jerry Moffatt, Lynn Hill and Leo Houlding. I was also pleased to see the opening pieces describing the early history of the valley; its native Ahwahneechee, the 'discovery' of the valley by white explorers and, later, the role of John Muir in the establishment of the national park in 1890.

In general, Huber provides a well-constructed, but brief history, and gets straight down to business with John Salathe and his influential development of modern steel pitons which opened the door for climbers to take on Yosemite's main challenges, the big walls. Although virtually all of the images come from modern day photo shoots by Heinz Zak, some of which are staged, the book also features several truly inspiring historical shots. Of these, first ascent shots of Royal Robbins advancing into a sea of overhanging granite on the headwall cracks of *Salathe Wall* and hanging out in hammocks 2000ft. up *North America Wall* in the early Sixties say more about the great courage and adventurous spirit of these pioneers than the writing manages on its own. This publication is so timely because the progress of styles and approaches to tackling these immense walls has come full circle over the last decade with the freeing of the most famous and grandest of challenges; *The Nose* by Lynn Hill and *Salathe Wall* by the Huber brothers.

Throughout, Huber grapples with the ethical twists and turns which went on from the early days of aid and the long expedition style sieges, through to the state of the art ascents such as *The Nose* free in 23 hours by Lynn Hill (with two pitches of 5.14a after 2000ft. of difficult climbing) or Leo Houlding's near-on-sight repeat of *El Nino* (5.13c). It is this logical and open-minded critique of the ethical statements of the pioneers through the ages and the way Huber tells the story of how circumstances, personalities and coincidences shaped them, that I feel is the sparkling highlight of the book. It is a remarkable insight into the mechanics of the evolution of the climbs as they are today and how the ambitions of the climbers of the day were balanced carefully with respect for the rock, the abilities of future generations and for the spirit of adventure.

The account by Jerry Moffatt of the equally-famous, though rather smaller, routes on the immaculate boulders in the Camp 4 campground in the valley basin was a welcome contrast to the endless exposure shots of El Capitan's headwall. An extended version of this published in *High* magazine in 1994 was partly what inspired me to become a climber. The shot of Jerry looking relaxed as he dynos across a roof on *The Dominator* (who would believe it is a British 7c move?). The book would also not be complete without the gut-wrenching accounts and images of Wolfgang Gullich's legendary free solo of *Separate Reality* in 1986 and Peter Croft's free solo on *Astroman.*

A large chunk of the section of free climbing is devoted inevitably to the Huber brother's ascents, with yet more jaw-dropping images which justify the exhaustive accounts of all four of their big routes on El Cap. However, the concluding article by Leo Houlding, rather fittingly, describes the early efforts towards a further progression in the direction of the purest and most demanding form of climbing yet undertaken on the big walls, onsight free first ascents of the 'new wave' lines which venture away from the security of Yosemite's famous cracks.

I found my concentration wandering throughout, however, this was only to ponder ways and means of making a pilgrimage to the valley myself, and which of the great climbs described I could muster the courage to attempt. Before picking up this book for the first time it was a matter of 'if' I might ever climb the great El Capitan. Now it's simply a matter of 'when'.

Dave MacLeod

Loose Scree: This is a small A5 booklet which, in the editor Barry Imeson's own words: "Is for, and intended to be by, seasoned climbers of all ages.

"Occupies the space between a club newsletter and the national glossies.

"Is free. Welcomes articles and short stories, letters, drawings, comments and reviews.

"Appears six times a year. Guarantees that your contributions will not be edited, unless authorised (The man's a saint. Ed.) except for spelling, libel and unamusing attacks on the management.

"If you have a story to tell, a view on the current climbing scene, an apocryphal story, an account of epics survived – on crag, hill or hostelry – and would be prepared to share it with others then please send it to *Loose Scree, 2 Highgreen, Tarset, Bellingham, Northumberland, NE48 1RP.*

"You will receive a free copy of the issue containing your contribution and an immediate surge of wellbeing."

An altruistic endeavour indeed and there is much good writing here from new as well as respected climbing authors. The next issue can be obtained from the above address by sending a suitable SAE (currently 34p).

The editor can be contacted by e-mail at barry@imeson6017.freeserve.co.uk

OFFICE BEARERS 2003-2004

Honorary President: William. D. Brooker

Honorary Vice-President: Douglas Scott

President: Peter F. Macdonald

Vice-Presidents: William S. McKerrow, Desmond W. Rubens

Honorary Secretary: John R. R. Fowler, 4 Doune Terrace, Edinburgh, EH3 6DY. **Honorary Treasurer:** John A. Wood, Spout Close, Millbeck, Underskiddaw, Keswick, Cumbria CA12 4PS. **Honorary Editor:** Charles J. Orr, 28 Chesters View, Bonnyrigg, Midlothian EH19 3PU. **Convener of the Publications Sub-Committee:** Rob W. Milne, Four Winds, Westfield, near Bathgate, West Lothian, EH48 3DG. **Honorary Librarian:** Ian R. Angell, The Old Manse, 3 New Street, Largs, Ayrshire, KA30 9LL. **Honorary Custodian of Slides:** Graeme N. Hunter, Netheraird, Woodlands Road, Rosemount, Blairgowrie, Perthshire, PH10 6JX. **Convener of the Huts Sub-Committee:** William H. Duncan, Kirktoun, East End, Lochwinnoch, Renfrewshire, PA12 4ER. **Custodian of the CIC Hut:** Robin Clothier, 35 Broompark Drive, Newton Mearns, Glasgow G77 5DZ. **Custodian of Lagangarbh Hut:** Bernard M. Swan, 16 Knowes View, Faifley, Clydebank, Dunbartonshire, G81 5AT. **Custodian of the Ling Hut:** William Skidmore, 1 Kirkton Drive, Lochcarron, Wester Ross, IV54 8UD. **Custodian of the Raeburn Hut:** Gerry Peet, 6 Roman Way, Dunblane, Perthshire, FK15 9DQ. **Custodian of the Naismith Hut:** William S. McKerrow, Scotsburn House, Drummond Road, Inverness, IV2 4NA. **Committee:** Rick Allen, Neil Marshall, Alastair P. Matthewson, Jamie R. Andrew, Heather Morning, Ronnie Robb, Donald J. Ballance, Adam Kassyk, Alex Runciman.

SMC Internet Address – http://www.smc.org.uk SMC e-mail: smc@smc.org.uk

Journal Information

Editor:	Charles J. Orr, 28 Chesters View, Bonnyrigg, Midlothian EH19 3PU. (e-mail: charliejorr@hotmail.com).
New Routes Editor:	A. D. Nisbet, 20 Craigie Avenue, Boat of Garten, Inverness-shire PH24 3BL. (e-mail: anisbe@globalnet.co.uk).
Editor of Photographs:	Alastair P. Matthewson, St Mungo's Lea, West Linton, EH46 7JA. (amatt@bgs.ac.uk).
Advertisements:	D. G. Pyper, 3 Keir Circle, Westhill, Skene, Aberdeen AB32 6RE. (e-mail: derek@pyper.fsbusiness.co.uk).
Distribution:	D. F. Lang, Hillfoot Hey, 580 Perth Road, Dundee DD2 1PZ.

INSTRUCTIONS TO CONTRIBUTORS

Articles for the Journal should be submitted before the end of January for consideration for the following issue. Lengthy contributions are preferably typed, double-spaced, on one side only, and with ample margins (minimum 30mm). Articles may be accepted on floppy disk, IBM compatible (contact Editor beforehand), or by e-mail. The Editor welcomes material from both members and non-members, with priority being given to articles of Scottish Mountaineering content. Photographs are also welcome, and should be good quality colour slides. All textual material should be sent to the Editor, address and e-mail as above. Photographic material should be sent direct to the Editor of Photographs, address as above.

Copyright.Textual matter appearing in the Miscellaneous section of the Journal, including New Climbs, is copyright of the publishers. Copyright of articles in the main section of the Journal is retained by individual authors.

SCOTTISH MOUNTAINEERING CLUB

SCOTTISH MOUNTAINEERING TRUST

HILLWALKERS' GUIDES

The Munros	£20
The Munros CD-ROM	£40
Munros GPS data disk – from SMC website	£10.48
The Corbetts and Other Scottish Hills	£18
The Corbetts and Other Scottish Hills CD-ROM	£30
North-west Highlands	£22
The Cairngorms	£17.95
Central Highlands	£17.95
Islands of Scotland including Skye	£19.95
Southern Highlands	£16.95
Southern Uplands	£16.95

CLIMBERS' GUIDES

Arran, Arrochar and Southern Highlands	£14.95
Ben Nevis	£19.95
Glen Coe	£18.50
The Cairngorms Vol. 1	£10.95
The Cairngorms Vol. 2	£11.95
Highland Outcrops	£16.50
North-east Outcrops	£18.50
Northern Highlands Vol. 1	£13.95
Northern Highlands North	£20
Scottish Winter Climbs	£17.95
Skye and the Hebrides (Two Vols)	£19.95

SCRAMBLERS' GUIDE

Skye Scrambles	£12

OTHER PUBLICATIONS

A History of Glenmore Lodge – e-book from SMC website	£5
Munro's Tables	£15.95
A Chance in a Million? Avalanches in Scotland	£14.95
The Munroist's Companion	£16
Scottish Hill and Mountain Names	£9.95
Ben Nevis – Britain's Highest Mountain	£14.95
Ski Mountaineering in Scotland	£12.95

Prices were correct at time of publication, but are subject to change.

Visit our website for more details and to purchase on line:
www.smc.org.uk

Distributed by:
Cordee, 3a De Montfort Street, Leicester LE1 7HD
Tel: 0116 254 3579 Fax: 0116 247 1176 www.cordee.co.uk
These publications are available from many bookshops and mountain equipment suppliers

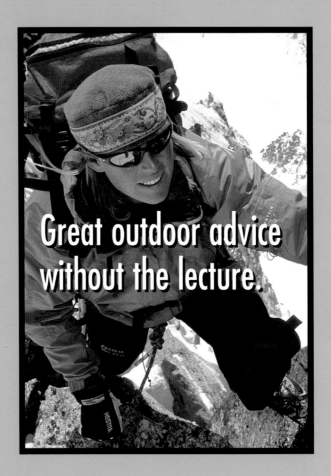